THE
GERMAN
CENTURY

Michael Stürmer

Picture Research by Sarah Jackson
and Franziska Payer

Weidenfeld & Nicolson
London

First published in 1999
Weidenfeld & Nicolson
Illustrated Division
The Orion Publishing Group
Wellington House
125 Strand
London WC2R 0BB

A CIP catalogue record for this book is available from the British Library

ISBN 0 2978 2524 0
Project Manager Franziska Payer
Picture Research Sarah Jackson with Franziska Payer and Sue McConachy
Editor Roger Hudson
Editorial Assistant Vicki Seaton
Design Paul Welti
Production Mary Osborne
Typesetting Peter Howard
Consultant Annabel Merullo

Typeset in Monotype Sabon
Origination by Jade Reprographics Ltd, Braintree, Essex
Printed by Nuovo Istituto Italiano d'Arti Grafiche SpA,
Bergamo, Italy

CONTENTS

EDITOR'S NOTE

Maritime ambitions: *rivetting the hull of a new liner for the German merchant marine, or one of the new warships for the high seas fleet, on a Hamburg slipway in 1911 (right).*
[PHOTO: JOHANN AND HEINRICH HAMANN]

As with the other titles in this series – *The Russian Century, The Chinese Century, The British Century* and *The Irish Century* – the photographs reproduced in this book are the result of extensive original research in archives, museums and private collections, mostly in Germany, but also in Great Britain, Austria and elsewhere as well. Additional material has been provided by contemporary photographers, many of whom have been introduced to us by Hansjoachim Nierentz of Agfa-Gaevert, and other friends. Our research began within the vast holdings of the Hulton Getty Picture Collection in London. It turned out to have key images which gave insights that were then to guide us in this project.

We are deeply indebted to the many archivists with whom we have worked over the past two and a half years. In particular, we would like to thank Heidrun Klein and Dr Karl Heinz Pütz at BPK in Berlin with its unparalled archive which includes the photographic holdings of seventeen museums in the Berlin area; Martina Caspers at the Federal Archives in Koblenz, founded in 1952, but with holdings going back to 1815, and merged with the former GDR archives in 1990; Beate Christians at Landesmedienzentrum Hamburg with its wonderful collection on the architecture and social history of the city and north Germany; Claudia Küchler at Deutsches Historisches Museum, Berlin. We are also very grateful that we have been able to include Max Ehlert's candid glimpses of Germany in the 1930s, 40s and 50s which we found safely resting in the archives of *Der Spiegel*, thanks to Christiane Gehner. *Der Stern* was equally helpful on many other aspects of the book. Sue McConachy's knowledge and enthusiasm were special on this subject and she was an invaluable part of the team.

We would also like to thank: Dr Christian Brandstätter, Austrian Archives, Vienna; Marion Gräfin Dönhoff and Wolfgang Wiese, *Die Zeit*, Hamburg; Inge Franklin; Ekkehard Kalusa, Berlin; Helga Heine, Rheindalen; Dr Marita Krauss, Munich; Dr Manfred Rasch and Heinz Dieter Rauch, Thyssen Stahl AG, Duisberg; Tina Schellhorn, Lichtblick, Cologne; Clarita von Trott zu Solz; Marion Wedekind, Transglobe Agency, Hamburg.

Half-title page: *A ride on a roundabout in Berlin, 1900.*
[PHOTO: HEINRICH ZILLE]

Title page: *Sunday afternoon, 1904, on the banks of the Grunewald Lake, Berlin.*

Copyright page: *The grape harvest above the Rhine, 1936.*
[PHOTO: MAX EHLERT]

Contents page: *A cabaret dancer at the Excelsior Hotel, 1936*

GERMANY AND ITS LÄNDER, 1990

SWEDEN

NORTH SEA

DENMARK

BALTIC SEA

GREAT BRITAIN

Helgoland

Kiel

SCHLESWIG-HOLSTEIN

MECKLENBURG-WEST POMERANIA

Schwerin

BREMEN

HAMBURG

Stettin

LOWER SAXONY

BRANDENBURG

NETHERLANDS

Hanover

River Elbe

Magdeburg

BERLIN

NORTHRHINE-WESTPHALIA

River Oder

BELGIUM

Essen

SAXONY-ANHALT

Düsseldorf

Cologne

Erfurt

Weimar

Leipzig

Dresden

Bonn

HESSE

THURINGIA

SAXONY

Wiesbaden

RHINELAND-PALATINATE

Frankfurt

Mainz

Former border between East and West Germany

CZECH REPUBLIC

LUXEMBOURG

SAAR-LAND

River Rhine

Heidelberg

Nuremberg

Stuttgart

BAVARIA

FRANCE

BADEN-WÜRTTEMBERG

Munich

River Danube

SWITZERLAND

AUSTRIA

SLOVENIA

ITALY

CROATIA

8

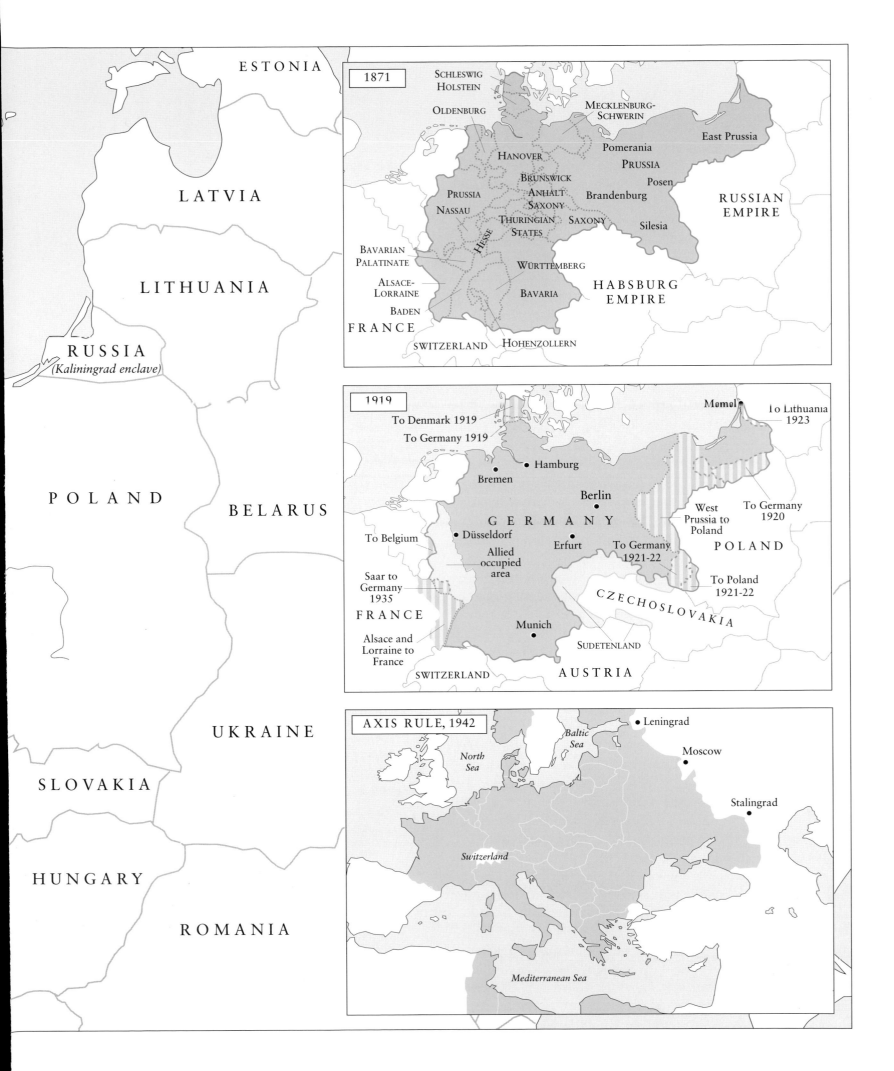

ESTONIA

LATVIA

LITHUANIA

RUSSIA
(Kaliningrad enclave)

POLAND

BELARUS

UKRAINE

SLOVAKIA

HUNGARY

ROMANIA

1871

SCHLESWIG
HOLSTEIN

OLDENBURG

MECKLENBURG-
SCHWERIN

East Prussia

HANOVER

Pomerania

PRUSSIA

BRUNSWICK

Posen

PRUSSIA

ANHALT
SAXONY

Brandenburg

RUSSIAN
EMPIRE

NASSAU

THURINGIAN
STATES

SAXONY

Silesia

HESSE

BAVARIAN
PALATINATE

WÜRTTEMBERG

ALSACE-
LORRAINE

BAVARIA

HABSBURG
EMPIRE

BADEN

FRANCE

SWITZERLAND

HOHENZOLLERN

1919

Memel

To Lithuania
1923

To Denmark 1919

To Germany 1919

Hamburg

Bremen

Berlin

GERMANY

West
Prussia to
Poland

To Germany
1920

To Belgium

Düsseldorf

Erfurt

POLAND

Allied
occupied
area

To Germany
1921-22

Saar to
Germany
1935

To Poland
1921-22

CZECHOSLOVAKIA

FRANCE

Alsace and
Lorraine to
France

Munich

SUDETENLAND

SWITZERLAND

AUSTRIA

AXIS RULE, 1942

Leningrad

Baltic
Sea

North
Sea

Moscow

Switzerland

Stalingrad

Mediterranean Sea

9

CHAPTER ONE

THE NEW REICH

After 28 years at the helm of Prussia and, subsequently, of the German Reich, Otto von Bismarck resigned from all his offices in 1890. An epoch came to an end. 'Dropping the Pilot' was the caption to the famous cartoon in *Punch*: the old man descending the gangway, supporting himself against the ship's side, making for a small rowing boat, while up on deck a young man with moustache and crown, his arms folded, watched him: Kaiser Wilhelm II.

Events in Berlin had a touch of patricide to them. They also reflected the uncomfortable truth that Bismarck's time had run out, that his system for containing the unsettling implications of industrialization and the strategic consequences of the creation of imperial Germany, had come to an end. The new generation no longer understood the world of its grandfathers, it no longer shared their hopes and their fears. Germany had ceased to be a 19th-century agrarian state, even if the 20th-century industrial society had yet to emerge. In terms of manners and way of life, mentalities, architecture and social hierarchy, everything continued as if nothing had happened. However, electricity and the telephone, rapid transport, bureaucracies and joint-stock banks had long become powerful engines of modernity. Berlin, at the beginning of the 19th century a town of craftsmen and soldiers, had, by the end of the century, become a sprawling industrial metropolis, the biggest on the European continent, a hub of capital, a turntable between north and south, east and west.

Bismarck had been called the 'Iron Chancellor' since the 1870s, and especially since his law 'against socialist intrigues' of 1878, but by 1890 he showed signs of rust. Two years before his fall, Wilhelm I had died in the spring of 1888, tired of life, at a great age, much mellowed and no longer the detested 'Open–fire Prince' of the revolutionary period and the 'mad year' of 1848/49. When Bismarck had stage-managed the creation of the Reich and the proclamation of the Kaiser in January 1871, the king had regarded this title as a cheap decoration and would have much preferred to remain the ruler of Prussia if Bismarck had only let him. He remarked wryly: 'Today we are burying the old Prussia.'

Crown Prince Frederick Wilhelm, along with his ambitious wife Victoria, the English Princess Royal ('Vicky'), had long waited for his father's death. Now he was brought back to Berlin from San Remo, terminally ill. He ruled his country for a mere 99 days, during most of which he was incapable of action. Yet those 99 days in 1888 held the hopes of a whole generation of German liberals. Frederick III, as he called himself when emperor, a name reflecting more the past glory of Prussia than the new magnificence of the Reich, left little behind but the

The Brandenburg Gate, *entrance to Prussia's political square mile, was completed when the French Revolution began in 1789. The Quadriga (chariot) and statue of Peace on top of the gate were taken by Napoleon to the Louvre and only returned after his final defeat. Here the Prussian troops celebrated another quicker victory over France in 1871 – Welch' eine Wendung durch Gottes Führung (what a deliverance through God's help) – here the remains of the imperial army straggled past in 1918. Here the Nazis staged their torchlight parade when they came to power in January 1933; here the last fighting in the battle for Berlin took place in April 1945. And here the Communists' Wall had its most conspicuous presence.*

East of the gate is Pariser Platz with the Adlon Hotel and the big embassies. North, hidden behind it, is the townhouse of Max Liebermann the painter (p.58), and out of shot on the left, a corner of the Reichstag. The gate links the wide 'Unter den Linden' (Under-the-Limes Street) and the Forum Fridericianum with the Great Western Road.

[PHOTO: L. L. ROGER-VIOLLET]

11

question whether, under better circumstances, his liberal beliefs and the influence of his English consort might have changed matters – in the direction of an alliance with England, of a liberal constitution, of civil society.

Now Wilhelm II, Imperator Rex, appeared on stage, spurs clattering. As a result of much psychological damage in early childhood he desperately tried to take a monarch's powers literally and to exercise them in defiance of constitutional practice and common sense, against tradition and public opinion. He was a highly talented, quick-witted monarch, but he needed to be loved and admired too much, to please

everybody. Bismarck, having shrewdly guided the old emperor with lengthy memoranda and, if necessary, an occasional threat of resignation, now made the mistake of investing almost unlimited trust in the grandson. There, on the one hand, was the vainglorious 28-year-old hothead and, on the other, the man of sorrow, the 73-year-old Chancellor with his load of experience and his heroic pessimism. The older man carried with him the burden of his century, while the younger suspected nothing of what the future held in store.

Among his intimates, who obsequiously reported back to the emperor, Bismarck mocked Wilhelm II, who in turn soon made

Pomp at Potsdam: *(Left) Crown Prince Friedrich Wilhelm and his wife Victoria, eldest daughter of Queen Victoria, receiving guests, c 1869, in front of Frederick the Great's Neues Palais. The tallest of their children beside them, with his crippled arm, is Prince Wilhelm. Within a year Crown Prince Friedrich Wilhelm led one of the triumphant German armies invading France, and in 1888 that boy was Kaiser Wilhelm II.*

The Crown Prince, *Friedrich Wilhelm (right) came to the throne in 1888, terminally ill of cancer of the throat. This was to be called 'the Year of Three Emperors' because he reigned for no more than a hundred days, taking with him the hopes and illusions of liberal Germany. One of his son's first moves on becoming Wilhelm II was to surround the Charlottenburg Palace with troops to prevent his English mother from removing any private or state papers.*

the map. His father, a Prussian landowner – a 'junker', a label suggesting a modest estate and rough manners – had been a military cadet under Frederick the Great. His mother, by contrast, came from a family of senior civil servants. Her father had been one of the Prussian reformers; she was shaped in an atmosphere of enlightened reform, when the rational began to be modified by the sentimental. All in all it was a very unequal marriage, and the incompatible character traits of his junker father and his intellectual mother had come together in Bismarck, generating creative energy, if not permanent conflict.

Having more or less stumbled into politics, he grew into a white revolutionary. He understood that, notwithstanding all the victories of the counter-revolution in post-1848 Europe – of the Prussians in Baden, the Russians in Hungary, the Austrians in Lombardy – the old order was doomed. Universal suffrage and parliamentary systems were the magic mechanics which the defenders of the old order would have to learn if they did not want to go under ignominiously. Above all, Prussia must not leave the national movement for the unification of Germany – which industry and banking urgently demanded and the students and their professors dreamed of – rudderless or, worse still, allow it to slip into the hands of others, such as the men of 1848, or a new Left, or the obstructing Austrians. 'We shall become the anvil if we fail to become the hammer', he wrote.

it clear that he would not be schoolmastered by the old man. Bismarck's fall, however, was not the result of combative temperaments or the perennial clash of generations, nor even of diverging views on what rights the constitution assigned to the emperor and what rights to the chancellor. The conflict was essentially political, encapsulated in the question whether Bismarck's Germany, trapped in crises and surrounded by potentially hostile alliances, still had a future or only a past.

Otto von Bismarck had been born in 1815, when Napoleon's 'Hundred Days' had ended in mud and misery at Waterloo and when the Congress of Vienna put a new balance of power on

Bismarck's chance came in 1862 when a passionate dispute between Crown and Parliament about the spirit and the organisation of the army reached a constitutional impasse. His advice to the king to risk a coup d'état if necessary won him appointment as Minister President. He then used the sword of German unification to cut the knot into which domestic policy had become tangled, and made no secret of it. 'The great questions of the day are not decided by speeches or majority decisions – that was the mistake of 1848/49 – but by iron and blood.'

In 1864 Prussia and Austria intervened in Schleswig-Holstein, ending many centuries of Danish rule in that part of northern Germany. Subsequently, however, they failed to share the booty amicably. The conflict with the imperial power of the Hapsburgs and most states within the Germanic Confederation had been carefully prepared for by Bismarck, not only militarily but more importantly, by an alliance with Italy and by sweeping the European financial markets clean. Prussia was also helped by the fact that the American Civil War was diverting Britain's and France's attention, and that Russia had no allies except Prussia. Napoleon III had been foolish enough to send an expeditionary force to Mexico which had defaulted on French government bonds. Thus, just when they were needed in Central Europe for a show of power and possibly war, the French armies were tied down in a hopeless overseas campaign.

The Prussian victory in 1866 over the Austrian forces between the fortress of Königgrätz and the village of Sadowa on the Elbe had the paradoxical result of not enlarging but diminishing Germany. It meant that the Austrian lands were excluded for good, so trimming the future Germany back to a format compatible with the views of the rest of Europe. But the question arose as to who would be the predominant power on the European continent, Germany or France. Napoleon III was bound to claim this role for France, not merely for domestic reasons of prestige, but also in view of France's tradition, going back to Francis I and Cardinal Richelieu, of preferring a divided Germany. A restless parliament and an unshackled press in Paris were increasingly driving him either to accept German unification under Prussia's leadership, meaning defeat for France – which would cost him his throne – or else to declare war. While Bismarck's North German Confederation, that had come out of the fighting of 1866, was nothing but a halfway house, the war offered itself as a powerful means to rally all of Germany behind the Prussian colours. In an act of brinkmanship, Bismarck opened a trap for French public opinion and for the Emperor who was unwilling to go to war – but finally had to.

In 1870 the vacant Spanish throne had been offered to a prince from the Catholic south-German collateral branch of the Prussian royal family, the Hohenzollerns of Hechingen. This had caused outrage throughout France, in parliament as well as among the wider public. It was assumed that France was now being encircled by the Hohenzollerns, as it had been by the Hapsburgs a mere 350 years ago. This was anachronistic and patently absurd, especially in view of the near total impotence of the Spanish crown at that time. What was at stake was not a European upheaval but a minor dynastic manoeuvre. But for the opposition in France it was a godsend with which to humiliate Napoleon, if he failed to accept the challenge, and perhaps even get rid of him.

The French declaration of war was followed by a sweeping attack by Prussia, masterminded by Field Marshal von Moltke, and the demise of the French Empire, after the bulk of its armies had been encircled at the fortress of Sedan on the Meuse. The French Third Republic, born out of these agonies, in spite of its willingness to fight 'à l'outrance', had to cede Alsace and Lorraine to Germany and pay five billion gold francs in war reparations. For good measure, the Prussian King was proclaimed German Emperor in the Hall of Mirrors in the palace of Versailles – not long before converted into a museum 'à toutes les gloires de la France'.

The fruits of victory were bitter. Bismarck now had only one concern – to save Germany from the consequences of its forced foundation. 'I continue to dream of what I think about when awake … Recently I saw the map of Germany before me; on it one rotten spot after another appeared and flaked off …' He had, as he once put in a diplomatic dispatch, the 'cauchemar des coalitions. This kind of nightmare will remain a very justified one for a German minister for a long time to come, and perhaps for ever.'

He felt that France was never to be wooed into an alliance with Germany – coexistence was the best that could be looked for: 'France is hopeless.' He therefore tried, in the great European game of the five powers, to be always allied with at least two, with Russia and Austria-Hungary, and possibly with Britain. But between Vienna and St Petersburg stood the issue of the Balkans, the Turkish straits and the inheritance of the Ottomans. Bismarck would have liked to make Britain the power guaranteeing the European Continent's equilibrium, playing much the same role as the United States of America in the latter part of the 20th century. But an active role in Continental Europe was one that Britain was historically very reluctant to play, and Bismarck had no desire to get involved in the Great Game between Russia and the British Empire, much further east.

Bismarck was at a loss what to do when republican France and Tsarist Russia were seeking an alliance in the 1880s: something that, for a long time, he had deemed impossible. 'We are pursuing a policy not of power but of security,' he wrote to the ambassador at the Tsar's court. External threats from the

The Iron Chancellor (opposite) in retirement: Bismarck at Friedrichsruh, his vast forested estate where he lived in an old inn which he never troubled to rebuild to better reflect his great national status and his huge fortune.

Balkans were now being joined by internal ones. The powerhouse at the centre of Europe worried not only its neighbours, who had come to regard a fragmented Germany as part of their birthright, it was also unsure about its own destiny, and driven by domestic forces of social change and ideology into restlessness and instability.

Bismarck would talk of equilibrium and contentment, but Germany could not be made smaller than it was, and there could be no return to the halcyon days of Metternich's order. Throughout Europe, expanding national egos joined with rapidly increasing industrial power and energetic new generations to prevent any equilibrium being achieved, and to make tradition and balance more and more irrelevant. People had to find work, which no longer existed in the countryside, and now, with universal suffrage and a collective memory of past revolutions, they might become rebellious. The powerful nation state was the natural form of life for the countries of Europe. But the modern state, even in its authoritarian version, had to be based upon industrial society. Bismarck realized that the alliance between the old Prussian elite and the rising industrial middle class, an alliance upon which the German Reich had been based, amounted to a Faustian bargain, and an unavoidable one at that.

In 1878 there were two attempts on the life of the Kaiser in quick succession. Bismarck exploited the panic and pushed his anti-socialist legislation down the throat of a reluctant Reichstag, in order to win loyal majorities in parliament. By 20th-century standards the repression of the socialists was mild, as it allowed them to continue their role in parliament. Furthermore it was combined with pioneering projects for obligatory social insurance for industrial workers against sickness and accident, and old age pensions. Yet the domestic tranquillity which Bismarck was seeking was not to be found. In 1889 there were extensive strikes in the Ruhr and in the Silesian mines: 145,000 striking miners gave the coal barons a lasting *angst*. A large consignment of rifles, labelled as fencing posts, was delivered to the Villa Hügel, the Krupp residence near Essen. Strategic coal supplies for the railways were running out. Bismarck wanted to send in the army, but the young Kaiser insisted on negotiating with workers' delegations. It was to be the beginning of the end of Bismarck's political career.

Bismarck was what his contemporary, the historian Jacob Burckhardt, called 'an individual of world history' – that is to say a man but for whom history would have taken a different course. His mode of thought was brinkmanship, not unlike, in the 20th century, Winston Churchill's or Charles de Gaulle's. He came from faraway, from the 18th century: 1789 was the founding event of the modern age, 1848 for him was still part of the present. He was not afraid of opening deep rifts: first with Austria and France; then with the old Conservatives who opposed secularization of the state and his bargain with the propertied and educated classes; then with the Catholics of the

Fuelling trade and industry *on the Elbe and in the Ruhr. Germany's economy boomed in the later nineteenth century. Colliers (opposite) return after replenishing the bunkers of a* *coal-fired steamship, in 1892, and Krupp steelworkers manoeuvre a steel ring at Essen in 1899 (above).*
[PHOTO, OPPOSITE: JOHANN AND HEINRICH HAMANN]

German Centre Party, whom he excluded as ultramontane 'enemies of the Reich' – i.e. followers of Rome; finally with the socialists whom he denounced as red-hot revolutionaries, and against the liberals whom he branded as being their clandestine allies.

He was capable of making compromises, but only in foreign policy, between one power and another. At home he believed in state sovereignty, and he feared that if he gave Revolution an inch it would demand a whole mile. His pride was closely akin to arrogance; he could charm if he wished and equally he could wound for ever. Alongside sparkling intelligence, sensitivity and poetical moods he displayed narrow-minded selfishness, not shrinking from personal enrichment or using official information for insider trading.

Human warmth and high politics were to him incompatible. He explained that in his carp pond, politics had killed all other fish. Bismarck was undoubtedly one of the great actors on the

Rural Germany *remained largely unchanged for this woman striding past Franconian plum trees (opposite) and for the* Baltic fisherman and his wife (above). Whilst he reads his newspaper wearing his cap, typical of northern Germany , *his wife peels potatoes in front of their house, which has been insulated with reeds. The Franconian plums, harvested in* the autumn, will be turned into the region's famous plum brandy.

[PHOTO, OPPOSITE: HEINRICH ZILLE]

Streets and gardens. *The menfolk of Berchtesgaden, deep in the mountains of Bavaria, gather round the fountain in the marketplace (above). A prosperous pharmacist poses with his family in the garden of his Black Forest home (right). People gather in an ancient narrow Hamburg street (opposite).*

[PHOTO, OPPOSITE: PAUL WUTCKE]

political stage of the 19th century – not because he was in tune with it but because he was so remote from it. He was as far removed from the simple faith of the liberals – that free flow of opinion and capital would keep the world in balance – as he was from the socialist idea of progress, which invariably saw the wheel of history at work. He had, because he saw it as inevitable, driven the old Prussia into an alliance with the liberal and national movements of his day, and was even prepared to concede 'whatever is justified about the socialist demands'. Just as Louis XIV once said that he was the State, so Bismarck could say the same: that he had tailored the German constitution to suit his own ends. In the long run, however, foreign affairs were no longer controllable from Berlin, nor indeed was domestic policy for Bismarck. The sorcerer's apprentice had called up the spirits to serve him, but then the word was lost with which to stop them. He probably suspected that the word had long ceased to exist, as had the old sorcerer. Pessimism was the keynote of his melancholy philosophy.

What did it mean to be a German in the time of Bismarck? Most of the 41 million people living between the Moselle in the West and the Memel in the East would actually have described themselves as Bavarians or Wurttembergers, Prussians or Saxons. The people of Franconia, for instance, still remembered that, after centuries of free cities, prince bishoprics, margraviates and independent lordships, their lands had been annexed by the Kingdom of Bavaria only in 1806, with the blessing of Napoleon. Rhinelanders resented being under the thumb of Berlin, 400 miles away in the East. In their carnival celebrations every winter the good people of Cologne loved to mock the Prussian soldiery, imitating their heel clicking, abrupt commands and their conspicuous *Zackigkeit* – parade-ground manner – while drinking, dancing and and merry-making.

In the West people still lived under the *Code Napoléon* introduced in 1804; in the East under the *Allgemeines Landrecht für die Preussischen Staaten*, dating from 1793 (and only replaced in 1900 by the civil code, the *Bürgerliches Gesetzbuch*). In the South people still counted in guilders, in the North in thalers, with a fixed relationship of two thalers to three guilders until, in the 1870s, mark and pfennig replaced all of the older coins.

Most people from the various German provinces, with their different vernaculars, would have encountered difficulties understanding each other. Only the educated classes more or less spoke high German, corresponding closely to Luther's translation of the Bible. Every valley, every city in Germany had its own lilt, its own idioms, its own linguistic store of historical memory, much as it had its own cooking recipes, local cheese,

An East-Prussian farmer (right) *drives his team briskly along a sandy road typical of the country north-east of Berlin.*

East Prussians were famous for their horses, hospitality and resilience – until 1945.

bread and beer. Local costume still prevailed in rural parts of Germany, *Loden* and *Lederhosen* in upper Bavaria for instance, or blue shirts for the men and wide black petticoats for the women in the central parts of Hesse, called *die Schwalm*. Houses looked different: checkered in the North, red brick in the West, and richly varied balcony-adorned wooden structures under gigantic overhanging roofs in the South, from lower Bavaria to the Black Forest. While red tiles were common in Germany, in the *Bergisches Land* between Cologne and Kassel roofs were covered in grey stone slates. Bavarian Catholics worshipped under onion domes, Franconian Protestants under graduated sandstone structures, and Northerners under church towers ending in green copper spires.

Even the way Germans ate and drank was – and is – different, not only among the various social classes, but in different areas too. It was Champagne, cognac and wine for the upper crust: in the North red Bordeaux coming in through the ports of Bremen and Lübeck, while in the South white wine prevailed, made mostly of Riesling grapes from the Rheingau, the Saar or the Moselle. *Frankenwein*, around Würzburg, in its

Beer for the masses, *wine for the classes. Every town boasted its own particular brew (left). The hop market in front of Hamburg's Nikolai Church, in 1905 (below). A mandolin players' club on* *an outing to a Bavarian beergarden rigged with Chinese lanterns for evening drinking: Krailing, 1904 (right).*
[PHOTO, BELOW: JOHANN AND HEINRICH HAMANN]

unusual bottles called *Bocksbeutel* was mostly made from Silvaner grapes. The lower classes enjoyed many hundreds of kinds of beer, mostly brewed locally, and different kinds of schnaps: a potato-based type of vodka in Westphalia for instance, fruit-based spirits in the Southern regions, or *Schwarzwälder Kirschwasser* distilled from Black Forest cherries, and plum brandy made from fruit harvested from the rolling meadows of Franconia.

Meat was, even for the middle classes, served only at expansive family lunches after church on Sundays. Venison still had the flavour of feudal elitism – or poaching. Fish was more popular in the North where herring was cheap and a daily staple, while in the South carp and trout, farmed since early monastic times, were too expensive to be served except on Fridays. The working classes had to rise early for their ten-hour workday, with a bite of crusty, darkish *Kommissbrot* – baked to the military standard – and then taking a container of soup with them, their day ending with supper at sunset to save on candles or, since the turn of the century, on electricity.

In the North, to this day, a kitchen has to look like a combination of an architect's office and a dental lab, while in the South the smoky smells and the flavours of a farmhouse are appreciated. Heating, until the early part of the 20th century, was coal-fired, mostly the compressed lignite (brown coal) briquettes, invented in the Rhineland in the 1860s and thrown

worker, a ten-hour day and a fifty-four hour week was standard. It caused an outcry among industrialists in 1912 when Robert Bosch in Stuttgart reduced working hours to forty-eight a week, justifying this radical departure because of higher efficiency in a technology-driven industry where quality mattered more than hours put in. It was only after the revolution of 1918 that the forty-eight hour week was to be introduced as the industrial standard.

The middle classes, in the age of comfortable railway travel, discovered the weekend trip from Berlin to the Baltic resorts, or from Hamburg to the sandy beaches of Sylt and Norderney. The rich, the aristocrats and the demi-monde would take the waters at Karlsbad in Bohemia, just across the Bavarian border, or in Baden-Baden, where Russian princes and French cocottes would join them at the gaming-tables. The Swiss mountains became popular among the rising middle classes who could afford the cosy comforts of Swiss hotellerie – the TB sanatoria of Davos, dramatised by the shadow of death, are forever

down from horsedrawn carts in front of the houses – or wood-fired. Real coal from the Ruhr was far too expensive to be much used in private homes. By the turn of the century Germans were no strangers to cold running water for cooking and washing. But few could afford the luxury of running hot water, let alone the comforts of central heating. In town and country, lavatories – indicated by a cut-out heart in the door or, in more elevated places, by a 'WC' sign – remained messy affairs, mostly outside the houses and shared by many.

The upper classes would call their breakfast, after riding out in Berlin's Tiergarten or in Munich's Englischer Garten, 'just a bite', while the real *Frühstück* would be a heavyweight matter, with champagne, at Borchardt's in the middle of Berlin's political square mile or at the Adlon Hotel by the Brandenburg Gate, opening to the Pariser Platz and a view of the major embassies. In the evening, children looked after by their nannies would have an early meal and, after prayers, be sent to bed. Their parents would regard any dinner commencing before eight o'clock as distinctly low-class. They would settle for a major spread later, rarely with less than six courses and three different kinds of wine, crowned with champagne, coffee and cognac at the end. One thing of course was common to the entire male population: the rich would smoke heavy Havanas or cigars from Sumatra, the lower middle class cigarettes. Virginia cigarettes were regarded as more modern, Egyptian ones as faintly decadent, as witnessed in Thomas Mann's incestuous novel *Wälsungenblut*. Pipe-smoking was almost the only habit uniting North and South, rich and poor. A woman who smoked was clearly setting herself apart from good society.

Holidays were unknown to the vast majority of the population. The old artisans' 'Blue Monday', devoted to recovery from the excesses of Sunday, did not survive the rigours of industrial discipline. For the average industrial

celebrated in Thomas Mann's *The Magic Mountain*. The vast majority, meanwhile, had no chance ever to see the Matterhorn or to cruise on Lake Lucerne, let alone spend the winter losing a fortune in the Casino in Monaco. But this is not to say that they did not have fun, too.

Sports became popular. But, once again, the nation was divided between the tennis-playing classes, who also rode horses or played golf, and the soccer-playing classes who also boxed or bicycled. For the people living in shabby *Mietskasernen* – the vast barrack-like living quarters of the poor – some fresh air and a little bit of greenery was available through the *Schrebergarten* – the colonies of neat little huts and

carefully tended vegetable, fruit and flower gardens on the outskirts of many an industrial city in Germany. They were a kind of safety valve where both rural nostalgia and a supply of vitamins from sour apples or black-currants were offered by the authorities to the labouring poor. In return, the *Schrebergarten* tenders developed their own, protective mentality, not caring about the great questions of politics, but about fences, water-supply, and an excess of regulations governing the shape and colour of roofs or the maximum size permitted to fruit trees.

The lot of women in Wilhelmine society depended very much on social position. Of course, farmers' wives and the wives of small businessmen had a large part in the family's endeavours;

Roller skating (above), introduced from the United States. To begin with it was a sport for middle-class adults, as this group testifies, not street children. Dressed in something like their best, these skaters are out to display their elegance and skill, not to work up a sweat.

Wind-assisted *ice skating (above) on the Müggelsee, one of the lakes near Berlin, in 1908.*

Self-portrait *(left) of the photographer Heinrich Zille, in striped trunks in the centre, with fellow-bathers at another Berlin lake in August 1901. He was an enthusiast for the open air and championed the cause of allotments - Schrebergarten - for the urban working classes. Zille's work strongly influences the picture we have today of turn-of-the-century Berlin – 'Zille sein Milljöh'.*

[PHOTO, ABOVE: RÖHNERT]
[PHOTO, LEFT: HEINRICH ZILLE]

Thuringian costume, *(above)* identifies card players wearing their Sunday best outside an inn near Weimar. A girl hands one of them a glass of schnaps while the others share jugs of wine. Each region was proud of its own distinctive wear. [PHOTO: HUGO ERFURTH]

A traditional night out *bowling for a group of young aspiring artists and sculptors (opposite), living la vie bohème in Berlin, 1900.* [PHOTO: HEINRICH ZILLE]

The Crown Princess *(right), wife*
of the future Wilhelm II, with
two of her children. Coming
from the princely house of
Sonderburg-Augustenburg, she
was married in 1881.
[PHOTO: E. BIEBER]

on the farm not only looking after the children and the farmhands but also producing everything from eggs and butter to wool and cloth. In a small business the wife automatically did the book-keeping, paid the taxes and dealt with the local authorities. The further down the social scale, the less defined was the place of women. A day-labourer's wife had to see how she, too, could scrape together a few *Pfennige*, rent out a bed to a traveller or a journeyman or help with the housework in a modest middle-class home without permanent servants. Sewing and ironing became important sources of income, and what the sewing machine did to enhance earnings, the bicycle did for mobility.

While courtship and marriage among the poor was left to chance, a Sunday dance or a carnival encounter and the efforts of friends and relatives, the finding of a suitable candidate for marriage became a major concern of middle- and upper-class parents, once a young girl was over the age of sixteen. Ten years later, it was assumed her chances were gone, the poor thing forever condemned to be a lonely spinster, a failure in terms of family fortune and prestige. The unmarried aunt became the laughing stock of comedy and novel. So every effort had to be made, while at the same time the girl's reputation had to be protected at all costs. There must be a chaperone for every outing, innocent reading-matter, but also clothing that would both proclaim purity of heart and display feminine appeal.

Upper-class girls should have a good education in French and English – the latter invariably spoken with a French accent –

read the expurgated versions of Goethe and Schiller, write an elegant hand, take piano lessons and sing. For good measure, a Swiss finishing school for *Höhere Töchter* would make them fit to face any dynastic challenge – including a bossy mother-in-law, almost permanent pregnancy and an occasional infidelity on the part of the husband. Anything was better than spinsterhood or divorce. This entire structure was built upon the assumption that fortunes would last forever, that the continuity of the family would remain unbroken, and that social norms would never be challenged. Thus, the Great War, although women were not sent to the trenches, ruined their lives almost as much as it destroyed their men's.

At the same time, the war ultimately broke down the walls around Ibsen's 'doll's house'. At the turn of the century the first female students entered universities, in spite of professors who never tired of exposing them to particularly tasteless jokes or embarrassing situations. However, they did not become members of student fraternities because of the heavy drinking, the dirty jokes and the patronising attitude towards the sweet little things. As women did not have the right to vote before 1919, their role in politics was less than marginal. One exception was Bertha von Suttner, an aristocratic pacifist; Rosa Luxemburg was another, a non-practising Jew from an orthodox family in the East. She was a left-winger, she had a university degree, and she campaigned first for the social democrats and later for their radical opponents; on all three counts she was the exception that proved the rule. Wilhelmine society, much as the rest of Europe, did not allow women to

Into male domains: *female students (above) at a life class at the Munich Academy of Arts in 1901, and training to be doctors (right) at an anatomy lesson. These are activities which only a short time before would have been unheard of for women.*

In the workplace *(opposite): a Hamburg factory producing fine bed and table linen. The work may be taxing, but this is no sweatshop.*
[PHOTO, OPPOSITE: JOHANN AND HEINRICH HAMANN]

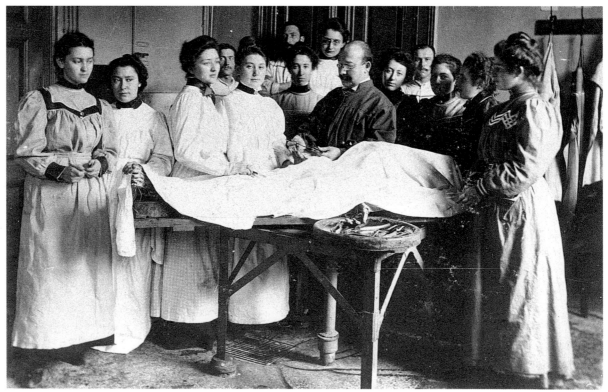

break free from the restrictions that tradition imposed on them. If they did, they paid a painful price, like Rosa – murdered by Freikorps soldiers in 1919.

At the time of Bismarck's fall in 1890 the German economy rose from the depths of a depression towards new heights. In terms of share of gross national product, employment and investment, industry assumed the leading role. The services sector began to expand with banking, insurance, management and training. The country and its people were changing rapidly. There were persistent conflicts between the government and the Reichstag, and at times a state of ungovernability ensued.

The delirium of those years, so long contained by Bismarck, did not exceed the general European level. But for reasons inherent in history and geography, and accentuated by population explosion, loss of tradition and the search for markets, it was more unsettling for Germany than it was for most neighbouring countries who were more set in their ways, had older traditions, and were not such powerhouses.

There was no shortage of obituaries when Bismarck departed. The predominant tone was one of relief, except in European cabinets where his regime was felt latterly to have been a stabilising force in international affairs. In Britain there was mainly regret, in France no jubilation, in Austria-Hungary deep concern, and even from Russia there came mainly worried voices. Yet in Germany it seemed as if an iron lid had been lifted. The widowed Empress Frederick wrote as if a new age had begun, and as if she did not know her triumphalist son:

'How we suffered under that regime! How his influence corrupted a whole school – his staff, Germany's political life! He made life in Berlin almost unbearable if one did not wish to become his depraved slave! His party, his followers and admirers are fifty times worse than he is himself. One would like to utter a cry for deliverance and it would be heard, what a deep sigh of relief would be the answer. It will take years to undo all the damage done. He who only sees the outside thinks Germany is strong, great and united, with a huge army ... If only the price were known that all this has cost ...'

At the turn of the century Germany was a restless Reich in a restless Europe. The dust raised by the revolutionary events of 1848/49 had not yet settled down when German industrialization began to take off. There had been setbacks, as in the first worldwide economic crisis of 1857/58. But industrialization, in the prosperous crescent from the Rhineland via the Ruhr to Berlin and on to Silesia, as well as in the older industrial centres of the south like Ulm, Stuttgart, Augsburg

Rosa Luxemburg, *future martyr of the Spartacist uprising in 1919, was from a pious East European Jewish family. Here she speaks at the Socialist Party* *Congress in 1907, flanked by icons of two founding fathers: Marx and Lassalle. The whole scene is one of the greatest respectability and restraint.*

The workers and their champion. *The dramatist, novelist and poet Gerhart Hauptmann (right) with his sons in 1907. The most famous of his social realist plays, akin to Ibsen's, was* The Weavers *(1892), and he won the Nobel Prize in 1912. These workers (opposite) in the Krupp foundry at Essen could have been his inspiration, if not his audience.*

and Nuremberg, was going on apace. Low wages, indifference to water and air pollution, political tranquillity and a stable investment climate, liberalized securities and stock-exchange regulations, high capital yields accompanied by speculation and the dream of quick and effortless wealth – all these forces reached their climax in the great boom that accompanied the establishment of the Reich in 1871. Towns spread, unplanned and uncontrolled, thanks to factory building or speculative housing, in Nuremberg, or in Berlin, in Silesia, and on the Ruhr; elsewhere they were planned and strictly controlled, as in Munich and Karlsruhe. In Potsdam the old Prussia of the Frederick Wilhelms and Fredericks was preserved almost as in a museum, enlivened by the splendid uniforms of the fashionable guards regiments. But Berlin, including the modern boulevard of the *Kurfürstendamm* in the west of the city, became the quintessential modern megalopolis. Surrounding farming villages now became dormitory towns. Fast railways, trams (after 1881), telephones and electricity provided ten thousand links with the centre. At the turn of the century the first underground railways tunnelled their way into the bottomless Brandenburg sand.

Germans were on the move. It was a period of mobility and of social change, driven by the great hope that life elsewhere would be better and fuller. During the first half of the century it was the rule that life's pilgrimage ended where it had begun, but this expectation was turned upside down by industrialization during the second half of the century. The great drift from the land was a long trek to better work, longer life, the right to a family, taking the road upwards.

The population total, from the ridge of the Vosges to the banks of the Pregel river in East Prussia, was only 41 million in

1871; a mere 20 years later it was 50 million; by 1913 it would be 67 million. The nation, concurrently, was getting younger day by day; by the time Bismarck died it was the youngest nation in Europe – with the exception of Russia. But all of these young men and women had to find work and make a living – each year half a million more people needed jobs. The internal drift was chiefly from east to west and from the countryside to the towns. The typical Berliner came from East Prussia or Silesia. The new arrivals went into industry, or became workers at the big construction sites, or entered domestic service. The old craft skills, rendered largely obsolete by machines and the division of labour, still produced the 'journeymen', who now became skilled workers after a long period of apprenticeship and an examination by their guilds. From this older tradition they brought with them their pride and organizational talent, as well as the desire for a middle-class lifestyle – which is why German social democracy spoke with a revolutionary voice but acted in an evolutionary manner. From Protestant vicarages and the former civil servant milieus came the new office workers, with and without higher education; these formed the 'new middle class' and demanded monthly salaries. They were not proletarian but not bourgeois either, eager to educate themselves and avid readers. Big firms such as Krupp in Essen or Siemens in Berlin described themselves, in imitation of feudal practice, as the 'House of Siemens' or the 'House of Krupp' and called their managers their 'officials'. The banks, both the many hundreds of private banks and the speedily rising joint-stock banks, did likewise.

A long deflationary period began in May 1873 with a stock-exchange crash; for the next 20 years it ensured that the economy remained subdued. Year after year more than a

German East Africa.

A colonial official (above) has armed himself well for a day's hunting. Rather than using the wildlife as targets, another has trained two zebra to pull his trap (right).

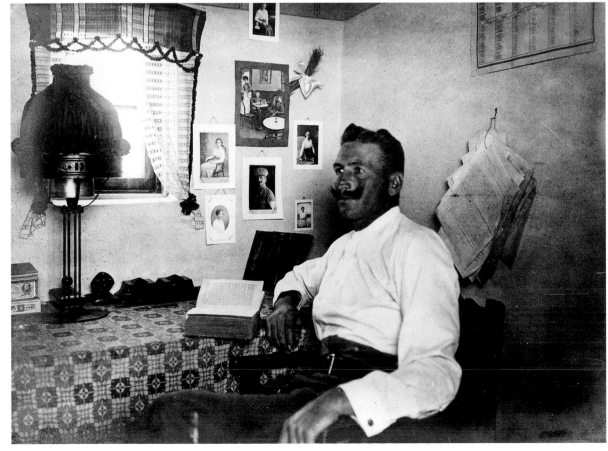

Tanganyikan train ride. *A party enjoys its hock and moselle on the train up to Mount Kilimanjaro, while a sergeant in the Protection Force cultivates his 'Kaiser' moustache.*

hundred thousand young people bought passages from Rotterdam, Bremerhaven or Hamburg to the New World. Many were young merchants or craftsmen who wanted to learn something useful – young Robert Bosch, for instance, who was to found a worldwide enterprise in Stuttgart, wanted to learn everything about dynamos on the eastern seaboard of the United States. There were also farmers' sons who were hoping that emigration would bring them land, as well as the prospect of marriage and family which, as a rule, they were denied at home.

But in 1893 emigration as good as came to a halt: in the USA there was 'the panic of 1893' while in Germany the new period of business expansion began. German industries took the lead in sectors such as mechanical engineering, dyestuffs and pharmaceuticals, chemicals and electrical engineering. New markets were opened up and the social climate became more relaxed. Life was easier again as wages rose from year to year, and the state's social insurance system provided a cover against the risks of urban life. The decadent charms of England in the 1890s or of France's *fin de siècle* were also reflected in Germany's elegant suburbs or in Austria's cafés.

With Bismarck gone, the Kaiser, using naval language, announced his 'New Course'. Domestically he aimed at reconciliation; and externally at confidence building. The new Reich Chancellor was 'a military man with a stiff back', as Bismarck approvingly characterized him. Infantry General Georg Leo von Caprivi, barely 60, had done good service as Chief of the Reich Naval Directorate and had been wise enough to confine German naval ambitions to troop transport and coastal surveillance, if only not to offend Britain. He was also credited with a dictum in tune with this policy: 'The less Africa the better'.

Such moderation was not universally popular. Caprivi sought a strategic arrangement with the British Empire as well as with Russia. The British coveted the fabulous island of Zanzibar and

Emigrants in Hamburg, *waiting to leave for North America (top left). The upbeat slogan above the door can be translated as 'The World Is My Oyster', and 100,000 left annually in the 1880s.* [PHOTO: JOHANN AND HEINRICH HAMANN]

Bound for Helgoland. *A flotilla of small steamers (above) takes holidaymakers in 1891 on the forty-mile trip to the North Sea island, acquired from Britain the previous year.*

exchanged Helgoland for it, situated in the middle of the Elbe estuary. With Russia he achieved what until then had always been blocked by Bismarck and the large grain-growing estate owners east of the Elbe – a trade agreement. The rapidly growing German market was opened to cheap Russian grain exports from the black-soil areas of the Ukraine, while in exchange the German electrical and mechanical engineering industries could make money from Russian industrialization, and German banks could invest in Russia. This did not prevent the Russo-French entente, many years in preparation, but it sapped its strength. In justification Chancellor von Caprivi said in 1891: 'We must export. We either export people or we export goods. With this increasing population we cannot, except by increasing industry, continue to live.' Rarely have the

Harvest time *(above) on an eastern estate. The women under the eye of the overseer are probably seasonal workers from Poland.*

Stettin *(opposite), Germany's biggest Baltic seaport until lost to Poland in 1945. The vast Gothic brick Nikolai Church is typical of this coast.*

driving forces of economic expansion and market conquest been defined more explicitly. And rarely, on the other hand, has the strategic dilemma in which Germany found itself been described more clearly.

What Caprivi, supported in the Reichstag by the Liberals and also by Catholics and Socialists, was aiming at was domestic reform and a peaceful foreign policy. For that, however, he needed the approval of the Kaiser, and this was increasingly lacking, as His Majesty found himself faced with the anger of the landed nobility, whose sons, serving in the Potsdam and Berlin guards regiments, felt the squeeze on agricultural incomes. Without their regular remittances from home they were unable to enjoy the lifestyle which as young lieutenants, pitifully paid by the state yet belonging to the top class of society, they wished to embrace. The Kaiser made Caprivi – mocked by the landowners as 'the man without an acre or a blade' – a count, but withdrew his support from him as massive Right-wing opposition was developing against the Russian trade agreement from the *Reichslandbund*, the Reich League of Landowners. This new body instantly mobilized over 300,000 members in its foundation year of 1893 and was not too particular about taking a leaf out of the socialists' book on matters of propaganda and mass organization.

High capital costs and the labour-drain, along with the prospect of declining profits because of cheap Russian imports, infuriated the big landowners who could not diversify into processed products. Farmhouse tourism had not yet been invented and deep-freeze lines not even thought of. Noisy propaganda was putting parliament, government, the court and the public under pressure. The government, the capitalists, the Jews, the export industry, were held responsible. Against them, but chiefly against the Reich Chancellor, the fury of the agrarians was directed.

Simultaneously the colonial lobby was making a big noise. Even Bismarck had not trusted them – in the end he had been willing, because of their unprofitability, to lease all the German colonies to a consortium of Hamburg merchants for the notional price of one mark. On one occasion he had dismissed a colonial enthusiast who wanted half of Africa with the remark: 'Here is France, and here is Russia, and we are in the middle – and that is my map of Africa!' But that was a long time ago. Now the 'Pan-German League' came into existence, representing German prewar nationalism in its most fanatical form. Its point of attack was the treaty with Britain trading Helgoland for Zanzibar – even though it handed Germany the strategic key to the Elbe, the country's most important waterway.

While the Kaiser's 'new course' in domestic politics did not result in eventual peace with the Social Democrats, it nevertheless inaugurated the second phase of the state's social policy: with its labour laws, in which the trade unions were recognised, it gave organized labour an official role, standing and influence. Bismarck's harsh regime, in which social security had been motivated by political rather than humanitarian considerations, was followed by a more open policy, resulting in more socially-orientated legislation, more industry, more growth and more jobs. But it did not bring internal equilibrium. The landed classes still rebelled and won the support of the court and the army. Caprivi, failing to achieve compromise at home and abroad, had to resign after four years.

His successor was Prince Hohenlohe, formerly Governor of Alsace, an affable southern German landowner, not greatly given to business or the study of state papers. Under his mild gaze the Kaiser's entourage hoped to develop what Wilhelm II – who loved acting the Great Elector and copying Frederick the Great's manner of speaking – regarded as his divine right of kings. The new form of government piled everything that Bismarck, as chancellor, foreign minister and Prussian minister-president, had kept in his own hands, upon a man who was a victim of his many gifts, of the sycophancy surrounding him and of the power which the nation was accumulating. The aim was a populist form of government, with much propaganda, vainglorious gestures and tempting horizons, something very ancient and very new, and none of it reality: just bread and circuses. In the end nothing was achieved except a paralysis of the administration and a dangerous loss of respect for the monarchy among many, including the landowners. At the turn of the century Germany had long become a pluralist industrial society with a thousand links – intellectual, cultural, technological and economic – with the rest of Europe and the USA. The country was ill-suited to be the stage for a populist-monarchist regime.

CHAPTER TWO

GLOBAL AMBITION

When the crowned heads of Europe came to London for Queen Victoria's Diamond Jubilee in 1897, to pay homage to the 'grandmother of Europe', the pictures showed nothing but harmony, the ladies in fine silks, the gentlemen in elegant uniforms, obligingly wearing each other's decorations. But in the widely ramified European family of the old lady, who for the past twenty years had also gloried in the title of Empress of India, everything was not as perfect as it seemed.

The widow with the disapproving mien certainly had every reason to view the future with concern. Her son Edward, Britain's ageing heir to the throne, notorious for his self-indulgence, despised his nephew Wilhelm Imperator Rex as a vain dunderhead, and Wilhelm returned the compliment. But the future Edward VII would be a constitutional monarch, not allowed any political extravaganzas, while Wilhelm II had the intention and the means to take his country's government, and especially its foreign and military policy, into his own hands. He regarded himself as God's instrument and 'by the grace of God' was, to him, not a pious historical formula but an arrogant assertion. To the daughter of the British Prime Minister, Lord Salisbury, he exclaimed, 'Thank God, I am a tyrant', when she ventured to explain parliamentary government. Volatile and highly gifted, irritable and arrogant, uncertain and unstable, he was the proverbial 'loose cannon on deck', an incalculable factor in a world apparently becoming more predictable, with its bureaucracies, industries and strategies, but in reality ever more dangerous and endangered.

'The most brilliant failure in history,' is what Edward VII called Wilhelm. Psychologically damaged by his crippled arm and a spartan upbringing, educated in a bigoted manner, inclined to rash judgements, disinclined to the thorough study of dossiers or profound analysis of the diplomatic chess game, a victim of his quick comprehension and brilliant memory, the Kaiser viewed the powerhouse at Europe's centre as a giant toy on an oversized parade-ground, and expected everyone to follow his word of command. Being born a cripple and having to pretend to be a hero, a supreme commander, even a demi-god, was too much for one man. His mother and father, stiff-upper-lipped and conforming to the detached aristocratic and military norms of the day, had not given him much warmth and never shown him that even in weakness there can be strength. It was only his grandmother, Queen Victoria, who seems to have accepted the boy as a human being – though she found his posturing unnerving and at times unbearable. His withered left arm drove him to pose for every virility test, and made his sense of humour crude and even cruel. A veteran general was made to dance in a woman's costume, until he literally dropped dead.

Playing at soldiers. *The Kaiser, left, walks with his sons to a military ceremony in Berlin on New Year's Day, 1913. The Crown Prince, Willy, wears the fur-covered head-dress of the Death's Head Hussars. In the background is the Stadtschloss, built two hundred years before to celebrate Prussia's rise to full royal status, a gesture of defiance towards the Hapsburg Holy Roman Emperors.*

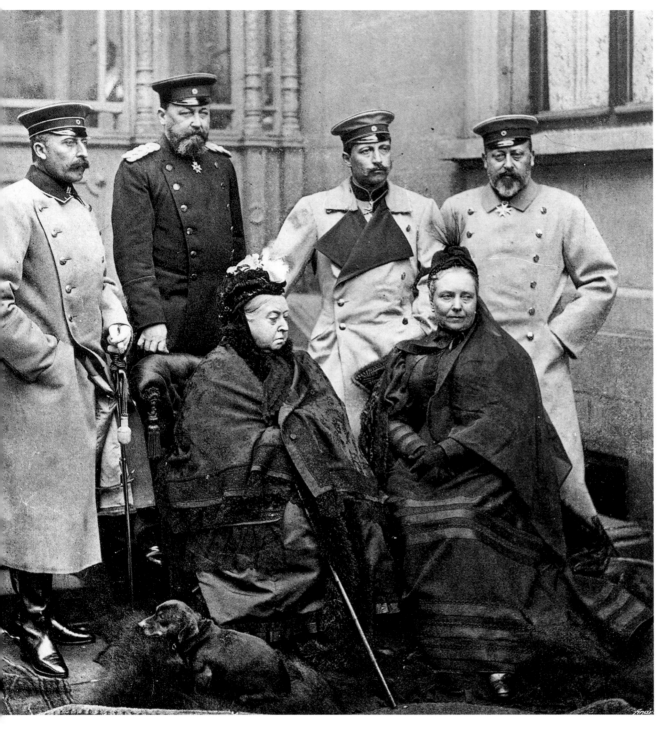

Family reunion. *Queen Victoria sits in Coburg with her eldest daughter Vicky, the Dowager Empress Friedrich in 1894 (left). Behind are the Empress's son, Wilhelm II (dark lapels), and the Queen's three surviving sons: Arthur, Duke of Connaught; Alfred, Duke of Edinburgh and now Herzog von Coburg; and Edward, Prince of Wales.*
[PHOTO: J. RUSSELL AND SONS]

After the battue *(opposite). The Kaiser, far right, and next to him, Nicholas II, Emperor of Russia, inspect the 'bag' at the end of a shoot in eastern Germany.*

One day in 1908, when a big political crisis broke in Berlin, Wilhelm had nothing to report except that he killed 162 red deer. His shortcomings would have been insignificant in a lesser man, but were fateful for the man who held the reins of power in Imperial Germany.

With all his irreconcilable qualities, however, the Kaiser was a man in whom large sections of the German élite recognized themselves, and this made him popular. He needed no script to act his various parts. A Prussian Guards' colonel even before puberty, a romantic beguiled by the most distant past and a technocrat in thrall to the far future, supreme war lord and eternal cadet rolled into one, he made his generals groan with his wish to see nothing but victory during manoeuvres, as if he did not understand the deadly seriousness of the colourful war

games. He loved the carefree tone of the regimental mess in Potsdam; sometimes he would act the pious Great Elector and sometimes the agnostic Fridericus Rex. Aboard the imperial yacht he had Viking songs recited to him. Some contemporaries were reminded of Caligula, others called him a monster.

Of Prussia, its external restrictions and domestic insecurity, His Majesty knew very little. He used Prussian history like a theatrical property room and, above all, as a picture book rich in scenes of martial boastfulness. He seemed not to understand Bismarck's warning that the German Reich must not act like the man who, having suddenly come into money, flashes it around and behaves loutishly. With his emotion and reason in irreconcilable conflict, Wilhelm II was a German nationalist of a common type. Pride in what had been achieved was allied to

fear that everything might be lost by standing still. The strangest of all his obsessions was his love-hatred of England.

In June 1889, a year after his succession to the throne, Queen Victoria granted her German grandson the honorary title of Admiral of the Fleet. The Kaiser was beside himself with joy. Herbert von Bismarck, State Secretary in the German foreign ministry, son of the Reich Chancellor, heard the Kaiser announce that he was now entitled to 'have a say in British naval affairs'. Young Bismarck records: 'I looked up in amazement, but H.M. had spoken quite seriously.' Old Bismarck had called him a 'complete Anglomaniac'. On the Isle of Wight the Kaiser personally commanded 1,200 German marines as they goose-stepped past the Queen and her entourage on the parade ground. 'Unworthy comedy', the

German officers muttered as they watched their supreme commander play soldiers. The Kaiser was a naive beginner in summit diplomacy and believed in simple solutions. If only the Prussian army and the British navy were sent in, order would be guaranteed around the world. Race and religion were to serve as the basis of a natural alliance.

Unrequited love turns to hatred, rejected admiration turns to destructive fury. In a regime governed by political interests rather than by emotions, temperamental urges would have played a lesser part. Things were different in Germany, given the economic rivalry with Britain, the international ambitions of the German élite and the notion that peace was best ensured by preparing for war. Moreover, the Kaiser held massive power, as the British ambassador had long warned: 'If we were dealing

Alfred von Bohlen und Halbach, *married to heiress Berta Krupp, shows off skills (opposite) as a cavalry officer in the reserve, already made obsolete by Krupp's products.*

The High-Seas Fleet *returns to Kiel (above) from exercises in 1909. Naval costs, 90 million marks in the 1890s, were up to 400 million marks. But the political cost was worse.*

with a country where foreign policy was conducted by the government and not by the sovereign,' he wrote, the personal feelings of the monarch would be 'a matter of slight importance, but this is not the case … His sentiments will count as an important factor in the policy he pursues towards us.' Nevertheless it took more than a decade before the conflict with Britain fully erupted. In 1892/93 Wilhelm II instructed the young naval officer Tirpitz to prepare the first draft of a new naval strategy and then entrusted him with the construction of a battle fleet to challenge the Royal Navy. In spite of the fact that since about 1880 new technical achievements – steel-hulled ships, torpedoes, fire-control equipment and long-range barrels – had opened a new maritime game with deadly stakes, this naval brinkmanship by a land power was being enacted in much the same flippant manner as boys and girls between Maas and Memel were then being put

into sailor suits. It seemed not to mean anything in particular.

Wilhelm had grown up as Crown Prince with the axiom of his mother, the Princess Royal, that anything English was always better than anything Prussian or German. It is hardly surprising therefore that he hated his mother, whose residence after his father's death he had ordered to be surrounded by troops, as an 'English colony'. The English doctors, he remarked, had not only killed his father, but they were also responsible for his crippled arm. The old Queen, he complained, treated him as a grandson rather than as the Kaiser, even though, when he felt in the mood, he described himself as her favourite grandson. When the Kaiser planned to visit Vienna he demanded that the Heir to the British Throne, who happened to be there, leave the city. Victoria reacted in her direct way and called this imperial presumption 'one of the greatest ignominies ever perpetrated', and Wilhelm's proposed visit to England was officially described as unwelcome. How all this fits in with the Kaiser's childish delight with his British admiral's uniform is a question for a psychiatrist.

There is no denying that at the turn of the century there was a realistic chance of an Anglo-German alliance – if the Kaiser's love-hatred had revealed its other side – when Britain stood desperately alone in the Boer War. But the German public was up in arms for the Boers, having long been manipulated into

Winston Churchill *and the Kaiser (left) at German Army manoeuvres in 1909. As President of the Board of Trade, Churchill was a member of the Liberal Cabinet, and in November that year he predicted to it that 'a period of great strain approaches in Germany. Will the tension be relieved by moderation or snapped by calculated violence?'*

King George V *(opposite) on a visit to the Kaiser in 1912. The King wears the uniform of the, Prussian Foot Guards, of which he is honorary colonel, while the Kaiser wears British uniform.*

profound hatred of 'perfidious Albion' by propaganda paid for by the Reich Naval Office.

When the *Entente cordiale* was established between Britain and France in 1904 – for the avoidance of colonial conflicts in North Africa, but soon serving to contain Germany – the opportunity for an arrangement was not yet lost. No matter how fiercely they were competing industrially, Germany and Britain still were each other's best customers, the City stood unchallenged as a financial centre, the trade links of the Empire remained intact, with the British navy supreme, both in equipment and operational experience. Nevertheless, Sir Eyre Crowe, Assistant Under Secretary in the British Foreign Office, penned one memorandum after another, warning Britain's leaders of Germany's ambitions and describing the containment of these as the British Empire's principal national interest. At the impressionistic, personal level British visitors to Germany were constantly amazed by militaristic and authoritarian manifestations they came up against. In Berlin in 1912 L.E. Jones took a tram ride when on a business trip. He did not speak German and when the conductor spoke to him could not understand what he was being told to do. The conductor

stopped the tram and ordered him off. Jones had paid his fare and stayed put. The driver joined in, then two policemen, who tried to remove him bodily, but he clung on.

'The policemen were little men; I was a big one; the struggle was unequal. They admitted defeat and left the car. Deserted by his allies, the conductor could do no more. The driver went back to his seat and we proceeded. Later, a German who spoke good English mounted the car. The story was told to him by the outraged passengers. He then explained to me that my legs were crossed, which was "verboten". I uncrossed them, and the incident was closed.'

In 1912 there was a major British offer of arms control, intellectually and politically far ahead of its time. This was presented by Lord Haldane, the pro-German Secretary for War, on a special mission to Berlin. Reich Chancellor Theobald von Bethmann Hollweg listened with rapt attention, the industrialist Walther Rathenau saw a future opportunity. But the Kaiser and Admiral Tirpitz indignantly rejected it, believing that German sovereignty would be compromised by the signature on any agreement imposing self-restraint. They probably also realized the difficulty of prescribing such a sobering process to a fleet-intoxicated nation. The increase in British 'Dreadnoughts' in 1908 had already marginalized large parts of the German battle fleet – glorified on the blue 100 mark notes of 1906 – especially as their coal-fired boilers severely restricted their radius compared to the British ships' oil-powered engines. Henceforward, the Germans placed their hopes on submarines.

Yet there was no inexorable fate at work: the Kaiser's moods were not all-powerful, the naval lobby was not invincible. In 1912/13, when the Balkan states confronted one another, it was chiefly the Germans and British who contained the fury of war, with an ambassadors' conference in London. At the same time there existed a tacit agreement between London and Berlin about the share-out of the Portuguese colonies in the event that Lisbon was unable to service its state loans. There was also agreement that the inheritance of the Ottoman empire was not worth a war between the great powers and that it was more important to keep the Russian navy out of the Dardanelles. The Germans were informally assigned the former Ottoman lands as a zone of influence, the British the sea.

Since 1905 the Schlieffen Plan had determined the German deployment in the event of a great war. It took its name from

the Prussian chief of the general staff, Count Alfred von Schlieffen, who had given instructions for it to be prepared in 1898. Until then the teaching of Moltke senior had been accepted – to avoid simultaneous war with Russia and with France at all costs, or at least to keep them separate as long as possible. The old field marshal had also realized that the well-equipped and highly mobile French army, intelligently led and probably reinforced by the British, would not be a walk-over. And finally he had believed that any strategic planning applied only as long as the first contact with the enemy; after that everything was 'a system of muddling through'.

Count Schlieffen saw the strategic situation differently; he believed Germany's prospects to be vastly better and the planning of war to have become much more of a technical challenge. He therefore based the defence of Germany upon a politically high-risk strategy, without any alternative. Schlieffen was obsessed with the idea of dealing the French a blow such as Hannibal had dealt the Romans at Cannae – but he overlooked the fact that ultimately the Romans had been the victors and not the Carthaginians, who lacked the strength-in-depth that would have allowed them to make the decisive advance on Rome.

The Schlieffen Plan envisaged holding a front from the ridge of the Vosges mountains to the Rhine valley, with a simultaneous vigorous sickle-cut through neutral Belgium and Luxemburg, and a final large-scale encirclement of Paris from the north-west. France was to be forced into rapid surrender before any British expeditionary force could deploy and before the Russian mass armies had time to thrust westward past Posen, cross the Oder and advance on Berlin. The German military machine would use the railways to wheel eastward after victory in the west and give the Russians a bloody welcome.

Clausewitz's warnings that in the fog of war no action can be executed according to plan, and that the craft of war must never be separated from the art of politics, were both ignored under the Wilhelmine regime. The Schlieffen Plan was an all-or-nothing gamble. It allowed of no alternative to the great war against east and west, whatever the source or the level of provocation. Disregard of Belgium's and Luxemburg's neutrality, although internationally guaranteed (including by Prussia), was bound to involve Britain as one of the guaranteeing powers, and certainly the guardian of the European equilibrium. But supposing the attack got stuck in the west, the sickle did not cut, the French army stood firm? It was characteristic of the authoritarian disorder in the German

More uniforms. *'Nicky', the Russian Emperor, and 'Willy', the Kaiser, in Berlin 1913 (right). As usual on such state occasions, they wear the uniforms of each other's countries.*

A peaceful scene: *a pleasure steamer on the Rhine (opposite) with a bridge of boats and Cologne Cathedral in the background. The second bridge with its twin towers, far right, carries the vital strategic railway to Belgium and France.*

leadership that the military commanders and the Reich Chancellor did not discuss such questions. Neither the Chancellor nor the State Secretary in the Foreign Ministry really knew what this strategic gamble was all about, nor did they insist on being told. As for the Kaiser, in whose hands all the reins should have come together, it was beyond him to comprehend the implications. When, in the last days of July 1914, he eventually understood what was happening and tried to change course, he was told by the chief of the General Staff that it was too late.

The *Entente cordiale* meanwhile was developing from a colonial standstill agreement into a grand European alliance between Britain and France. From 1907 onwards the Russians became full partners, having concluded a bilateral alliance with France in 1892/94. The French wanted revenge for 1870, to regain Alsace and Lorraine, and, in the event of conflict, not to have to face Germany alone; the Russians desired the break-up of the Hapsburg monarchy, whose last support was its alliance with Germany, so as to gain the Dardanelles and play the leading role in the Balkans. In 1911 talks began between Britain's Imperial General Staff and France's military leaders about transferring troops, and the allocation of battle zones, in the event of war with Germany. Asked how many British troops he needed, Marshal Joffre is reported to have replied: certainly one, and he would make sure that the Germans encountered him first.

On the German side there was concern that, as Italy sooner or later had to incline towards the powers controlling the Mediterranean – Britain and France – Austria was the only ally left, and a very wobbly one at that; in 1909 Moltke junior

therefore assured the chief of the Austrian General Staff that the Germans would go through thick and thin for their Austrian allies. This meant that Bismarck's warnings against unqualified support of Austria had been forgotten. The Austro-Hungarian generals were given a free hand to sever relations with Serbia or with Russia whenever they felt the old empire would benefit from a test of virility. A major crisis in the Balkans would inevitably drag the German Reich into the contest; in fact war was regarded as inevitable sooner or later.

A similar situation existed amongst the *Entente*. London and Paris feared that Russia might drift into the German camp – there was the meeting at Bjorko in 1906 of the Kaiser and the Tsar ('Willy' and 'Nicky') who swapped uniforms, toasted each other as 'Admiral of the Pacific' and 'Admiral of the Atlantic' and organised the world. So Britain and France granted the Russians more support than was perhaps advisable in the interests of European peace.

Ernst von Weizsäcker, one-time naval officer and subsequently State Secretary in the German Foreign Ministry under Ribbentrop, observed in his memoirs that in 1914 the war, 'came not from hardship, but rather from a surfeit of strength in the old continent.' A very dissimilar character, the Viennese Jew Stefan Zweig, one of the great writers of the century, came to a similar conclusion in his memoirs:

'If today one asks with calm deliberation why Europe went to war in 1914 one finds not a single sensible reason and not even an excuse. It was not about any ideas, it was scarcely about the small border regions; there is no other explanation than this surfeit of strength, as a tragic consequence of the inner dynamism which had accumulated over

forty years of peace and now had to discharge itself violently.'

Had the 'latecomer nation', as Ludwig Dehio called the Germans, not come too late for a global role? German naval ambitions certainly expressed the determination to gain 'our place in the sun', the threatening phrase of Bernhard von Bülow, the Foreign Minister, in the Reichstag in 1897. It was an ambitious bourgeoisie and the landless nobility who were behind this drive, not the old ruling families of Prussia, instinctively aware how easily the map of Europe could be imagined without Frederick the Great's state. Those conservatives also realised that Prussia had just about fitted into the continental scheme of things, but Germany perhaps did no longer.

The cracks in the political facade were, fundamentally, a manifestation of deeper fissures in lifestyle, culture and class structure at the turn of the century. The eruptions which, a generation later, disfigured the face of Weimar culture could already be felt in a less violent form about 1900. Fathers and sons did not share much of their experience, their illusions, and

their fears. 'Hitler's Vienna', to borrow the title of Elisabeth Hamann's vivid description, was certainly not the Vienna of the Hapsburgs and their court, or the Vienna of the Rothschilds and Sigmund Freud – and yet it was the same city at the same period. *Fin de siècle* weariness, decadence and the cult of violence, a dismal fear of the future and at the same time a firm belief in progress, were all part of an epoch that had long lost a sense of unity and an organising principle. The path of progress skirted the abyss.

The voice of the epoch was most clearly perceptible in art and literature, and perhaps the key events at the turn of the century were not described in the language of politicians, industrialists and military men at all, but in the idioms of artists, poets and scientists, of the theatre and architecture, by the groups of painters known as the *Sezession*, the Expressionists, the *Neue Sezession*, the *Blaue Reiter* [Blue Horseman], the *Brücke* [Bridge], and in experimental magazines such as the Munich

The Berliner Sezession *group of artists (left), founded in 1899 to get away from the academic tradition, consider a painting submitted for inclusion in one of their exhibitions: (left to right) Kurt Hermann, Oskar Frenzel, Walter Leistikow, and Max Liebermann.*

Lovis Corinth *in his studio (opposite). He was naturalistic rather than impressionist in his style, with a weakness for lush allegorical and religious subjects, until he had a stroke in 1911. Thereafter he became more expressionist in his technique.*

Jugend [Youth] which gave rise to the *Jugendstil*, the style called *art nouveau* elsewhere.

One painter whose work, as well as life, strikingly reflected this revolutionary period at the turn of the century, was Max Liebermann. His parents had moved to Berlin from West Prussia, entrepreneurs who owed their respected position to a combination of economic achievement and moral probity. They were assimilated Jews, typical both in the success of the symbiosis as in its failure. Liebermann died in 1935; his wife Martha had the misfortune to survive him and was driven to suicide in 1943. In his apprentice years Liebermann had made the acquaintance of Courbet and Millet in Paris, and his early pictures reflect the Barbizon School Later he turned, intellectually and in his painting, towards the Dutch artists of the Golden Age. His work around the turn of the century echoes the early impressionism of Manet and Degas. He painted bathers on the Baltic and scenes on the Wannsee, as well as portraits and flower-pieces. In his openness towards Holland and France, and in his fondness for everyday life at home, he searched for that authenticity which was so sadly absent from the official art of Imperial Germany, as displayed in city halls, regimental messes and annual academic exhibitions.

In 1899 the artists of the Berlin *Sezession* elected him their first President. He was then living right next to the Brandenburg Gate, in an elegant town house which, Thomas Mann recorded, was the focus and gathering point of good entertainment and strong characters. With his income from painting Liebermann purchased a villa on the Wannsee and delighted in convincing his sceptical parents that one could make one's way in life with brush and canvas. Liebermann was a *grand seigneur* of art, engaging in intellectual dialogue with the great figures of his day – artists, scientists and policy makers.

Had the revolution of sentiment begun with Richard Wagner's music drama that, up on the Bayreuth hill, tore wide open psychological worlds which might otherwise wisely have remained closed? 'It is better than it sounds', was Mark Twain's judgement on Wagner's music. But the enthusiasts making the pilgrimage to Bayreuth summer after summer were looking for more than the excitement afforded by the sound and the fury. Searching for one's soul or for the meaning of life was a stronger urge than mere aesthetic edification. The distant past, or what passed for it, as conjured up by the surf of miraculous music and strange words, merged with violent visions of the future. Wagner, the 1849-revolutionary from Dresden, and Ludwig II, the eccentric monarch from the Bavarian mountains, known locally as good king 'Wiggerl', formed a spiritual alliance manifested in smoke and mirrors. The audiences were given cues that they could not yet understand, but whose dark intimations intoxicated them. There is some irony in the fact that Wagner's suggestions of steamy eroticism found an academic echo a generation later in the Viennese psychologist Freud – the former an anti-Semite, the latter Jewish, and no Wagnerian.

No discovery of this epoch, fascinated and overburdened with discoveries as it was, has changed human beings more in their daily – and nightly – lives than that of sexuality. For many generations before, amorous adventures were for shepherds and shepherdesses, for gods and goddesses, for the rich and powerful. The ordinary man and the ordinary woman, on the other hand, were made to pay dearly if they transgressed the standards of a static society. A dramatic expression of sexuality was scarcely possible before the First World War. The paintings of Lovis Corinth, showing himself and his half-naked mistress, and the plays of Ibsen and Strindberg, were exciting exceptions. Divorce was made possible by secular laws and regulations, but was apt to result in social ostracism and material ruin. Meanwhile there were those small concessions to human nature, described by Thomas Mann in *Buddenbrooks*, where the Lübeck patrician Thomas Buddenbrook visits the suburbs for relief from the good-tempered affection of his angelically beautiful but rather cold wife, though at the price of an uneasy conscience.

There was a suspicion that if this most awesome of all barriers was breached all others would inevitably fall. Guilt and responsibility would merely be outdated formulas, cause and effect would blend into each other, heaven become indistinguishable from hell, and man, having eaten of the tree of knowledge, would be God and devil at the same time. There was also the dark warning of the Vienna psychologist that great cultural achievement only came with the continued suppression of the base instincts.

In physics Albert Einstein's theory of relativity was overthrowing the accepted laws of science, so beautifully confirmed by their industrial application, and Max Planck's quantum theory left it open whether the world was held together by waves or by matter. But what was all this compared to the discovery of the forbidden garden of human sexuality and the adjacent lands of brutal violence? All of a sudden the ambiguous message from ancient Greece found its true meaning once more: Mars and Venus, Aphrodite and Hephaistus, love and death, heaven and hell, beginning and end, the bed and the battlefield.

Three writers and a Muse:
Theodor Fontane (above far left), a witty observer in his novels of the crumbling of the old order; Lou Andreas-Salomé (above left), friend of Nietzsche, Freud and Rilke and an important voice for the rights of women; *Friedrich Nietzsche (above), rejecter of Christian morality and seeker after the blond beast; Rainer Maria Rilke (above right), a poet of deep sensibility who progressed from romanticism, through symbolism to a final mysticism.*

Who could withstand the radical contradiction between a rebellious inner world and a conventional external one? The hints of human desire and hence the memory of wild natural forces, and their revelation through the indiscreet inquisition of psychoanalysis, were threatening everything at the turn of the century. Freud's writings undermined the foundations of the entire system of norms governing guilt and responsibility.

One did not have to understand the expert literature and its incomprehensible technical jargon in order to sense what was at stake. There was a promise of liberation: no more suppression of nature and the darker desires, but rather emancipation from parents, from the past and from convention. 'Up to the mountains in the morning dew,' the *Jugendbewegung* (youth movement) followers sang to the guitar – young men with open-necked shirts and young women without prudishness, who at night leapt through the camp-fires together on the hilltops, promising one another that they would never be like the old ones down in the valley: a Jugendbewegung song that even made it to zionist Israel. Rainer Maria Rilke's *Kornett* became the cult book which united those in the know, the 'Song of love and death' including passionate and anonymous adultery on the eve of the ultimate battle in which the young officer meets his destiny.

Youth, until then nothing but a transitional phase automatically disposing of itself with time, now became a revolutionary, superior form of life; the 'Youth Movement' was intoxication without champagne, an elite devoted to gentle

Wandervogel. *Middle-class boys (left), 'wandering birds', seduced by the message of the Jugendbewegung, the Youth Movement, take a pause from their hikes through the hills to refuel on bread and butter. The guitars are the badge of membership of this movement for which the qualifications are youth and an educated background.*

revolution, whose members, whether young men or young women, recognized one another by an emphatic openness, willingness to lead, and idealism. For them the periodical *Jugend* was published in Munich, promoting the new organic style called *Jugendstil*. It bloomed everywhere from bodies to buildings and avoided all associations with the past – unless medieval book illumination was seen as an inspiration. It reflected the new spirit of spontaneity, rejection of history and permanent revolt. In Munich it was the beautiful Countess Franziska von Reventlow, from the top drawer of the German-Danish nobility, who celebrated the new age in the bohemian quarter of Schwabing. In Murnau in Upper Bavaria Wassily Kandinsky and Gabriele Münter were painting abstract pictures which nobody understood; it was only to earn a crust that they decorated the Murnau railway station, where the painting can be seen to this day. Franz Marc in nearby Kochel painted blue horses, even though everyone in the Bavarian mountains and throughout Germany knew that such animals did not exist.

Gustav Nagel *(1874-1952) (above) was an eco freak and hippie before his time, wandering through Germany preaching the simple life and the importance of being in tune with nature. He wore simple, monkish garb and sandals, when not barefoot, and lived in a cave in Brandenburg on a vegetarian diet. One of his campaigns was against the use of capital letters.*
[PHOTO: LOUIS HELD]

Was the world about to reinvent itself – or was it becoming a madhouse?

'During the 19th century, Germany experienced a population movement, a population redistribution, a migration of peoples compared to which the movements of past centuries, including those referred to as the age of migrations of nations, shrink to paltry events.' This is how Werner Sombart saw things in 1912, in his great conspectus *The German National Economy in the 19th Century*. People moved from east to west, from the countryside into the towns, from Germany to North America. The rise of the agricultural labourer to skilled industrial worker and mechanic in one or two generations, and then, in the second or third generation, to schoolmaster, pharmacist, or bank official, created a climate of confidence, self-assurance and hope. At the same time, there was a dark side. The epoch of growth and promise brought with it a loss of identity, disorientation and homelessness, a loss of tradition and of belonging. Every experience of and all advice from the fathers, was lost on the sons.

The family, formerly a comprehensive social organism with unmarried aunts and uncles, three or four generations living under one roof, with servants and apprentices, wet-nurse and general handyman, now shrank and became a private refuge.

Industrial paternalism *filled the gaps in Bismarck's state socialism. A worker's gym (below left) built by the House of Krupp in Essen for the use of their employees. The figures in the foreground are fencing with sabres. Housing in Essen (right) built specially for Krupp pensioners from the steelworks there.*

The great flight from the land in the 19th century resulted in each life becoming a quest and a venture. The sound and fury of political events were mere sideshows compared to this ever accelerating pulse-beat of a restless nation.

At the time of its foundation, there were some 41 million people living in the German Reich, including the annexed 'Reichsland' of Alsace and Lorraine. In 1913 the figure had risen to 68 million. To these should be added the lost army of emigrants: during the first 20 years of the Reich's existence an average of 100,000 young people went overseas every year. Until 1906 population growth still increased year by year. Each year almost a million more were born than died. In 1906/07 statistics recorded an industrial recession and, for the first time, a stabilisation of population growth: just as in the old days when the price of bread had determined the pace of marriage, procreation and birth, so it was now industrial employment which dictated acceleration or deceleration of the birth rate. During the last prewar years the population increase was still around 800,000 annually. After August 1914 the Grim Reaper had his harvest among the young men and during the lean war years marriages were deferred, millions of children never born.

People lived longer than their forebears, they were better

nourished, they lived cleaner and healthier lives. Infant and child mortality declined drastically. The number of illegitimate births also declined, probably the number of abortions too. This was due not to stricter morals, but to the fact that marriage was no longer controlled by guilds, magistrates or the rural economy. This swept away a great deal of personal misery and hardship.

Meanwhile, rural Germany was being drained of its population. Towns were filling up and industrial suburbs with their surrounding tenement blocks created a new pattern of life, as did garden suburbs such as Grunewald near Berlin or Grünwald near Munich with their convenient urban rail and tram connections with the city centre. After 1860, Ludwigshafen, a small riverport on the Rhine where BASF (*Badische Anilin-und-Sodafabrik*) became a powerful complex, grew into an industrial city in a few years. Berlin, for some generations the largest city in Germany, was the biggest industrial centre in Europe on the eve of the First World War, a hub of banking and of railway lines, with not far short of four million inhabitants.

In older capitals like Munich and Karlsruhe, the alliance of the princely dynasty and the administration for a while resisted the advent of major industries with their thousands of workers

– and their conspicuous ugliness. Industrial enterprise was promoted instead in Augsburg or Rastatt. But the turn of the century marked the end of most attempts to halt change. The aim then was to provide work, get industrialists to invest and find tax payers for the city coffers. Property sales on the edges of towns turned small tradesmen or modest farmers into wealthy men of independent means. Neighbouring villages and urban districts often bore the stamp of one single enterprise, and indeed a single product. In Dortmund and Gelsenkirchen it was coal, in Kassel locomotive construction, in Griesheim and Höchst near Frankfurt, just as in Leverkusen near Cologne or in Ludwigshafen, it was chemicals for fertilizers, dyestuffs and pharmaceuticals. Proximity to river or rail was a decisive advantage, as was proximity to the ever-hungry consumer centres. Thus entire landscapes were dug over – in the literal sense in the regions of lignite strip-mining on the Lower Rhine, on the Oder and near Halle.

Other landscapes, however, looked as though history had passed them by: Rothenburg ob der Tauber had, as it were, been touched by a magic wand and frozen to appear as it had at the end of the 18th century. The railway kept a good distance, people drifted away from the town, and tourism had

Outdoor Life. *The Krupp von Bohlen und Halbach family pose (top left) in front of their villa at Badenweiler near the Black Forest. A Berlin family (left) enjoy their allotment on the fringe of the city.*

Black Forest farmhouse *(above).*
Barn, stabling, cattle shed and
living quarters are all under one
large roof, part thatch, part
shingles.

Berlin *became the hub of Germany's transport and banking systems after unification, but before that it was already the largest industrial city on the Continent, a magnet* *drawing in people from the eastern provinces. At the turn of the century garden suburbs were developed in the west while large open spaces were reserved to link the parks and palaces of* *Potsdam and Berlin. Spreewald (above) was an area of backwaters, marshland, woods and canals enjoyed by Berliners at weekends, often as an accompaniment to hearty food.* *Grunewald (opposite) was another open space where the population of the capital could refresh itself among the woods in summer or winter: soon also a fashionable suburb.*

not yet been invented. It was a *cul de sac* of development. The same applied to Kronach in Franconia and to many ancient market and craftsmen's towns in south-west Germany. Strasbourg, in the Middle Ages the second largest town in the Holy Roman Empire after Cologne, despite the 'Reich university' set up there in 1871 and the renown this won, managed to preserve its historical charm at the expense of commercial vitality.

In the 19th century nothing changed the land and its people more than the railways – comparable to the change brought by the motor car after the Second World War. The old Germany was oriented around its rivers, but none of these was regularly navigable all the year round. Their channels changed, their water levels dropped in the summer, and ice-floes threatened shipping in the winter. The great canal projects were all directed at creating a network. At the turn of the century the most

important constructions were the *Mittellandkanal*, which linked the Rhine with the Oder, and the *Nord-Ostsee-Kanal*, which allowed rapid passage from the Baltic to the North Sea for cargo boats – and medium-sized warships. Canalization of the Neckar was backed and partially financed by Robert Bosch senior, but not until some time after the turn of the century. A canal link between the Rhine and the Danube was started by the Bavarian administration about 1900 but not accomplished until nearly the end of the 20th century.

The United States and the vast Russian empire only achieved political and economic unity through their railways in the second half of the 19th century. Matters were not as dramatic in Germany. But there was a reciprocal effect between the growth of industry, economic interests and technological communication by rail and telegraph, which created a new concept of space and time. The fact that the railway was laid in

The Nord-Ostsee-Kanal.
The ceremonial opening of this link (left) between the Baltic and the North Sea in 1895.
[PHOTO: M. ZIESLER]

Monorail overhead tram
(below) avoids non-existent traffic jams in Barmen-Elberfeld (Wuppertal), 1905: technology for its own sake.

such close proximity to Cologne Cathedral had nothing to do with a lack of piety but stemmed from the wish to link what was seen as the greatest work of the Middle Ages with the greatest work of modern times.

The 19th century, regardless of its anxieties, nightmares and troubles, was an age of great innovation driven largely by one great hope – that life had more to offer than in the past. People did not just move from the countryside into the towns out of hardship, but from a conviction that they would find a better life. In the 18th century, the pursuit of happiness had been the great leitmotif of the Enlightenment; in the 19th it became the small change of everyday life: freedom to conclude contracts, freedom to pursue a trade, freedom to move, freedom to marry, the opportunity to study, to be the architect of one's fortune, with the promise of prosperity through hard work. In this vision of happiness great and small lay the main force which, despite all the breathless haste, change and alienation, stabilized German society, gave it direction and objective, and legitimized the state and the social system as a whole. In exchange for hope and improvements, better wages, greater security, more warmth, and always having enough to eat, people were willing to accept a lot – the faceless tenements without trees or garden, the long walk or bicycle ride to the factory, fourth-class travel

'for travellers with loads', the discipline and not least the firm hand which directed it all. If people measured their situation against past experience, and not by visions of the future, the present was not so bad. It was this pragmatism based on a million small satisfactions, along with the craft rather than factory-derived tradition of their leaders, that shaped German social democracy – a 'party of resolutions' rather than the spearhead of revolutions (Erich Matthias).

The army, too, was an engine of change. Of course, there was no German army. Instead there were Prussian, Bavarian, Saxon, Württemberg troops. However, while retaining local allegiances, traditional regimental structures and family loyalties, they were all trained and organised by the Prussian *Grosser Generalstab* in Berlin under its legendary chief Count Moltke. The Berlin demi-gods, with their broad red stripes down the side of their breeches, set the standards of military training, of technology and of efficiency. The chief responsibility of any Minister of War, Prussian or Bavarian, was

First Footguards *on parade in Potsdam, 1896 (opposite). The boy is Crown Prince Wilhelm, eldest son of the Kaiser. After 1918 the successor to the Footguards would be the Infanterieregiment Neun, also known as 'Graf Neun'. No less than eighteen of its officers died for opposing Hitler.*
[PHOTO: SCHERL]

Sitting on the fence. *These boys, (right) in Werder near Düsseldorf in 1908, are enjoying a more normal childhood than the Crown Prince's, though they will be lucky to avoid death or maiming in the deadly years ahead.*

to shield the armed forces against any intrusion from outside, whether from the press or from parliament. While the size of the army was average by European standards, less than one percent of population, ever since the troubled days of 1848 it was seen as the last resort against parliamentary democracy. That is why conscripts served for three years though the simple manoeuvres they had to perform could easily be learned within a few months. That is also why the officer corps of every regiment was allowed to co-opt young men whom they found suitable and reject others for being too poor, too rich, of Jewish family background or left-wing convictions. That is also why the military budget – in the beginning up to 90 per cent of the state budget – was regularly set for five or seven years so as to preempt any undesirable parliamentary interference in the meantime. Young officers were poorly paid and therefore constantly in need of support from home, yet land-owning fathers preferred to send their younger sons into the army

rather than to university. To study economics, medicine or science would have caused a lot of raised eyebrows and needed much explaining. To find an educated aristocrat or even a mere 'von So-und-so' in a commercial or industrial profession was the exception – and sometimes followed by a demand from the authorities to retire from the register of nobility. However, agriculture-related trades such as brewing, schnaps-distilling, wine-making or even mining were acceptable, as was the law, since the country needed educated governors. The Prussian nobility, after heavily investing in joint stock companies and enjoying the fat growth rates of the 1860s, had found their fingers burned when bust followed boom in 1873. This had confirmed all their prejudices against *Börsenschwindel* (stock market fraud) and its promoters both Christian and Jewish.

The ruling elite of landowners, diplomats, senior ministerial officials and senior civil servants was derived from perhaps 5,000 families, connected by club, marriage and lifestyle, many

A steam hammer *(left) about to descend on a white-hot length of steel at the Borsig-Werke foundry in Berlin-Tegel.*

Robert Bosch *(right), by perfecting electrical technology for the fast-emerging motor-car, built up a huge industrial concern in and around Stuttgart. Politically liberal, he was a philanthropist who built hospitals, financed left-wing newspapers, and also protected Jews from the Nazis.*

of them aristocratic or with links into the nobility. (Of East Prussia it used to be said that only three families counted – the Lehndorffs for their beauty, the Dohnhoffs for their intelligence, the Dohnas for their simplicity.) They were local government *Präsidenten* or *Oberpräsidenten* and had, preferably, as young men served in the 1st Foot Guards Regiment, whose tradition was to be continued in the Weimar Republic by the 9th Infantry Regiment, the IR 9, nicknamed 'Count Nine'. But these commanding heights of society were not impossible to climb. Wealth could be acquired, a scholarly reputation could lead to the Prussian Upper House, and Jewish origin was no bar to access to the royal court. In 1866 Prussia, by absorbing Frankfurt, acquired its first Jewish baron, von Rothschild, and in 1868 Abraham von Oppenheim, the Cologne banker, was ennobled by the King of Prussia, as was his brother Simon by the Austrian emperor. Admittedly the fashionable regiments were slow to grant commissions to Jews, and much the same was true of the civil service. But generally speaking there is no doubt that the number of Jewish bankers, lawyers, scientists and physicians was increasing about the turn of the century – suggesting opportunities for promotion and acceptance rather than closed doors or innate distrust. There was no Dreyfus Affair in Germany.

A student of Imperial Germany focusing only on the old, largely land-owning elite, or those who had married into this elite, could easily overlook the many other roads open to those ascending the social ladder. Rarely was the rise from peasant boy to industrial patriarch accomplished in a single generation, as in the case of Robert Bosch; but over two or more generations such achievements were possible. Konrad Adenauer was the son of a Catholic Prussian non-commissioned officer, born in 1875, who studied law and married into patrician society, in 1916 becoming Lord Mayor of Cologne and in 1949 Federal Chancellor of Western Germany. Such a career was not the rule, but neither was it a rare exception, apart from the *pater patriae* role at the end. Theodor Mommsen, classical scholar and winner of the Nobel Prize for Literature, came from peasant stock, as did many others.

The expansion of the universities, and even more so that of the technical universities, provided opportunities for gifted young people. Technical occupations had been virtually non-existent in the first half of the century, or only as part of the armed forces, or the universities. Werner Siemens was a Prussian first lieutenant of artillery when he invented the telegraph, Reiniger a university mechanic in Erlangen when he applied electrical engineering to medical problems.

The Friedrich Wilhelm University in Berlin was regarded as the 'intellectual Guards regiment of the Hohenzollern'. This innocent mockery from the provinces was an acknowledgement that a professorial chair in Berlin carried more weight, standing and pay than one at any other university, not excluding Heidelberg. Mannheim and Nuremberg had ancient commercial colleges, where hard work was done but without much social distinction. The student fraternities represented a kind of secular monastic order, where the yardstick was not the mortification of the flesh but a man's singing and drinking capacity and his readiness, even for the sake of mere trifles, to hand out or accept a challenge to a duel – always assuming

A bus on tour *round Berlin and Potsdam (below) in front of the Café Bauer on a corner of Unter den Linden.*

The Bavarian royal family, *the Wittelsbachs (above), on an outing in 1908 near the Schliersee, one of the lakes in the Bavarian Alps. The onion-domed church tower, balconies and overhanging eaves are typical of the region.*

that the other party was in a position 'to give satisfaction'.

There were about a thousand private banks in Germany, though few of the standing or reputation of Sal. Oppenheim Jr. & Cie in Cologne, Arnhold in Dresden, Warburg and Heine in Hamburg, or Bethmann in Frankfurt. There had also been, since the middle of the 19th century, the people's banks and *Raiffeisen* banks, organised as cooperatives deeply rooted in rural lower-middle-class Germany. Since 1860, however, the most vigorous element in the financial markets was the great power houses of the joint-stock banks – above all Deutsche Bank, Disconto-Gesellschaft, Dresdner Bank, Commerzbank, Nationalbank and Darmstädter Bank. These and the big insurance companies needed a new class of qualified staff with sophisticated and specialised technological and administrative skills.

Germany at the turn of the century meant not one society, but several. The Berlin court was the most elegant, but it was not the only one that counted. To be seen at court, whether Munich or Dresden or Karlsruhe or Stuttgart, not to mention lesser centres like Weimar or Meiningen, both great cultural magnets, ensured social status. For the banker it was proof of his standing, for the officer it implied eligibility for higher rank. But the pomp and circumstance did not greatly impress the Hanseatic cities and their patrician leaders. The southern German princes, from the Wettins in Saxony to the Wittelsbachs in Bavaria, jealously guarded their rights and rank. The only exception was the court in Karlsruhe, traditionally linked with Prussia politically and by marriage. Bavaria, Württemberg, Saxony and Baden had their own armies and diplomatic corps, as well as their own postage stamps and coinage. It was only through the great equalizer, the Great War, that old-fashioned German federalism, with all the princes and free cities, was swept away and a genuinely unified state was called into being. Even then, Germans still bore a marked regional or even tribal stamp. The political centre might be Berlin, but culturally and economically the provinces were just as proud and important.

French soldiers *among corpses killed by shelling in the middle of the war, June 1916. In August 1914 the flower of the French Army had flung itself at the German fortifications in the Ardennes, suffering its heaviest casualties of the war, worse even than at Verdun. As the French forces reeled back at least it allowed Joffre, the French Commander, to redeploy enough of them eastwards to stop the German offensive at the Marne. With each side's initial thrusts contained, trench warfare could begin.*

CHAPTER THREE

THE BLOODBATH

Gᴇɴᴇʀᴀʟ ᴅᴇ Gᴀᴜʟʟᴇ, ʟᴇᴀᴅᴇʀ ᴏꜰ ᴛʜᴇ Fʀᴇᴇ Fʀᴇɴᴄʜ, in his London exile in 1944, spoke gloomily of the 'Thirty Years' War of our century'. It was indeed a European civil war on a world stage, in the end decided by the United States of America. But perhaps it is more accurate to compare those three decades to the age of the French Revolution and the Napoleonic wars. Not only the empires of the Ottomans, the Romanovs, the Hohenzollerns and the Hapsburgs collapsed, but also ancient social hierarchies, the gold standard, belief in progress and a liberal world order. It was as though European culture, which through competition and nervous energy had conquered the globe, now had only one task left – that of its own destruction.

Yet before the shots fired at the heir to the Austro-Hungarian crowns in Sarajevo echoed around the world, there had been no shortage of warning voices. Walther Rathenau, industrialist and outstanding writer, head of the AEG company founded by his father Emil Rathenau, was not only fascinated by the dynamism of modern industry, as it far outpaced the nation state, but also foresaw the danger that the modern industrial Behemoths, driven by ancient passions and run by traditional elites, might clash in battle. He had an unparalleled ability to understand political and economic interdependence and to take the long view. Engineer, chemist and banker that he was, he had learned to think in terms of interlocking systems. He saw in the future 'a single indivisible economic community'; he wanted to create synergies and release them through superior organization. Nation states, formed through history, did not fit into this strategem – though Rathenau expressed his insights with restraint or disguised them behind the goal of Germany's economic hegemony over Europe. He was concerned not with monopolies or profits, but with efficiency, synergy and full utilization of capacity.

In 1912, he drafted core elements of arms control, arms quotas, budget limitations, supervision by an international court of accounts, and regulation of troop strengths in accordance with population figures: what in modern terms would be called confidence- and security-building measures. Politically Rathenau was aiming to keep Britain neutral, to enhance interdependence, and thus to deactivate the looming Franco-Russian coalition. But there was more behind this – the idea that the power and weight of a country was based not on armaments, but on economic and moral potential. No means to that end was more important than the integration of Europe's industries, and Rathenau therefore drafted a plan for an economic merger among central and west European countries at the end of 1913: *Mitteleuropa*.

In 1914 Dr Kurt Riezler, a close adviser of Reich Chancellor Bethmann Hollweg, published an essay which concluded that both the facts of economic integration and the horrors of modern warfare would contribute to permanent 'postponement of warlike conflicts'. At the same time Bethmann Hollweg spoke out against any frivolous gamble involving war. He had seen the Haldane mission of 1912 fail in the face of the Kaiser's arrogance. Under no circumstances must 'a war be provoked unless our honour and our vital interests are infringed.' Anything else would be a 'sin against German history ... even if, according to all human judgement, we might expect total victory.'

A little later, sensing the crisis to come in 1914, Bethmann Hollweg warned against what loose talk about a lightning war and easy victory would lead to: 'In no case has Germany's honour and dignity been infringed by another nation. Anyone wishing to wage war without such a cause must identify vital national tasks that cannot be fulfilled by means other than war.' Bismarck had waged war for precisely such objectives. After that, however, preservation of peace had become his supreme goal. Bethmann went on: only 'total lack of political judgement' or 'ill will' could allow anyone to call on Bismarck as a witness in favour of lightheartedly going to war. 'In any future war undertaken without compelling cause not only is the Hohenzollern crown at stake, but also the future of Germany.'

Nations and governments were caught in a vicious circle: as alliances tightened their grip, the scope for diplomacy was diminishing; as armament costs rose the questions became when, not if, the war would come, and how one could secure the best initial advantage. In 1912 Wilhelm II learnt of the British intention that in a future war Britain would from the very beginning stand by France, so he summoned his advisors. For such an alliance, anchored in the *Entente Cordiale* of 1904 and in the two countries' agreements with Russia, there could be but one adversary – Germany. Seen from London the *Entente Cordiale* was a deterrent; from Berlin it looked like a pincer movement and a vast strategy to undo the Reich at the heart of Europe.

The Kaiser either forgot to summon the Reich Chancellor and the Foreign Minister to Potsdam or, so as to avoid their 'if and when', did not wish to have them present. Tirpitz was there; Moltke junior, chief of the general staff; Admiral von Müller, head of the naval cabinet; and Vice-Admiral von Heeringen. The Kaiser pronounced his view that Austria, in order to remain a great power, must 'put its foot down'. As Russia would support the Orthodox Serbs against the Hapsburg armies, war was now 'inevitable'. The Austrians should fight against Russia, Germany 'with all its force against France ... and the navy, naturally, must get ready for war against England.' The chief of the general staff supported the Kaiser: he considered war unavoidable, 'and the sooner the better'; however, war against Russia would first have to be made popular. The navy was more reluctant; Tirpitz spoke in

Field Marshal von Hindenburg *(opposite), who had been on guard as a young lieutenant at Versailles when the German Empire came into being there in 1871, presided at the end of his life over Hitler's seizure of power. His military reputation was established by his defence of eastern Germany against Russia in 1914.*

Admiral von Tirpitz *(right). He might have been a non-political technocrat, but he was also instrumental in the creation of the German battle fleet, so must take much of the blame for the growth of distrust between Germany and Britain prior to 1914.*

[PHOTO: E. BIEBER]

81

favour of 'delaying the great struggle by a year and a half.' Moltke took the view that Germany was getting 'into a progressively unfavourable situation because our opponents are arming more vigorously than we.'

Was this, as some historians believe, in effect the master plan for war? Was this improvised meeting, confirming long-standing plans for an emergency, a 'war council'? In reality it was inconsequential and was followed neither by a propaganda campaign nor by economic mobilization. As to withdrawing gold coins in circulation for the purpose of financing a war, the Banque de France was years ahead of the Reichsbank. 'The outcome was more or less zero,' was Admiral von Müller's sober summing up when he asked himself what had been achieved.

The German Navy manoeuvres *in 1911 in the 'German Ocean', the North Sea, watched by the Kaiser, who is on the ship's bridge in the foreground (above). The construction of the fleet meant plenty of work for firms like Krupp (left), in which the Kaiser had a large shareholding.*

In the Balkans in 1913, German-British crisis management worked as it had often done before. Why not again? The reason was that the Balkan war of 1912/13 was yet one more blow to the prestige and viability of Austria-Hungary, Germany's last ally of any importance. Colonel Ludendorff, a technocrat and the chief planner in the German General Staff, demanded an immediate increase in the army's strength of 300,000 men. The defence associations, generously funded by industry, called for a major effort. Bismarck had concluded the alliance with Vienna (the 'Zweibund') in 1879 to bolster Austrian morale and secure an ally against Russia, but he was loth to extend the strictly defensive character of the alliance in case it encouraged Austrian brinkmanship. Three decades later all that seemed to matter was to extend the lifespan of the Austrian monarchy, to allow the Austrian generals an easy triumph somewhere in the Balkans, and if necessary to wage the Great War. As for the alternative – to call a European congress to keep the peace, control armaments and secure open markets – it was one century too late or half a century too soon.

Thus Germany's existence, without any alternative even being considered, under a leadership no longer adequate to the task, was chained to Austria-Hungary. This ancient empire seemed to most of its nations – wrongly, as they were to realize two world wars later – a great prison, but to the Russians and their Serb protégés it was simply an obstacle to Slav greatness. Decline and decadence were perceptible everywhere – a kind of collective death wish and noble rot which Arthur Schnitzler portrayed in his day, and Robert Musil, in his *Man Without Qualities*, in retrospect.

The great *renversement des alliances*, Berlin's dream of moving with the British Empire against the Euro-Asian landmass of Russia, had long been blocked by German naval construction. Therefore nothing remained but the fatalistic gamble on the Great War, not for the sake of specific aims, to gain territory or economic wealth, but for Germany to break out of its geostrategic prison in the centre of Europe, before it was too late. If this was a rationale for preventive action, it was born of fear and weakness, of the rejection by the military state of its decline, and in the hope of rediscovering in war the nation's magic unity lost in peace.

Schon im Auto zur Todesfahrt

Graf Harrach steht zum Schutze auf dem Trittbrette

W.TAUSCH, SARAJEVO. 1914.

After the fatal shots in Sarajevo on 28 June 1914, all the actors seemed to be driven by forces beyond their control – in Berlin, in Vienna, in St Petersburg, in London and in Paris. Anyway, what did the great powers have to do with the bloody deed in a god-forsaken Balkan city? In the strict sense nothing, but by the standards of the time, everything. Austria-Hungary's role in Europe, indeed the existence of the Danubian monarchy, were at stake. Tsarism, on the other hand, was doomed if it let down the Slav brethren in the Balkans, threatened by Austrian revenge. Tsar Nicholas II dared not resist the pressure from the public, the military and the Pan-Slav press. If the German leaders in Berlin were now to issue a stern warning, Bismarck-like, and restrain Vienna, then her alliances with Austria as well as Germany's entire future standing would be in jeopardy. France was focusing on her alliances that one government after the other had cultivated since 1890, while the British had forgotten how to think and to act in terms of European equilibrium. Indeed, on all sides there was a fatal contraction in thinking about the war. It was about to become feasible because it seemed inevitable – while, at the same time, its grim reality remained utterly unimaginable.

Once the harvest was in from the fields in the last days of July, the Great War became inescapable, as the Russian mobilisation began its inexorable progress. At the beginning of July, the Austrians had received the Germans' 'blank cheque', which made them feel under an obligation to put on a show of strength. However, Austria-Hungary's mode of government was much too complicated to deliver a lightning strike, the corridors

Sarajevo, *28 June, 1914. Austrian Archduke Franz Ferdinand and his wife have just got into the car to drive through the streets of the Bosnian capital (above). They will die at the hands of a Serbian assassin not many minutes later, thus setting in train the outbreak of war.*

A troop train *(right) with an optimistic slogan – Paris & back – chalked on its side. The whole Schlieffen Plan was geared to the railways, but when the Belgians put theirs out of action it inflicted an unforeseen yet crucial delay on the German advance.*

of power too long, resolve too scarce a commodity. Valuable time was lost, and once the Russian steamroller had got into motion it was too late for a surgical operation.

Bethmann Hollweg suspected that all the meticulous calculations of the Schlieffen Plan were of little use. After the first step, the rest was bound to be 'a leap in the dark', he said on 14 July 1914. The French ambassador to the court at St Petersburg, Jules Cambon, spoke of his country dragged along on the road to disaster: '*Et la France, victime de son alliance, suivra le destin de son allié sur le champ de bataille.*'

Rarely has so much clairvoyance been coupled with so much futility as in the final days of July 1914. Wilhelm II, suddenly scared at the horrid thought of real war, wanted to give orders for deployment solely towards the east. However, his military leaders informed him that there no longer existed a plan for such a move, and that the war had to be fought, come what

may, on two fronts. Meanwhile, crowds were dancing on the boulevards. The departing soldiers were garlanded with flowers like the sacrificial oxen of antiquity. A few weeks later they were floundering in the blood-soaked fields of Flanders and the swamps of Galicia.

For the German high command success depended on seizing and keeping the strategic initiative. This meant a massive thrust westward. But the attack did not have sufficient strength in depth, and serious mistakes were made by the commanders. The French divisions deployed forward were defeated but not annihilated. While taxis were ferrying the last available troops from inner Paris to the defences east of the capital, the first German patrols arrived at the Marne. What for the French became the miracle on the Marne, was for the Germans the beginning of the end. The strategic initiative was lost forever. The war, having started so furiously, after less than six weeks went into the trenches, where rain, cold and vermin plagued the troops just as much as the ever-lurking snipers or the artillery barrages which preceded every infantry assault. The machine-guns tore the attacking troops to ribbons and turned the heroic charge of earlier days into a macabre dance of death.

With cavalry rendered obsolete except in the east, lending new thrust to massive infantry charges became the key tactical

August sunlight *falls on soldiers (right) as they march to entrain for the front, decked with flowers, flattered by the attentions of the womenfolk and with the only fear for most that the fighting might be all over before they get there. It falls too on the children watching an artistic soldier (above) seizing a quiet moment to do a sketch.*
[PHOTO, ABOVE: EUGEN HEILIG]

Uhlans, *German cavalry, make a fine show (opposite top), but many of the officers will soon switch to flying, once they realise how useless they are on horseback.*

A small field piece *and its limber are manhandled by troops wearing the model of helmet introduced later in the war (opposite below).*

German trenches *(above) were reckoned much better than Allied ones. Here, one in the Argonne is being repaired in November 1915.*

problem for commanders. Concentrated artillery fire, gas, and ultimately tanks were answers developed in the course of the war. The Second World War in the European theatre would be characterized by the aggressive combination of armour and airforce, but in the First World War defence was vastly superior to attack. However, there were unimaginable losses in the trenches and fortifications as well as in no man's land, as artillery pounded the concrete and the defenders burrowed into mud and soil. More ammunition and men were consumed than any planner could have imagined. Medical services collapsed in many places. Losses through typhoid and dysentery were heavy, influenza resulted in mass deaths.

'Back home when the leaves fall', the Kaiser in his military innocence had called out to the departing troops. In East Prussia, in the battles of Tannenberg and on the Masurian Lakes, the Russian masses had been halted and defeated – thereafter, Hindenburg and Ludendorff were regarded as saviours of the country. But the German leaders had to admit to themselves in November 1914 that the strategic initiative had been lost, that France had not been defeated, that the Austrians were in mortal danger in Galicia, and that ammunition supplies were dramatically inadequate.

Two deeply entrenched front lines extended from the coast of Flanders to the Swiss frontier, sometimes approaching each other to within range of a thrown hand grenade, protected by mines and barbed wire. And behind the trenches, as though the chaos had some hidden order, were the long rows of crosses above the bodies of young men pierced by bullets or bayonets, torn by shrapnel, tortured by tetanus, or choked by gas.

In the east, the badly mauled Austrians soon showed signs of disintegrating and had to be beefed up by German divisions. As the main thrust of the German effort continued to be in the west, distrust of the German ally began to grow in Vienna. Without a joint supreme command, without significant strategic or diplomatic coordination, the alliance revealed all the weaknesses of coalition warfare. Matters were not much better between Paris and London on one side and St Petersburg on the other. Military and political objectives were at cross purposes. The German relief offensives towards the Carpathian mountains became bogged down. The Russians were weak in attack, but strong in defence. So in the east, too, an equilibrium of deadly exhaustion emerged at the turn of 1914/15.

If the politicians had been strong and sensible enough, they would have sent out peace feelers. But they were not. Hate propaganda would have had to turn into a dialogue of reason overnight, but military and political leaders would also have

Early victims. *French refugees from the battlefields find shelter in a Catholic church under the eye of German guards in the first weeks of the war.*

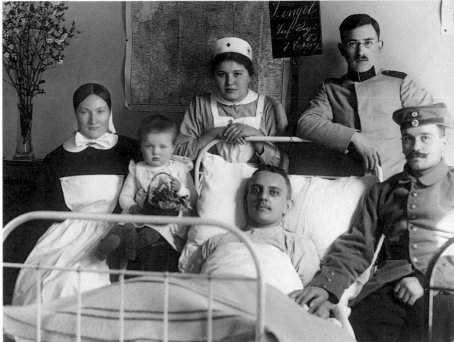

Over the top, *(left) the most vulnerable moment, out of the shelter of the trenches. After the smoke of preliminary artillery bombardment troops were fodder for relentless machine-gun fire as they struggled through barbed wire.*

A wounded man *(above) has reached a hospital back home, only to die three days after this picture was taken.*

had to explain why such a vast disaster had been unleashed so irresponsibly and so inconclusively. That would have sparked unrest, crisis and revolution. The war was continued out of material strength and political weakness. There were good grounds, therefore, why all efforts were directed at extending the war and gaining new allies. In the end the Entente powers proved greatly superior to the Central Powers on both counts. Despite the previously unimaginable losses, the material hardships and the technical bottlenecks, the war was kept going for years and years. This was due to the resilience of the industrial countries, their age-old social discipline, the trusting belief of the people, the charisma of leaders and the vast adaptability and capability deployed in mobilizing all forces.

General von Clausewitz' classic teaching *On War* (1831) had warned against 'absolute war' and insisted that the craft of war be never detached from the art of diplomacy. Ludendorff, by contrast, in his book *Total War*, demanded that war and its requirements be supreme over any civilian considerations. His war would end in triumph or disaster; there was no other way.

German industry was soon short of nitrogen, previously imported as saltpetre from Latin America. Without the Haber-Bosch process for obtaining nitrogen from air, implemented as soon as it had been invented, the German armies would have run out of ammunition by the end of 1914. Walther Rathenau became the organizer of Germany's war economy. The first day of the war saw the end of Germany as a constitutional monarchy with all its checks and balances. What followed was economic and military dictatorship by the Supreme Command, based on hope of victory and fear of defeat. The Reichstag voted itself almost out of existence, granting itself a long recess, and some of the younger members went to the front; many, including SPD deputy Bruno Frank, were killed in action for the Fatherland. It would have been better if parliament, instead of just giving up and ritually approving the war loans, had compelled the government and the military leaders to accept a political pact – a say in decision-making in exchange for shared responsibility. But the myth of the military was too great, respect for the demi-gods of war was boundless and the politicians full of self-doubt, only too ready to off-load responsibility. The German Reichstag admitted that it existed

An early sacrifice. *A body awaits burial at Ypres (left) in 1914. As the war went on coffins were to become increasingly rare.*
[PHOTO: EUGEN HEILIG]

Behind the front line. *Troops are redeployed (above) in May 1916 at the Chemin des Dames ridge north of the river Aisne, between Reims and Laon, one of the great bloodbaths of the war.*

only for the marginal, at best for the normal, but certainly not for the extreme.

Politics were paralyzed, diplomacy was silent, the total mobilization of forces producing its own ideological furore. Four hundred professors at German universities voted for a rabid renunciation of the West, dictated by hatred, disappointed love and blind enthusiasm for the war; they extolled German high-mindedness over western shallowness,

idealism over materialism, and accused the 'age-old enemy' France and 'perfidious Albion' of allying themselves with Russian barbarism. The vague war aims of the two sides were not the cause of war, they merely fostered it: on the one side the vision of Central Europe under German control, economically self-sufficient and militarily unassailable, on the other the vision of a vastly different map of Europe, with Germany carved up as in centuries past. The finances of the war, too, were based upon

victory – in Germany war loans were contracted one after the other, which could not otherwise be redeemed; on the side of the Entente loans came from US banks, to be paid for by Germany on the day of victory. Victory meant the moral and material destruction of the enemy, yet this same enemy was expected to pay up. Had the consequences of the American Civil War been forgotten, when the South needed two generations of retrenchment and reform to recover?

Both Entente and Central Powers ceaselessly sought new means of war and new allies. Turkey entered the war on the side of the Central Powers before the end of 1914: Serbia was quickly occupied, supplies and troops were moved to the south-east, German commanders and instructors reinforced the Turkish troops ill prepared for a modern technological war. Winston Churchill, First Lord of the Admiralty, hoped to break the deadlock on the Western front by a landing on the Gallipoli peninsula, the key to the Dardanelles, and a rapid advance on Istanbul, taking Turkey out of the war and opening a sea link to Russia. The plan was too bold; French, British and ANZAC forces were mown down by Turkish defensive fire directed by German reinforcements.

Meanwhile the Entente gained Japan as a distant ally. More important was the fact that Italy in 1915 entered the war against its old central European partners. Large sums changed hands, annexation of the Tyrol and dominance in the Mediterranean were promised. But the Italians paid for it with colossal losses on the mountain front and in many Isonzo battles.

The coal-fired German battle fleet lacked the range for bursting open the paralyzing British blockade in the Atlantic. A half-hearted attempt was made to seek a confrontation in coastal waters, but the Battle of Jutland denied victory to either side. The lesson the British learned was that waiting and

A bow on her tunic, *a defiant feminine touch by one munitions worker in a Krupp plant in Essen (above). Total war brought with it the direction of capital and labour from above, by the state. Its demands, not moral principles, won women a way out of their homes, even if only into a factory.*

The ladies of Munich *(right) set to in the first months of the war sewing undergarments for the wounded in the Bavarian royal family's palace – the Residenz – in the centre of the city, surrounded by wall paintings of stirring moments from Bavarian history.*

blockading were more useful than costly engagements, and to hell with heroism. The Germans next staked everything on the U-boat war, which aimed at disrupting supplies for Britain's economy and undermining British morale. But this never succeeded in sweeping the convoys from the Atlantic, while it soon amounted to an informal declaration of war on the United States, an open-ended strategic gamble. The German military leaders persuaded themselves that the Americans would be incapable of projecting power across the watery wastes of the Atlantic and that, anyway, troops from the New World would arrive too late to deny the German armies their certain victory. From now on the war over the future of Europe became a global affair.

In 1916 the German High Command had brought in the 'Auxiliary Service for the Fatherland' law, mobilizing men and women and all available material for the war effort. As compensation the military granted the trade unions co-determination through works councils. Both from the military and the trade union viewpoint this was an attack on the liberal economy of the 19th century. 'The proper mean between military dictatorship and social democracy' is how General von Seeckt characterized and idealized the bargain. (During the Weimar period he was to be chief of the *Reichswehr*, Germany's elite postwar army.) There was no answer to the only question which more and more occupied the public – how to get out of the war. It needed a shock from outside to unblock the impasse.

When the horrors of the Western front and the privations of the Home Front are remembered, it is easy to see why this one question predominated. Karl Gorzel, a law student from Breslau, serving on the Somme, wrote home in October 1916 about what was, on the face of it, the successful repulse of a British attack, what he called the 'horrible affair at Thiepval':

'Suddenly the barrage lifts ... and there, close in front, is the first wave of the enemy! Release at least! Everyone who is not wounded, everyone who can raise an arm, is up, and like a shower of hailstones our bombs pelt upon the attacking foe! The first wave lies prone in front of our holes, and already the second is upon us, and behind the English are coming on in a dense mass. Anyone who reaches our line is at once polished off in a hand-to-hand bayonet fight, and now our bombs fly with redoubled force into the enemy's ranks. They do their gruesome work there, and like ripe ears of corn before the reaper the English attacking columns fall. Only a few escape in full flight back through the bayoux (communication trenches). We sink down, dazed, upon the tortured earth, and tie up the wounded as well as we can, while awaiting the coming of a second attack or of the night ... I light a cigarette and try to think – to think of our dead and wounded; of the sufferings of humanity; to think back to – home! But away with such thoughts! The present demands its rights – it requires a real man, not a dreamer...Reinforcements arrive, things are cleared up and the dead buried, and a new day breaks, more horrible than the last!

Such is the battle of the Somme – Germany's bloody struggle for victory. This week represents the utmost limits of human endurance – it was hell!'

Gefreiter Fritz Heinemann of the 165 Infanterie Regiment suffered if anything an even worse nightmare when his position was overrun by the British in the same offensive, and he and a few others took refuge in a dugout. A shell then exploded, blocking the entrance, and entombing them.

'The man who was wounded twice was the only one among us who could speak English well. He had not lost consciousness so we moved him to the dugout's blocked entrance. Then we began banging on the steps, hoping someone would hear the noise and investigate. Suddenly we heard faint English voices. It was difficult at first for him to shout and hear through the earthen barrier, but he made those on the other side understand that we were completely exhausted and could not dig out by ourselves. With that we heard the sound of shovels hacking away at the ground. Thinking of the fresh air outside, I was flushed with newfound strength and tore at the earth with my hands. In the meantime, Leutnant Liebau collected letters and other papers from the men and ripped them into small pieces. At last, a plate-sized hole was punched through the entrance, letting in light and flooding the dugout with air. Soon the hole was enlarged sufficiently for each of us to crawl out, one after the other. Two soldiers wearing khaki stood waiting with their rifles levelled. Several of our men ignored the weapons upon seeing some grass growing from the wall of the trench. They ripped clumps out and immediately stuffed as much as possible into their mouths. Watching this, one of the enemy soldiers removed his water bottle and passed it around. I will never forget this gesture as long as I live.'

Civilians did not face hand-to-hand fighting or being buried alive, but they came close to starvation in the 'turnip-winter' of 1916-1917. Grain and potatoes were increasingly scarce and the only substitutes were turnips. These too were rationed, with the weekly allowance in Berlin down to between two and six pounds (or two pounds of bread if it was available), less than two ounces of butter and an ounce of margarine. By the summer of 1917, 837 nonmeat substitutes for sausage and salami had been patented.

In response to the revolution of February 1917 in Russia, Wilhelm II promised in his 'Easter Message' far reaching domestic reforms for Prussia and Germany, while he was careful not to alienate the Conservatives or the military by providing detail. The tacit presumption was that the greater the victory, the less democracy and parliamentary control would have to be conceded. One of the items high on the reform agenda was Prussia's 'three-class electoral law' introduced in 1849, which weighted votes according to tax revenue and thus rendered lower-class representation virtually impossible.

In the summer of 1917 the Reichstag, in view of gloomy news from the Austrian front and from the U-boat campaign, all of a sudden asserted its weight. A centre-left majority, the future constitutional base of the Weimar Republic, put together a 'peace resolution' demanding an early end to the war 'without annexations and reparations'. This was to furnish the government of Chancellor von Bethmann Hollweg with a mandate for peace feelers and, perhaps, negotiations. It also reinforced the conviction in Germany that the war, thrust upon the nation, was a just cause. But the government was more and more subservient to the Military High Command under Hindenburg and Ludendorff. The Chancellor had to resign, the military made sure that the parliamentary initiatives led nowhere in particular, and the Reichstag resolution remained a dead letter. For young men like Gerhard Gürtler, a theology student from Breslau fighting in the early stages of the Third Battle of Ypres – Passchendaele – this was a sentence of death. He wrote home on August 10, 1917, four days before he was killed:

'Nothing is so trying as continuous, terrific barrage such as we experienced in this battle, especially the intense English fire during my second night at the front ... Darkness alternates with light bright as day. The earth trembles and shakes like a jelly ... And those men who are still in the front line hear nothing but drum-fire, the groaning of wounded comrades, the screaming of fallen horses, the wild beating of their own hearts, hour after hour, night after night. Even during the short respite granted them their exhausted brains are haunted in the weird stillness by recollections of unlimited suffering. They have no way of escape, nothing is left them but ghastly memories and resigned anticipation ..."Haven't you got a bullet for me, Comrades?" cried a Corporal who had one leg torn off and one arm shattered by a shell – we could do nothing for him ...The battle-field is really nothing but a vast cemetery.'

There were few who could find any redeeming features among all this, but one of them, Ernst Jünger, the archetypal storm trooper, wrote of his experiences. *Storm of Steel* became something of a bible to the Right in Germany after the war.

'Chivalry here took a final farewell. It had to yield to the heightened intensity of war, just as all fine and personal feeling has to yield when machinery gets the upper hand. The Europe of today appeared here for the first time on the field of battle. [It] seemed that man on this landscape he had himself created, became different, more mysterious and hardy and callous than in any previous battle ... After this battle [the Somme] the German soldier wore the steel helmet, and in his features there were chiselled the lines of energy stretched to the utmost pitch,

New weapons of destruction *confront each other in the closing months of the war. A British tank is attacked by a German flame thrower team. The circular container for the latter's fuel can be seen on the back of one of the soldiers. Tanks were first used effectively in November 1917 at Cambrai when 381 advanced five miles and punched a hole four miles wide in the German line. But no-one knew how to coordinate them with supporting infantry and the advantage was thrown away. The mistake was not repeated in August 1918.*

lines that future generations will perhaps find as fascinating and imposing as those of many heads of classical or Renaissance times.'

In the east, the collapse of the last Russian offensive under Brussilov broke the back of the Russian army, already weakened by the February Revolution, so victory there seemed within Germany's grasp. In late summer 1917 the German High Command allowed Lenin, leader of the Bolshevik revolutionaries, to travel to Russia in a sealed railway carriage from Zürich across German-occupied territory, so that he could plunge the Bolshevik dagger into the seething heart of Russia. The German generals and the Bolsheviks – theirs was a pact with the devil if there ever was one.

In November 1917, having won control over St. Petersburg, Lenin pronounced a pompous appeal 'To All', calling for comprehensive peace without annexations or reparations, world peace through world revolution, 'war to the palaces, peace to the cottages'; there was no reference to national states, only to a great alliance for peace and the proletariat. In January 1918 President Woodrow Wilson's riposte came in a message to both Houses of Congress, his 'Fourteen Points ... to make the world safe for democracy'. This meant world peace through self-determination of nations, democracy and free trade, with a 'League of Nations' to supervise international affairs and, if necessary, right any wrongs.

The Social Democrats, who accepted the *Burgfrieden* – harmony on the Home Front – as a patriotic duty and who saw the 'Auxiliary Service for the Fatherland' law and the Kaiser's Easter Message as a promise of a better Germany, were alarmed by the horrors and summary executions of Russia's Bolshevik revolution. They tried to gain control of the widespread 'January strikes' of 1918, born of hunger, cold and anger, and simultaneously preach moderation. They feared a Russian contagion. After 1918, this ambivalence was to give rise to the 'stab in the back' legend. Since 1917 the party had been divided between opponents and supporters of the war effort, radicals and moderates.

By March 1918, the Soviets had no choice but to grit their teeth and sign whatever the German generals threw before them at the negotiating table in Brest-Litovsk. But Trotsky and Lenin were confident that the German military colossus had feet of

clay and that social revolution would soon break out in Germany and then spread all over Europe and indeed the world. A million German soldiers were meanwhile transported from the eastern front to the west to snatch victory by a last-minute all-out offensive, designed to forestall full deployment of American forces. After some initial successes, this offensive failed – ammunition was too scarce, the troops too weary, supplies too scant.

In August 1918 the British mounted a counter-attack at Amiens, using the tanks they had first introduced – and squandered – at Cambrai the previous November – huge steel monsters bridging the trenches on their caterpillar tracks. Against them the German infantry was virtually powerless – quite apart from being paralyzed with terror. Discipline broke down. In the south-east the Austro-Hungarian army disintegrated into irreconcilable national elements. It was now only a question of lending the defeat a suitable form; and of finding a new beginning. This had to be looked for over the

Fighting famine: *soldiers man a soup kitchen (opposite) in December 1918 and it is not urchins but well dressed children who queue with their bowls. Women scavenge among the rubbish (below) for something to eat.*

barricades being put up in many cities of central Europe.

Those prewar worlds, which a swift war was to have saved, were irredeemably destroyed by the long war. Management of shortages and compulsory service at the front and in the factories transformed the states and societies of Europe more thoroughly than the most merciless revolution could have done. War had become the organising principle, while the war effort opened social rifts, ruined hundreds of thousands of independent, small-scale livelihoods and, through allocation of capital and raw materials, promoted that industrial concentration which continued unchecked through inflation and depression. Through the compulsion to put all money into war bonds, and through the blocking of any other investment possibility, the behemoth state gobbled up all capital. Inflation was made invisible by price regulations, but the shortages continued. Despite all prohibitions, 'hoarding' of farm produce by townspeople, to be exchanged for gold and valuables, became a way of life, in fact a means of survival. In order to secure something to eat, people had to beg from farmers or resort to the black market, or both. The average industrial income nominally more than trebled during the war, but no one could eat his fill from that. A barter economy and the black market were the answers. Exploitation, hardship and shortages arose such as had not been known in human memory. Protest was brewing among farmers, and even more so among industrial workers, (the latter inspiring the 'Spartacus League' from which, at the turn of 1918/1919, the Communist Party was to emerge), and the 'revolutionary floorleaders'

Sailors from Kiel *(above) spread the revolution in November 1918. Here they slouch down the Friedrichstrasse in Berlin, with their rifles defiantly upside down.*

Street fighting. *The army take on Communists in Berlin (right) at the behest of the Social Democrats, then forming the government, at the end of 1918.*

(*Revolutionäre Obleute*) in the factories.

The 'Fourteen Points' of US President Wilson were now grasped like the roadmap to the promised land, both by politicians in Berlin and by the men in the trenches. After all – in defiance of the threats to partition Germany coming from the Entente – the US president seemed to guarantee the existence of European nation states, including Germany. And was not the road to democracy inevitable one way or another? What point was there in fighting on and dying when victory was impossible and defeat no tragedy?

Faced with the strategic superiority of the Entente in the west and the dissolution of the Hapsburg monarchy in the south, Hindenburg and Ludendorff called on the politicians of the Centre-Left majority in the Reichstag to form a new government, request an armistice in the west and enter into peace negotiations with the Entente. In the Reichstag the

Centre-Left candidate for Reichskanzler was Prince Max von Baden, a non-party man, a southern-German *grand seigneur* of moral integrity, but with little political experience and, more important, without that hardness and decisiveness that distinguish a leader in a time of crisis. Valuable time was lost in Berlin with coalition talks. The prince, though well-intentioned and well-advised by Kurt Hahn and a number of southern-German liberals, was in poor health. Instead of real action there were laborious negotiations to rewrite a few, albeit important, points in Bismarck's constitution. For a few weeks Germany, having gone through four years of military dictatorship, became a constitutional monarchy.

However, before negotiations even began with the Entente – the diplomatic links between Berlin and Vienna had long been severed – and while the land forces were collapsing, the German Admiralty ordered the battle fleet out to sea for a final engagement – not in order to correct the course of events but to create a heroic myth of steel, fire and blood for the future. The sailors, fed up with strict discipline, patronizing arrogance, disgusting food and the endless privations of the war, turned against their officers. Threats of arrest and court martial proved ineffective. Discipline broke down. Red flags appeared.

The Imperial Navy was no more. Radical slogans, fathered by the Bolshevik Revolution, emerged. Revolutionary sailors travelled from Kiel through the length and breadth of the country, as emissaries of despair and rebellion. Officers, if encountered, had their insignia of rank torn off. The insurrection spread like wildfire into armament plants and then to the whole country. Workers' and soldiers' councils were set up in most cities, and soon also in front-line units, in the latter case often with tacit complicity between officers and men.

Discipline was maintained only among front-line troops. This is where Heinrich Brüning, to be the last democratically created chancellor of the Weimar years, had his formative experience. All in all, however, what happened was not a revolution to soak the country in blood, to change it from top to bottom. It was the breakdown of a defeated army and of a worn-out nation. In the Rhineland the middle classes welcomed British troops, since the foreign adversary seemed preferable to home-grown revolution. In Berlin an observer of a march by soldiers and workers noted that a few soldiers 'had taken off their tunics and hung them loosely over their shoulders like capes, and inside out at that. To increase the effect they had actually turned the sleeves inside out, so that they hung loosely, showing their lining, like empty sausage skins. This was the only touch

of the picturesque in the whole procession, a picturesque bit of disorderliness to show that there was now an end to war and discipline.'

The Kaiser, to whom the generals had suggested a hero's last stand, instead went to Holland by train and asked the Queen for asylum – which was granted. Who would give shape and direction to the chaos ensuing from the absence of any legitimate authority? Karl Liebknecht proclaimed the Socialist Republic from one of the balconies of the Berlin Stadtschloss, while Philipp Scheidemann proclaimed parliamentary democracy from the Reichstag. Liebknecht was an able Communist leader, Scheidemann a middle-of-the-road Social-Democrat politician. These were symbolic acts, competing with each other, designed to define the road to the new legality,

Triumphant Freikorps *stage a victory parade after crushing the 'red republic' of Munich in Spring 1919.*

German Republic. First, Ebert and the People's Deputies received the support of the trade unions which wanted no truck with the Spartacus League or with the standard bearers of the red flag; they were afraid that these were out, Bolshevik-style, for a bloodbath, and they feared the fate of the Mensheviks. Second, trade unions and employers jointly, at top level, established the 'Central Working Committee' which together made every effort to channel the political revolution into a wages movement and to contain it by means of welfare policy. Finally, the generals appreciated that they had found responsible politicians in Berlin, able to deliver order and authority, with large sections of organised labour behind them, who would prevent violent revolution and establish a firm base of law and order.

Thus an axis was forged between the military and the politicians, between the Supreme Command at Wilhelmshöhe Palace near Kassel and the new central power in Berlin. Although the latter's title suggested that it was a body of people's commissars after the Russian model, in reality it wanted nothing better than to hand over its awesome powers to an elected and properly constituted Reich government. The basic geometry of power was clearly laid out. In the triangular relationship between army, trade unions and employers each needed the others, no one group could manage on its own. This compromise would prevent a Communist seizure of power, bring the troops back home, convert industry to peacetime production, provide food for the starving urban masses, prepare for early elections and, together with the Allies, find a way out of the war, even a kind of peace.

Fortunately for the new provisional authority in Berlin the Allies refused to negotiate with any revolutionary force. Meanwhile the (by now armed) uprisings and the persisting unrest in the country increasingly forced the Social Democrats, whether they liked it or not, into closer alliance with the old powers of the civil service and the army. 'Someone's got to act the bloodhound', said the Social Democrat Noske, the people's commissioner responsible for the military. Months of civil war followed, with Red forces against the Social Democrats and later the National Assembly in Weimar, a war that witnessed the rise and fall of the Munich Republic of Councils, Soviet supplies of weapons and propaganda and, not least, the Communist Party's all-out boycott of parliamentary elections – historically on the model of 1848.

Among all the gloom and doom many vast changes took place, especially in industrial relations. The eight-hour work-day was enacted, works councils were confirmed and strengthened, the minimum wage was introduced. General elections were held on 19th January 1919, an astonishing organisational feat, but even more astonishing was the fact that the parties of the Centre-Left coalition, responsible for the 'Peace Resolution' of 1917 and for the October reforms, collected three-quarters of the vote. The revolution now turned into a movement for better pay. There was no question now of expropriation without

though in fact they merely outlined the fronts of the civil war that was soon to embroil the country. Prince Max von Baden at the last minute entrusted the Social-Democrat leader Friedrich Ebert with executive power, even though Ebert regarded the overthrow of the monarchy as an unwise and unnecessary break of continuity. Ebert immediately established the 'Council of People's Deputies' made up of six moderate men, majority socialists and independent socialists. Thus, during the violent weeks of transition, the country was provided with a source of authority, especially for the military. Whether the 'Executive Council of Workers' and Soldiers' Councils' existing in parallel in Berlin was an opponent or an ally was, for the time being, not quite clear.

There were three main factors that helped establish the

compensation, either of big industry or of large agricultural estates, just as there was no question of immediately introducing a socialist comprehensive school system for all. This was no mean achievement, taking into account that the government was weak and inexperienced, that authority had all-but broken down, that revolt from the Left was well armed and that in the last resort there were nothing but dishevelled army units hastily brought together, and a wide array of Freikorps.

These independent military units of the immediate post-war era filled the gap between the collapse of the Kaiser's armies in 1918 and the creation of the Reichswehr in 1919. The average age of the soldiers was around 20; the only trade they had known was war, and peace exposed them to an empty future. Manfred von Killinger, chief of staff of the Freikorps called the 'Marinebrigade Erhardt', drew a parallel: 'The Landsknechte [16th-century mercenaries] did not much care why they fought and for whom. The main thing for them was that they were fighting. War had become their career.' The officers were not much older than the men, and all were survivors of the great blood-bath of the Western trenches and, more often than not, the Eastern campaigns. They were an all-volunteer force, held together by loss of purpose and resentment against the revolution and its protagonists. Some dreamt of a piece of land somewhere on the eastern plains of Europe; most wanted to become part of the future German forces, and in fact many of the Freikorps were merged in 1919/1920 into Reichswehr battalions and brigades. Their only loyalty was to their officers, charismatic or brutal, or both, who were their masters next to God. Most of those were in fact former officers and NCOs, and leadership counted for more than hierarchy. Freikorps commanders had to keep their people together by a balanced diet of patriotism, elitism and stiff discipline. Some of them, like the Brigade Erhardt, adopted the Swastika symbol, but this was more to distinguish themselves from Imperial Germany and its Iron Cross than to anticipate the lure of Nazism – in 1919 not even a marginal force.

Freikorps soldiers, after having defended the legitimate government, shot the captured Communist leaders Karl Liebknecht and Rosa Luxemburg in Berlin in 1919 and threw the corpses into the Landwehr Kanal. But Freikorps soldiers of the Maercker Battaillon were also the ones to protect the National Assembly in rural Weimar against unwelcome surprises. Freikorps soldiers, finally, gave support to the Kapp-Lüttwitz Putsch in March 1920. As they entered Berlin Erhardt's brigade sang

Hakenkreuz am Stahlhelm
Schwarz weiss rotes Band
Die Brigade Erhardt
Werden wir genannt.
Swastika on helmet
Black white red brassard

A peace to end all peace. *Allied staff officers and diplomats at Versailles crane to watch the actual signing of the treaty which settled the terms imposed on Germany in 1919. The Galerie des Glaces, the Hall of Mirrors, in which it is done is where the German Emperor was proclaimed in 1871, after Prussia's defeat of France.*

The Erhardt Brigade
is what we are called.

(In years to come, line three was altered to 'Sturmabteilung Hitler'.) When, defeated, they marched out of Berlin later, they sang defiantly:

What do we care if a putsch goes wrong?
We will make another one before too long!

This botched attempt at seizing power in Berlin marked all too clearly the distances already existing between the Reichswehr commanders, who wanted authority, order and obedience, and

the anarchic strain in the Freikorps, who throve on turmoil. Those who failed to be selected and transformed into the highly disciplined and elitist Reichswehr cadre were disbanded and left to their bitterness. It did not need much to convert them to the gospel preached by many prophets of disaster, among them a certain Adolf Hitler, that the new republic and all it stood for meant nothing but shame, decline and dishonour.

It is easy to argue that the use of the Freikorps had its price, that it corrupted the course of liberal democracy and ultimately led to the fall of the Weimar Republic and, thus, to the rise of Hitler. But anyone criticising the Weimar politicians with the wisdom of hindsight should bear in mind that they had little choice, attacked from inside and under threat of an Allied invasion. Weimar was a symbol of this ambiguity, this epitome of German Geist. It had been chosen to be the seat of the National Assembly, not as a tribute to the great minds, Goethe, Herder, Wieland and Schiller, who had flourished there, but because it was a small town, little damaged and easily defended by two battalions of loyal troops.

CHAPTER FOUR

THE WEIMAR YEARS

EVERY CONSTITUTION REFLECTS THE FORCES shaping it, and this was certainly true of the Weimar Constitution of 19 August 1919. It aimed to give everybody what they wanted: to the supporters of direct democracy it gave the referendum; to the champions of Westminster-type democracy it gave the Reichstag, without whose approval the government could not adopt a budget or pass laws. And to those who trusted neither referendum nor parliament and who wanted a substitute Kaiser, it gave the Reich President: directly elected, a guardian of the Constitution. It was in his hands that the supreme command of the armed forces, the right to dissolve parliament, and to proclaim a state of emergency, were united, making him a real Ersatzkaiser, more powerful in a crisis than Wilhelm II had ever been, now reading P G Wodehouse at Huis Le Doorn in rural Holland.

The parties which in 1917 had adopted the 'Peace Resolution', and in 1918 agreed on constitutional reform, and supported the government of Prince Max of Baden, had received a deceptively large vote of confidence in the elections of January 1919, when they won three-quarters of the seats in the National Assembly. The Social Democrats (SPD) and their centrist allies were anxious to create a new legal basis as quickly as possible, to exorcize the spectre of a Bolshevik takeover with its revolutionary councils, and to ensure maximum continuity through the constitution. In this way they were hoping to reconcile the past with the present, the basic rights of 1848 with a strong civil service, parliamentary freedom with presidential authority. They overlooked the fact that the double-headed eagle is a monster because its heads either look in different directions or peck out each other's eyes. This was amply manifested during the fourteen years of the first German Republic. Time and again the political parties shunned the responsibilities of government in order to gain strength in opposition, until by 1930 there was neither governmental responsibility nor a powerful political party left anywhere across the dwindling democratic spectrum. After a decade of fragile parliamentary government, mostly characterized by minority cabinets, the presidential system came into play over and above political parties.

The Centre-Left majority dominating the National Assembly in 1919 moved Germany into the western tradition of liberal democracy, based upon guarantees of property and freedoms, the rule of law and a measure of social welfare. It preserved, simultaneously, the German tradition of a strong pluralism of interests and of social intervention – what the constitutional lawyer Ernst Forsthoff was to call the 'all-embracing welfare

A modern dance routine, *complete with bare-breasted chorus, to entertain guests at an ultra-smart art gallery called 'The Tempest' belonging to Herwarth Walden in Berlin's not-so-fashionable Potsdamer Strasse, 1923. The paintings behind are by Sonia Delaunay who together with her husband Robert had been combining cubist ideas with their particular interest in colour. Three of the elements which were to characterise the city in this decade are clearly present: artistic experiment, a determined decadence, and an international café society.*

The German Hogarth *was what the painter and caricaturist George Grosz (above) wanted to become. His targets were the arrogance of the middle classes and the brutality of the army. His Berlin profiteers, prostitutes and military thugs revolt and fascinate us. He deliberately set out to preach and reform; if art was not didactic, it was nothing – hence his involvement with Dada. When Hitler came to power he sought exile in America.*

A Dada fair *in Berlin, 1922 (right). The Dada movement was founded in Switzerland in 1916 and its artists used the illogical and absurd to deflate complacency, conventionality, pomposity. As well as paintings by Otto Dix, left, and Grosz, right, slogans such as 'Take Dada seriously, it's worth it', 'Dilettantes, rise up against art', and 'Dada is political' can be seen. Grosz is the one wearing a hat.*

supported by industrialists like Robert Bosch and brilliantly represented in parliament by the national-social pastor Friedrich Naumann. This was the only party unconditionally constitutional, invariably the cement of coalitions, but in an ever-diminishing minority position. Immediately after the war there was a brief opportunity for overcoming the division among German liberals, which went back to the formation of the Reich half a century before. But the founders of the German Democratic Party in 1918 did not wish to take on board Dr Gustav Stresemann, who had been an enthusiast for excessive war aims and an admirer of the Ludendorff-Hindenburg Supreme Command. So Stresemann led the remnants of the old National Liberal Party into the new German People's Party (DVP), representing the interests of small and medium-sized business and heavy industry. While never committing fully to the Weimar compromise, the DVP became a vital link between democratic politics and the captains of industry. From 1920 onwards there was no government in which the German People's Party did not participate. Indeed, it had to participate if a majority was to be ensured.

The nation was deeply divided, despite the fact that three out of four voters had wanted the Weimar compromise in 1919; the basis of the Constitution remained fragile. The political parties trusted each other even less than they trusted

state'. The Social Democrats intended, once the voters had given them the absolute majority which they assumed to be their birthright, to go much further. They clung to the slogan, concealed behind much verbiage at their Heidelberg conference of 1925, that 'Democracy is but a half-way house – socialism must be built'. The party therefore tried hard to play down its socialist rhetoric, to win the middle-class vote and to have a major say in shaping the new Germany.

The German Centre Party, still the fortress of political Catholicism, similarly pursued an agenda aiming beyond the present and the Weimar Constitution. Although it found bridges to social democracy in Catholic social teaching, it never abandoned its fascination with the authoritarian state of the past, which had given the Catholic part of the population a share in bureaucratic power, equal rights and concessions to its educational interests. The Bavarian People's Party – rural, petit-bourgeois and monarchist – held similar views. Reich Chancellor Heinrich Brüning's authoritarian vision of the early 1930s sprang from these left-wing Catholic authoritarian roots. This vision, projected by Field Marshal-President von Hindenburg, was finally to break the back of democracy, though proving unequal to the violent assaults of Communists and National Socialists.

Then there was the German Democratic Party, holding radical liberal views, strongly rooted in the old Prussian Progress Party and in the Württemberg People's Party,

Gustav Stresemann (above, centre), the foreign minister 1923-29, was, with Walther Rathenau, the most distinguished politician of the Weimar period. He did much to heal the wounds left by Versailles. Other wounds, like this ex-serviceman's (below) could not respond to treatment, while many of the working class sought solace with open-air nature worship and folk revivals (opposite), learning from middle-class youth movements.

the administration and that is why, not unlike their predecessors, they left crisis management – control over the armed forces and over civil rights – to the president. But he was a guardian of the Constitution under no obligation to them, as he was directly elected by the people. In consequence, the president held the keys to a different republic. With those wide powers Reich President Ebert guided the wavering republic until 1925, through the turmoil of civil war, inflation and the pain of the French occupation of the Ruhr. But his successor was the octogenarian former field marshal, Paul von Hindenburg, his roots deep in imperial days and his formative experience the World War, who saw himself keeping the throne for the return of a Hohenzollern monarch. In sharp contrast to his SPD predecessor in 1923, Hindenburg was to use his powers to push the tottering republic over the edge while giving Hitler's dictatorship a legal facade. The Nazis did not even trouble to abolish formally the Constitution and, by implication, the republic that had been set up in the idyll of Weimar in 1919 and was to end, only

fourteen years later.

In Paris meanwhile, the peace conference, with France the host and Britain and the United States the main participants, enshrined the new European map in the Treaty of Versailles. When Philipp Scheidemann, a former mayor of the city of Kassel and now prime minister of the Reich, received the text of the treaty from Paris, he was shocked: 'This treaty is so unacceptable that I am unable today to believe that the earth could tolerate such a document.' This was bombastic, and politically unwise, but it reflected the mood in Germany about the 'shameful dictate'. Scheidemann failed to realize that there was virtually no way of negotiating over, let alone mitigating, Allied demands. He also ignored the fact that future governments would have to implement the treaty as best they could. After all, what was the alternative? Military invasion by the western Allies, followed by implementation of the treaty's demands under worse conditions.

The impassioned protest in Germany, extending from the Communists to the nationalists, was directed against the

attribution of sole responsibility for the war to Germany, against the unlimited and certainly unfulfillable reparation demands, against the cession of Alsace and Lorraine, and in particular against the fact that the new Polish Republic was carved out of the flesh of Germany's eastern lands as well as incorporating West Prussia, the province of Posen and parts of Upper Silesia. What was overlooked in this mood of despair was that the substance of the German nation state had been

preserved in spite of all the French plans for partition and Clemenceau's dreams of re-establishing older German divisions. Cardinal Richelieu's ancient plan was denied fruition firstly because the British wanted some chance of the war debts being paid by the Reich and therefore needed continuity, secondly because the Americans wanted a stable Germany as a dam against Bolshevik Russia. Also overlooked in Germany was the fact that neither White nor Red Russia had participated in Paris

Street violence. *Brawling in Berlin in the 1920s (left). Walther Rathenau (right), visionary, technocrat and democratic foreign minister, became the target of ultra-nationalist propaganda and was shot dead on the way to work in Berlin in 1922. The dedication is to Gerhart Hauptmann's wife (see p. 39).*

unimportant by comparison. Germany and Russia may have been the pariahs of the world system in 1919, but together they had the potential for unhinging the peace of Paris. When the American Senate in 1920 refused to ratify the accession of the USA to the League of Nations, no world system was left, merely a system of collective security in Europe almost indistinguishable from a system of collective insecurity. In 1922 the German Foreign Minister Walther Rathenau signed the Treaty of Rapallo with the Soviet Union under which the two countries recognised each other and agreed to let bygones be bygones. But, depressed by defeat, by economic hardship and the loss of the eastern provinces, the Germans could hardly have been expected to realize the vast potential in the situation and to congratulate themselves on how much worse things might have been.

Was Weimar, as the saying goes, a republic without republicans? Was everything bound to happen the way it did? As early as March 1920 a right-wing coup was staged in Berlin, led by the East Prussian banker Kapp and Reichswehr General von Lüttwitz. For this action a Freikorps of 5,000 men, 'Brigade Erhardt', withdrawn from the Baltic as a result of Allied pressure and earmarked for demobilization, had made itself available. The coup was improvised and executed in a haphazard fashion; it found little support and petered out. Kapp dissolved the Prussian State Legislature and reinstated it within a day or two; arrested the Prussian cabinet and then reinstated it; abolished all university exams. The senior officials of the Berlin ministries stayed aloof. The trade unions called for a general strike. Berlin was paralyzed, the government hurriedly moved to Stuttgart. The army waited, and after three days the drama turned into farce.

in the reshaping of Europe and that the new Polish state had also been carved out of Russia's western provinces. So Russia was unlikely in future to support the treaties of Trianon, St Germain and Versailles, making her a potential ally.

For the first time in a generation, Germany no longer had Russia as an enemy and, in consequence, almost had a chance to become arbiter of the Continent. France's 'Little Entente' with Romania, Czechoslovakia and Yugoslavia was

Bavarian Freikorps *recruits march into Munich in 1919 (right) to wrest it from the Communists. Their hakenkreuz (swastika) armbands and flags* *show that the National Socialists were not the first to use that symbol to distance themselves from Imperial Germany and its iron cross.*

However, the right-wing parties in parliament realized that the wind had changed in their favour. At once they demanded new elections for the Reichstag. When the votes were counted the three pro-republic parties had lost their majority. Now was the chance of those who called themselves 'republicans by reason', implying that their hearts were elsewhere. Gustav Stresemann, an industrial manager, a protégé of Ludendorff's and a late convert to Anglo-Saxon democracy, was to be their leader.

It was not merely nostalgia for the past splendour and glory of imperial Germany that was the driving force on the Right. There was also now the myth of the 'stab in the back', administered to a victorious army by a home front of little faith and by timid politicians. This myth unfolded in countless variations and was to play a role in the rise of the Nazi Party. Little was achieved by the Reichstag's efforts to conduct an inquiry into the causes of the German collapse in September 1918; though it interrogated numerous witnesses and meticulously documented the events in extensive reports, the myths invariably re-emerged triumphant later.

More than anything else the Bolshevik revolution in Russia was a formative influence on democracy and party politics in Germany. To some, like the Communists and the protagonists of Soviet-type Councils, it was a dream come true. To the vast majority, however, it was a nightmare, which terrified the Social Democrats, made them lose their support, politically disoriented and paralyzed them. For the Right the Russian horrors became both a trauma and a mobilising force. In 1919 the short-lived Munich 'Republic of Councils' under Kurt Eisner, a pacifist dreaming of a socialist world, drove the legitimate government under the Social Democrat Hoffmann out of Munich to the idyllic small town of Bamberg. But then, after a few weeks, the Räterepublik of Munich partly died a natural death and partly collapsed under the counterattack of Bavarian home-guard units reinforced by Freikorps. One Freikorps officer was quite clear in his instructions: 'You know what to do: shoot, and report the prisoner attacked you or tried to escape.' Munich chimney sweeps traditionally had red flags on their carts and a number were shot before the Freikorps realised their mistake.

The wild speeches of Eisner's men, among them gifted intellectuals and writers, and more especially their execution of hostages towards the close, made Munich fertile soil for radical prophets at the other end of the spectrum. One of these was a thirty-year-old Austrian, a former soldier decorated with the Iron Cross, who had attracted his superiors' notice by his

passionate eloquence and hatred of the Left – a Reichswehr agitator named Adolf Hitler.

The French occupation of the Ruhr in 1922/23, to safeguard 'productive securities' for France and to encourage Rhineland separatism, proved unsuccessful. The British and Americans at the same time, for fear of losing Germany to the Bolsheviks, went over to supporting the country at Europe's strategic centre. Inflation, which had begun during the war but had been kept under control until 1920, reached vertiginous heights in the course of 1922 and 1923. Tax revenue was nowhere near

sufficient for reparation payments, to pay the Reichswehr and the police, to keep the Rhineland above water and to calm the population. So the Berlin government financed the state by means of the printing press. In November 1923 the infernal spiral eventually reached its climax – more than four thousand billion marks had to be paid for one US dollar.

Banks had given up counting out notes and issued them by weight. Notes were issued on leather, porcelain and even lace in an attempt to give them value. Barter took over, with cheap theatre seats costing two eggs and the most expensive a few

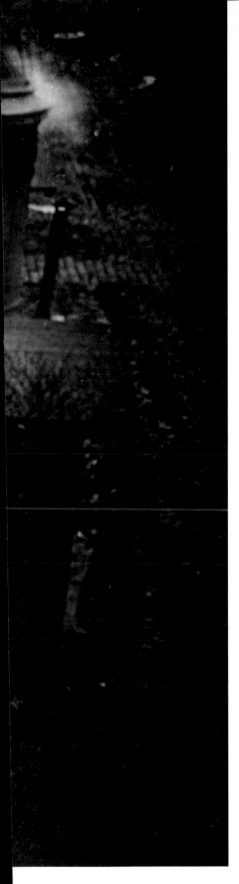

The Ruhr occupied. *A Belgian tank guards an entrance (above) to the Thyssen steel works in 1923.*

Selling their treasures *(right). Members of a Berlin association of pensioners hit by inflation are forced to part with their possessions.*

ounces of butter. A pound of butter bought a pair of boots. Mail boxes were robbed for the stamps, lead stolen from roofs, door handles from doors. Rail fares were fixed so one could get across Germany for a few copper coins.

The history of the first German Republic does not deserve to be invariably viewed as an irreversible voyage down some Stygian pit. It was surely a miracle that the German Reich held together in 1919 and was not partitioned from outside. And it was a second miracle that, four years later, when inflation unleashed the apocalyptic horsemen of angst, speculation, poverty and despair, neither the French occupation of the Ruhr, nor the Reichswehr-based dictatorship of the centrist government, nor the surgical strike against the 'Popular Front' governments in Thuringia and Saxony, nor Hitler's putsch in Munich led to the overthrow of the government in Berlin or to civil war in the country at large.

In the firefight on the Odeonsplatz that saw the ignominious end of Hitler's attempt at a Bavarian coup d'etat, Hitler avoided

New banknotes *(left) being carried from the printers to the banks at the height of the 1923 inflation. In the time it took to transport and issue them they would have lost much of their value.*

injury by throwing himself flat on the cobbles, though he did dislocate his shoulder. Ludendorff, a fellow-conspirator, simply walked unscathed through the police lines, while Göring was wounded in the groin. This was to lead to his lifelong addiction to morphine. Hitler was arrested a few days later. His trial before a sympathetic judge resulted in a sentence of four years *Festungshaft*, fortress arrest. This had been something reserved, typically, for students or officers who killed someone in a duel, and was as much a compliment as a punishment. It certainly did no harm to the image of the ex-corporal, who put his time in prison to use, writing *Mein Kampf*. In October 1925 Joseph Goebbels was able to record in his diary: 'I am finishing Hitler's book. Thrilled to bits! Who is this man? Half plebeian, half God! Really Christ, or only John?' A few months later he echoed the theme, after one of Hitler's speeches: 'Deep and mystical. Almost like Gospels. Shuddering we pass together with him along the edge of life's abyss.' Goebbels would also have read and marked passages in *Mein Kampf* such as: 'An effective propaganda must be limited to a very few points and must harp on these in slogans … As soon as you sacrifice this slogan and try to be many-sided, the effect will piddle away.'

As well as the Beer Hall Putsch, November 1923 brought the

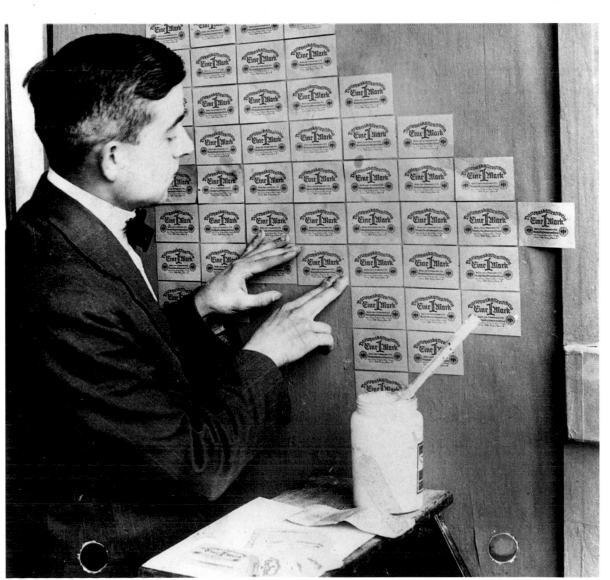

Papering the walls *with banknotes (right), cheaper than using real wallpaper, thanks to the effect of inflation.*

A new voice. *Hitler (opposite) speaking in the Hofgarten at Munich at the first National Socialist Party Day demonstration of 6000 SA stormtroopers on 25 January 1923: 'The betrayers of the German Fatherland [the Republican Government] must be done away with... We must always remember that in any new conflict in the field of foreign affairs the German Siegfried will again be stabbed in the back.'*
[PHOTO: HEINRICH HOFFMAN]

A new face. *Marlene Dietrich in top hat and tails (right), typical Berlin 1920s cross-dressing. She established herself on the stage and in silent movies but her big break-through was* The Blue Angel *talkie in 1930.*

'Rentenmark', based on the fictitious overall yield of the German soil, but in fact maintained by the prospect of American and British loans to government, industry and banks. The Reichswehr handed back its extraordinary powers, largely because of the need for American goodwill and capital. A new Reichstag was elected: provided Stresemann's German People's Party co-operated, it would actually ensure a majority loyal to the constitutional compromise of 1919. The government was again in the hands of elected politicians, and things seemed to return to normal. The constitutional spectrum was extended towards the middle classes, and the partisans of civil war were relegated to the red and brown margins of parliament and society.

After the trials and tribulations of the early period the Weimar state went through a phase of consolidation. But only for a small minority were these golden years. The cultural fragmentation of the Weimar Republic suggested tensions and rifts in society, hatred and the prospect of catastrophe ever-present. In 1921 finance minister Matthias Erzberger, a Catholic from the Centre Party, was murdered; in 1922 Walther Rathenau, a Jew from the Democratic Party, was assassinated. The inflation of 1923 undoubtedly gave a kick-start to the new decadence that transformed Berlin and made it internationally a magnet for those seeking sexual and artistic freedom. That year was the first in which the Hotel Adlon made professional male dance partners available for its female clientele. Hotels like this, and embassies, were the centres of social life, no longer the town houses of members of the Imperial court. Film stars had become the new aristocracy of a rootless society whose biggest event was the Press Ball, a subscription dance for six thousand. Another big spectacle was the six-day bicycle race, where even at two in the morning there was a large crowd, many in white tie and furs.

Nudity in the nightclubs was commonplace: 'On stage at the Bonbonnière, nothing above the waist is de rigueur ...' At Resi, in Neumanstrasse, 'the chief attraction is the table telephones. The tables are numbered and on every one is a small telephone. If you see a lonely little thing at table 25 and you are feeling romantic, you ring up that table ...' All tastes were catered for by, for instance, such places as the Topkeller, a working-class homosexual nightclub: 'Gemütlich fifty-year-olds, salt of the earth, with rounded bellies and threadbare evening clothes, wiping the Pilsener foam from their citizenly moustaches, asking another moustache for a dance'.

Film making, theatre and cabaret were all outstanding. Leni Riefenstahl and Billy Wilder cut their teeth making documentaries at the same time as expressionist works like *The Cabinet of Doctor Caligari*, or Fritz Lang's *Metropolis* and *M*, were setting new standards. Cabaret techniques spoke loudly in the film *Blue Angel* and in the greatest theatrical piece of the time: *The Threepenny Opera* by Bertolt Brecht and Kurt Weill. The greatest cabaret MC or '*conférencier*', Werner Fink, at the Katacombe in the Bellvuestrasse, survived into the Nazi era, giving the Hitler salute and saying, 'That's how deep we are in the shit?' Another of his lines was, 'No, I'm not Jewish, I only look intelligent.'

Actors and scenes *from the expressionist masterpiece* Metropolis *(1926) set in a city in the year 2000, made in the UfA film studio which dominated German production. Its huge crowd scenes of submissive slaves, and its scientific devices still astonish. (Top) Gustav Fröhlich, (opposite) Brigitte Helm as the robot Maria, (right) Rudolf Klein-Rogge straps Maria into his fiendish machine.*

Fritz Lang *(above), director of* Metropolis. *In 1931 his* M, *in which Peter Lorre played a child-killer, caused a sensation. His Dr Mabuse, aimed against dictatorship, appeared in 1933. He fled to Hollywood in 1936.*

Actors: *Emil Jannings (above),
who specialised in pathetic and
tragic roles, applies his make-up.
He was Marlene Dietrich's
elderly lover in* The Blue Angel.
*Gustav Gründgens (above right)
as Mephisto in Goethe's* Faust.

The Swiss clown *Grock (right)
with actress Trudi Schoop in
Berlin in 1932. He was also a
masterly acrobat, tightrope
walker and juggler.* [PHOTOS,
ABOVE AND RIGHT: LOTTE JACOBI]
[PHOTO, ABOVE RIGHT: WILLI SAEGER]

Ballet costumes *(above) by Oskar Schlemmer for a 1926 revue at Berlin's Metropol Theatre. Schlemmer, a painter and sculptor, was also head of the department of theatrical* *design at the Bauhaus(p.132). Clear-cut geometric lines and shapes, and simple patterns, mark a conscious move away from expressionism.*

Bertolt Brecht *taken in 1927, with the leather coat and cigar which became his trademarks. His aim was to fight out the class war on stage, and he made his name the following year with his Dreigroschenoper (Threepenny Opera), an updated version of John Gay's* Beggar's Opera *about the early eighteenth-century London underworld. Meeting him in October 1928 Count Harry Kessler recorded in his diary his 'strikingly degenerate look, almost a criminal*

physiognomy… a peculiarly suspicious expression; very nearly a typical twister.' When Hitler came to power he took refuge in Scandinavia and then in the USA.

Other exiles *(opposite).* **Lotte Lenya** *whose haunting rendition of the ballad-style songs in* The Threepenny Opera *owed much to the example of Berlin cabaret chanteuses (top).* **Kurt Weill** *(below left), husband of Lotte Lenya and the composer who collaborated*

with Brecht on The Threepenny Opera, The Rise and Fall of the City of Mahagonny *and other pieces. There was a riot at the premier of the latter in Leipzig in 1930. This couple went to the USA, as did the physicist* **Albert Einstein** *(below centre), transferring from Berlin to Princeton University, and the Nobel Prizewinning novelist,* **Thomas Mann** *(below right).*

[PHOTOS, ABOVE: KONRAD RESSLER]

[PHOTOS, RIGHT: LOTTE JACOBI]

Outside the performing arts, and elsewhere than Berlin the other outstanding cultural movement of the Weimar period was Walter Gropius' Bauhaus group of architects, painters and designers. As well as evolving what we know as 'modernism' they had a deeply-held countercultural aim: to dispense with distinctions between function and aesthetics, art and craftsmanship, bosses and workers. They stressed instead the cooperative and the collective within the workplace. It is therefore understandable that Krupp were reluctant to supply Marcel Breuer with his raw material when he was about to make his prototype tubular chair.

The years from 1923 to 1929 proved that post-war Germany, taking a respite from violence, was economically viable. With the aid of the big banks on New York's Wall Street and from London's City, financial and political stabilization

The Bauhaus: *the new premises (above and opposite) erected for the 'House of Building' after the move from Weimar to Dessau in 1925, designed by Walter Gropius (top) with his staff and students. The Bauhaus under his leadership had developed from the Weimar School of Arts and Crafts founded in 1907 by the Belgian Henri van de Velde*

(bottom) who was keen for architecture to go in the direction suggested by new techniques and materials. Paul Klee (middle) the outstanding Swiss-born artist who had been a member of the Blaue Reiter group (p.56) taught at the Bauhaus from 1920 to 1933.

[PHOTO, ABOVE LEFT: LUX FEININGER]
[PHOTO, TOP AND BOTTOM: LOUIS HELD]
[PHOTO, CENTRE: HUGO ERFURTH]

began in Germany, soon to be followed by economic recovery. The British government, which had distanced itself from the French call for revenge ever since the Paris peace conference, continued its detachment. It was John Maynard Keynes, the

Berlin Society *(left) during an interval at a gala performance in 1929. George Grosz caricatured scenes like this. The Great Depression is just around the corner.*

[PHOTO: ERICH SALOMON]

Queuing for jobs *that don't exist outside the Hanover labour exchange in 1932 (opposite). By that time there are seven million out of work. The slogan on the wall behind, 'Elect Hitler', is strategically placed.*

[PHOTO: WALTER BALLHAUSE]

economist, who, as an expert at the side of the British delegation, had observed in 1920 that the Treaty of Versailles, imposed upon the Reich, contained the seeds of another war. Whatever such foresight was worth the British government did not wish to have German hegemony in Europe replaced by French predominance. Nor could London in the long run disregard the interests of its overstretched Empire, now greater than ever, in favour of permanent intervention on the continent of Europe. The Labour Government under Ramsay MacDonald was ready to transform those long-term interests into rapprochement and indeed reconciliation with Germany.

The Dawes Plan, named after the Wall Street banker and US Vice-President who instigated it, adjusted German reparations to the German economy's actual capacity to pay. For the first time an end to the payments was proposed – admittedly not before the mid-1980s. Simultaneously the Dawes Plan closely linked American and German interests. US policy was to turn Germany into a stabilizing factor in Europe, chiefly against the Soviet Union, officially regarded by the US government as an outrage. Wall Street realized that British and French payments to the super-creditor, the USA, would come in only if Germany remained efficient and financially sound. The American bankers also saw that France's policy was trapped in the past of the European power game and that, unless something decisive was done, French intransigence and German nationalism were bound, one unhappy day, sooner or later, to clash and settle accounts through another war.

Germany's economic health was a key factor in the stabilization of international financial markets. Linked with the Dawes Plan was an informal tie-up of the rentenmark to the US dollar, as well as a string of loans which banks in New York, London, Amsterdam and Paris granted to German debtors. Inside Germany, regardless of right-wing clamour against a 'second Versailles', heavy industry, large-scale agriculture and the banks were supportive of this stabilization. Stresemann's German People's Party, and even the successor to the Prussian Conservatives, the German National People's Party, ensured that a Reichstag majority adopted the Dawes Plan, though only after protracted and tortured discussions.

By the mid-1920s, according to official statistics, the gross national product once more reached the 1913 level. One of the bright spots in Germany's economy during those years was the British general strike of 1926. Britain's industrial centres seemed on the verge of civil war. The Germans were able to deliver, the British were not. Thus 1926/27 became one of the best years for German industry. Why then did the new times not become the good times? The plain statistics should not be allowed to conceal the fact that the war and the post-war period had ruined large sections of the middle classes, that inflation had spared the owners of material assets while it had robbed the owners of savings and bonds of their hopes and claims, that there were virtually no retirement pensions for large portions of the middle classes and that one worker out of ten was unemployed or on short time. In 1927 the Centre-Right government of Chancellor Dr Hans Luther created the Reich Labour Office to help the unemployed and to secure unemployment benefits. But the country's economic strength and the political time available were not sufficient to build up adequate financial reserves for the disasters waiting to happen.

Since the Dawes Plan, Germany in fact was enjoying a greater influx of capital in the shape of loans than France and Britain, in their turn, were receiving in the shape of reparations. Moreover, the monetary policy of the Reichsbank had been removed from control of the Reich government, with the result that the rentenmark was on the way to gaining international confidence. But structural weaknesses were not overcome. There was insufficient capital formation by industry and through private savings, extreme dependence on foreign trade, while short-term low-interest foreign loans were being invested long-term at high interest – so any recall of money across the Atlantic would of necessity trigger disaster. And that is what happened in 1931/32. Besides, Germany's high wages – inevitable result of the purchasing of internal peace in 1919 – made it hard to compete internationally. Any devaluation of the rentenmark, however, was prohibited by the creditors from abroad. The sudden and drastic devaluation of sterling against

the dollar in 1931 found Germany burdened with the disadvantageous exchange rates of the past and exposed to overpowering British competition, so German products flopped in the market.

For most Germans the Weimar republic was their second choice. At best, like foreign minister Gustav Stresemann, they accepted the form of government thrust upon them by defeat and its aftermath. In 1928, on the tenth anniversary of the republic, books appeared striking a note of cautious optimism: the worst was over. Germany again had become a player in the international concert. In 1925 the Dawes Plan was followed by the basket of treaties at Locarno, at their centre the Rhine pact between France and Belgium on one side and Germany on the other. Next came an abrogation of forcible change of borders. Border disputes both east and west were henceforth to be decided by arbitration. 'Locarno' was seen as the end of 'Versailles'. But subsequently Stresemann was unable to sign an 'Eastern Locarno' with Poland, and France's foreign minister

A mark a load. *A human beast of burden gets his payment for hefting two sacks (left).*
[PHOTO: ERICH ANDRES]

A homeless bag lady *(right) outside the Marienwerdersche Church in Berlin.*

Briand had to offer Czechoslovakia and Poland treaties of assistance in the event of German attack, in order to offset the modicum of détente with Germany.

One result of Locarno was that Germany joined the League of Nations and became a member of the Council. Gustav Stresemann and Aristide Briand were awarded the Nobel Prize for Peace. In a meeting at Thoiry, close to Geneva and the League of Nations, the two statesmen went so far as to talk of an overall settlement. Heavy industry in Germany and France began to discuss cooperation, in fact integration. This would not just be a case of cartel creation, of a kind then practised nationally on a large scale, but a move with far-reaching political implications, involving as it did mutual interlocking through swapping shares and hence mutual control of the great arms factories. Briand and Stresemann conceived their vision of a united Europe not from high-flying idealism, but in painful awareness of European resentments and with the intention of sparing the nations a repeat performance of the World War.

Stresemann's success in overcoming 'Versailles' was due to the western powers, and the United States in particular, regarding the Soviet Union under Lenin, and later under Stalin, as far more sinister than the German Republic under its patient,

reasonable, democratic leaders. But Stresemann, instead of unambiguously and irrevocably backing the West, tried also to keep the Soviet markets open to German industry, to put pressure on Poland, and to remind the West that Germany had other options. Besides, there were still substantial German grievances which the West had left unanswered, from the occupation of the Rhineland to reparations, from Allied military control to the continuing French occupation of the Saar region.

Stresemann acted in line with what he believed history and strategic geography dictated to Germany. But a great opportunity was perhaps missed as a result. Konrad Adenauer, Germany's first Federal Chancellor, twenty years later, never ceased to criticize Weimar's foreign policy as weak and vacillating. But the time was not ripe for an exclusively western option, nor was there, as in Adenauer's day, an overwhelming imperative in the shape of the Cold War and Germany's division. Adenauer himself had, in the Weimar era, been mayor of the city of Cologne and President of the Prussian State Council. But when, in 1927, he was offered the Reich Chancellorship, he coldly declined. He was thus spared the decision on which way to orient German foreign policy.

Stresemann's policy achieved a lot, but not everything. Arms reduction Europewide to reflect the low state of the German forces remained a pious wish; the peaceful border revision in the east, a dream. Instead there was an attempt to extend the frontiers of German influence both towards the east and the west through a daring balancing act. Germany's new great-

power role became symbolically apparent in the part which Stresemann played at the conclusion of the Briand-Kellogg Pact for the proscription of war on 27 August 1928. His last foreign-policy success was the Young Plan of 1929, which once more reduced German reparations – even though they were still to be paid for the next 59 years. French and Belgian troops were given definitive dates by which they would have to withdraw from the Rhineland, foreign control of German monetary policy was to be abolished, payments would henceforth go through the new Basle-based 'Bank for International Settlement' (BIZ).

At a last meeting on the shores of Lake Geneva Briand told the League of Nations that a 'united community of European nations' would have to be created, and he spoke of the 'états unis de l'Europe'. Stresemann, already marked by death like the state he represented, 'his face ashen grey' as the British historian G.P. Gooch reported in retrospect, spoke of a European coinage, which would have to come, and of European postage stamps. In political terms, however, he did not go beyond the idea of a European economic space. Briand's bold vision of the 'United States of Europe' found no echo in Germany. Briand maybe was more courageous, but the German foreign minister was more realistic. On 3 October 1929 Stresemann died of a heart attack.

It is said that no one is irreplaceable. But there are exceptions, and Stresemann was such a man, at a time when the German Republic was painfully short of democratic leadership, diplomatic skill and international standing. Walther Rathenau and he were the two politicians indispensable to the Weimar republic. A high flyer from a modest background, who had studied economics and gained his doctorate with a dissertation on the Berlin bottled beer trade, he allowed himself, even while foreign minister of the German Republic, to be impressed too much by the old ruling classes of Prussia, especially those in uniform. In 1923, the year of crisis, Stresemann had been Reich Chancellor for a few months. After that, throughout each shifting coalition, he remained Minister of Foreign Affairs. Certainly until 1932 such arrangements as were made would have been unthinkable without the store of goodwill that he had built up.

Ten years after the bitter harvest of 1918/19 Germany again enjoyed a spring of hope and the country regained a front place among the nations of Europe. But Europeans were still too trapped in their incompatible nightmares, economic interdependence was too fragile, the United States of America too far away. In 1929, the Great Depression, having long cast its shadow ahead, stifled a policy which had aimed, with a boldness flying in the face of reality, to close the chapter of the Great War. It began to dawn on people that what they had

experienced lately was merely a short break in the drama.

The end-game began, as end-games do, in surroundings of deceptive security. The Reichstag elections of 1928 produced a majority for the coalition of parties from the Social Democrats to the German People's Party, embracing both the large industrial trade unions and heavy industry, i.e. the principal forces of the German economy. But this last grand coalition was soon adrift in the vortex of the world-wide depression – declining yields, declining demand, declining investments, declining employment, declining tax revenue. It fell apart when the Social Democrats declined to vote for cuts in unemployment-benefits. Once out of government, they soon had to support measures even less to their liking.

In the spring and summer of 1930 the Weimar republic found itself not just in crisis but entering its final agony. What remained was already a different kind of republic, based on the authority of the Reich President with parliamentary proceedings short-circuited under Article 48 of the Weimar Constitution. This was to be the preferred instrument which the government, under Dr Heinrich Brüning, the Centre Party leader, used whenever it seemed appropriate. His strategy was not only to steer the ship of state through the storm but also to

reach port in a restored Bismarck-state. Meanwhile the presidential regime was tolerated by a parliamentary majority, with the Social Democrats thankful they were not themselves responsible for the cruel social welfare cuts, while most captains of industry welcomed the wholesale undoing of the revolution of 1918.

Brüning was a withdrawn and private person, a thin-lipped financial expert and strong man in the Catholic Social movement, a World War One captain despising revolution. In him, a man had now risen to the peak of politics who believed in traditional values, thrift and paternal commonsense, responsibility and reason, a man to whom the commonwealth

was not empty fiction but the anchor of all politics. Simple remedies like credit expansion by the state, inflation or deficit budgets were no option for this believer in enlightened absolutism. Instead he attempted to make a virtue of necessity and use the crisis as a means of reining back the welfare state. Moreover he needed the goodwill of the Allies for any revision of the treaty of Versailles. In the spring of 1932, the customs union with Austria, sought by Brüning for economic reasons but also as a tonic for the nation, failed in the teeth of fierce French opposition.

Economic crisis and sterling devaluation made it virtually impossible for German industry to compete internationally, not

Communist militants (left) *march under a banner proclaiming 'Fascism means hunger and war'. Many of these members of the Roter Frontkämpferbund - the Red Front – will soon exchange one set of uniforms and slogans for another and join the Nazi SA. What really matters is the sense of belonging, the meaning which marching, brawling and beery choruses give to what would otherwise be a life without hope.*
[PHOTO: ERNST THORMANN]

Food first, rent later *says a slogan between these Berlin tenements (right). The flags show both Nazi and Communist sympathisers live here, but all agree with the message.*

is an unending vortex of mutual deceit and self-deceit through ideologies.' His lecture was published immediately and became a bestseller, number 1000 in the popular Goschen series.

Civil war, the fundamental pattern of political discourse since the French Revolution, had been checked in the Weimar republic by large-scale social and political compromise and by the constitution. A decade later, however, compromise was exhausted, while the extremist parties under hammer-and-sickle and the swastika were lying in ambush for each other. This happened in parliament, in the streets, in pamphlets and newspapers, in people's minds. There was an eagerness to seek salvation in a messianic movement from the Left or a messianic leader from the Right. Were the Communists the answer to the crisis of liberal Europe? Or a political general? Or a mixture of Right and Left, a Duce as in Italy? Mussolini's fascism had, since 1922, been a strange and unorthodox combination of the old and the new. Italy still had its monarchy and traditional state structures – and it would be in the name of these that in 1943, when the Allies had already landed in southern Italy, Mussolini

only because of high interest rates and high wages, but also because Germany was forbidden by the Allies to follow the path of devaluation. The state budget was weighed down by welfare payments. National Socialists and Communists were engaged in street battles in all the major cities, and the police were, time and again, drawn into conflicts bordering on open civil war. Salaries and wages were cut, prices were frozen. The philosopher Karl Jaspers, in his Heidelberg lecture theatre, spoke of a crisis of confidence and identity that had become a feature of the epoch well beyond Germany: 'There seems to be a widespread feeling that everything is failing, that nothing is left that is not questionable; nothing authentic is reliable; there

Franz von Papen *(left), the Catholic right-wing lightweight whom Hindenburg made Chancellor for a few months in June 1932, before his morning ride in Berlin's Tiergarten in 1925. Von Papen joined Hitler's cabinet in 1933, thinking he could handle him, yet before long counted himself lucky to have escaped alive.*

[PHOTO: HERBERT HOFFMANN]

Chancellor Heinrich Brüning *(seated, right) in conversation with the Italian dictator, Benito Mussolini, in Rome 1931. The figure in between them is Julius Curtius, German foreign minister (opposite).*

[PHOTO: ERICH SALOMON]

was overthrown and his regime brought to an end. Mussolini's 'March on Rome' in 1922 had been a farcical event, heroic theatre, *bella figura*. But the new creations – *dopo lavoro*, the black uniforms, his youth militia, the party army, the concentration camps – all these definitely pointed to the future.

Hysterical accusations of 'fascism' were regularly thrown at the Right and the Centre, including the Social Democrats, by Communist stalwarts. Yet those expecting a German Mussolini were indulging in the illusion that Hitler was nothing but a copy of the Duce, to be controlled by the powerful forces of the German establishment. They overlooked the fact that Hitler with his ruthlessness and murderous energy was incomparably closer to the man in the Kremlin than to the man in the Palazzo Venezia – an elective affinity nourished by mortal enmity. What linked the movements of the extreme Right and the extreme Left in Germany was not only the concept of the final battle between good and evil, not only hatred of the bourgeoisie and liberal culture, but their dependence on a unique and irreplaceable charismatic leader, who knew everything, commanded everything, and was responsible for nothing. Hitler's ideology of annihilation echoed Stalin's murderous pursuits, not Mediterranean rhetoric. With the Hitler movement a wild concoction of fear and hope, of anarchy and alienation and totalitarian cleansing was administered to Germany. Using the streets and beer halls, unnerving their opponents by killings and by mass rallies, by pipes and drums, Hitler's brown battalions provided the infernal accompaniment to the death throes of the republic. And they were doing so in shrill concert with the Communists.

In Berlin's Wilhelmstrasse, meanwhile, Chancellor Brüning stood aloof, preaching nothing but classic financial policy; indeed, he had an unequalled command of the budget and budget legislation but he failed to understand what was going on in the nations's guts and gutters. When the Social Democrats and German National People's Party opposed his economies, he got the Reich President to dissolve the Reichstag in the summer of 1930. Little did he suspect that he had opened the floodgates of anger and desperation. After the elections of 14 September 1930, there were now, instead of the earlier fourteen, over a hundred roaring, whistling, howling, stamping brown-shirted people's representatives in the house, directed by Hermann Göring from inside and by their 'Führer' from outside – as Hitler held Austrian citizenship, he was legally not eligible until 1931. Brüning's idea of the autonomous presidential authority above party had gone astray. From then on he stumbled from one emergency decree to another, a man driven rather than driving. He could govern as long as the Reich President was willing to sign documents and as long as a Left-Centre majority in the Reichstag regarded him as the lesser evil and, from fear of the extremists, accepted whatever he put on their plate. Ultimately, it was the Reichswehr on which law and order depended.

In the summer of 1932, however, Hindenburg's seven-year term of office would come to an end – this ancient field marshal who, as a lieutenant in 1871, had attended the proclamation of the German Reich in Versailles. Brüning did all he could to field a credible counter-candidate of the Centre to oppose Hitler. It was not a bad idea to trump the First World War private, first class, with a field marshal and to win Social Democrat and

Centre Party support. Thus the 80-year-old man was re-elected by a wide margin. Brüning hoped that Hindenburg would repay loyalty with loyalty, but he soon learned that gratitude is not a political commodity. 'One hundred metres from the finish' – as he subsequently put it, bitterly but calmly – the last halfway-democratic Reich Chancellor was dismissed. Brüning, architect of presidential re-election, had become too powerful. Also, he stood in the way of the great national right-wing rapprochement sought by the Reich President and his sinister entourage. Brüning's opposition to this plan was his undoing. He had wanted authoritarian leadership, so as to be able to oppose 'the drummer' – Hitler – and his desperate hosts. Now he had served his purpose and was unceremoniously cast aside.

Brüning was succeeded, by fiat of the Reich President, by Franz von Papen. The latter had not risen through parliament but belonged to the far Right wing of German Catholicism, a vain and empty ex-officer whose experience was confined to aristocratic clubs and elitist journals. No sooner was he in office than he gave orders to depose, through a coup d'état, the government of the state of Prussia, still headed by the 'Red King of Prussia', the East Prussian Social Democrat Otto Braun. On 20th July 1932 the most powerful among the German states capitulated to a little force, the proverbial lieutenant with ten men. To send the Prussian police into action and bare their teeth at the Reich government, let alone mobilize the republican militias, seemed inadvisable to Braun and his minister of the interior Severing. They knew the widespread sympathy for the Nazis and the admiration for the Reichswehr existing among the ranks of the police. They feared bloodshed and civil war, and they could not imagine the consequences of their credulity bordering on weakness.

For good measure Papen dissolved the Reichstag, in order to free himself for a few months from parliamentary interference. A British writer, E Mowrer, witnessed the election campaign that followed:

'A state of virtual anarchy prevails in the streets of Germany … Brown shirts were everywhere in evidence again, and now four private armies, equipped at the very least with jack knives and revolvers, daggers and brass knuckles, were shooting in the squares and rampaging through the towns. Processions and meetings, demonstrations and protest, festivals and funerals, all wore the same face but a different uniform – except that the SS and SA of the Nazis, and the Red Front of the Communists marched more obstreperously, the Sozi Reichsbanner more fatly, the Stahlhelmers more sedately. The Reichswehr, the only legal force, was least in evidence, even though it was, in a sense, the private political tool of Hindenburg.'

These new elections gave the NSDAP (the Nazi Party) and the KPD (the Communist Party) a virtual majority, though the totalitarian twins were united only by their hatred of Papen and the republic. Hitler's success fed on itself. A young man, out of work, would join the SA and receive a uniform, badges and boots, hot soup and pocket money. Thus he would join a rough

men's club that was half socialist and half military, he would become somebody, armed with his fists and his boots and a desperate hope one day to be delivered from all evil by his devilish messiah. Marching in columns generated a sense of unity as well as a thirst for vengeance, blood lust and hunger for loot and promotion. Once more Papen gained the Reich President's support for dissolving an absurd parliament. As if Germany had looked into the abyss and shuddered, the elections of November 1932 reflected a change for the better. The slump had evidently bottomed out and this glimmer of hope cost the Nazis so many votes that their leaders, not least Hitler, feared the movement might lose its revolutionary appeal and material support, and crumble. The liberal *Frankfurter Zeitung* was not alone when, towards the end of 1932, it claimed that the worst was over and Hitler in decline.

So far the Reichswehr had kept in the background, but there were more than a few Nazi sympathizers among the young officers. In the 'Ulm Reichswehr trial' Colonel Beck – one of the main figures in the attempt in July 1944 on Hitler's life – spoke out for two lieutenants who had openly supported the Nazi Party, thereby infringing the Weimar Constitution's ban on political activity in the forces. It was a warning signal for commanding officers that there were limits to loyalty and obedience and that it would be wise not to test the cohesion of the forces in fire.

The Wandervogel tradition goes on (above) and boys continue to sing away in huts and round campfires in the hills.
[PHOTO: AUGUST SANDER]

Student duelling (right), with the object of acquiring as many scars as possible, but no serious damage, was a highly formalised rite of passage. Protective clothing and goggles to shield the eyes were worn, but the rest of the face and upper body were left bare to receive the desired sabre cuts. White-coated medical attendants wait to sew them up, not too neatly so these will be visible proof of youthful bravado. The student bodies which organised the fights were suppressed in 1935.
[PHOTO: JOSEPH SCHORER]

A Hitler Youth and a Young Fascist from Italy in fraternal embrace (far right). The innate Italian sense of style is clear from the much smarter Fascist uniform.
[PHOTO: MAX EHLERT]

Papen, even for Hindenburg's taste, was too much of a lightweight. To succeed him, General Kurt von Schleicher was appointed Reich Chancellor. He was not popular among the ranks as a military commander, as he was rather a political general. His strategy was to keep emergency measures for a limited period, rally all men and women of commonsense, from the trade unions to industry, and prevent open civil war. As for the radicals, he hoped to deal with them by threatening to dissolve parliament. Otherwise he aimed to gain time by emergency decrees, wearing down the Nazis and the Communists. If this was a dangerous gamble, what else was left?

But Schleicher failed to gain confidence and broader support. To the trade unions he was too much of a general, to the nationalists he was too much of a politician, to the landowners he was someone who wanted to carve up estates in the east. Moreover, the President refused to sign the dissolution order for the Reichstag through which Schleicher hoped to hold Hitler in check. Meanwhile the wily Papen, representing the Hindenburg interest, the condottiere Hermann Göring standing for the Nazi Party, and the press lord Alfred Hugenberg for the German Nationalists were jointly intriguing in favour of a Hitler coalition, which they intended to manage and use. Such an alliance would draw a line under trade union activity and parliamentary rule and would, at the same time, fence in and tame the loudest voices among the Nazis. By the end of January 1933 they had succeeded. Schleicher had served his purpose and was told to go. Exactly seventeen months later he and his wife were shot dead by Hitler's henchmen.

It was a chilling scene when, on 30 January 1933 just before noon, the new Reich cabinet, Chancellor Hitler in morning coat and top hat, took their oaths on the Weimar Constitution. None of those present doubted for a moment that now the final convulsions of the first German Republic had ended in its death. At the climax of a long day, when the triumphal torchlight procession of Brownshirts had passed through the nearby Brandenburg Gate, one Berliner felt something in particular puzzle him. The SA were not doing the Prussian goose-step but marching with the long stride of the Deutschmeister, Vienna's crack regiment. This was the replacement of the north by the south, Austria's revenge for defeat at Königgrätz in 1866. Another noticed that as each band passed the French embassy on the Pariser Platz they broke into 'Siegreich wollen wir Frankreich schlagen – Victorious we will crush the French'. Göring asked Hitler what he would have done if he had been the French prime minister. He replied instantly: 'I should have marched'. Joseph Goebbels, clear-sighted and determined as the devil, remarked to those present: 'No one will get us out of here alive.'

CHAPTER FIVE

THE THOUSAND-YEAR REICH

ADOLF HITLER WAS OBSESSED BY POWER. HIS TOOLS of tyranny were seduction and violence. He combined the threat of concentration camp, torture and lonely death with the promise of the new community, the glories of the master race and the end of history in the 'Thousand-Year Reich'. André François-Poncet, French Ambassador to Berlin in the 1930s and one of the great chroniclers of the decade, described the Führer:

'pale face, protruding eyes, the distant gaze of a medium or a sleepwalker. At times excited, fidgety, shaken by passion and violence. Not accessible to any control, bold, cynical, energetic. Sometimes with an expression of violent aggression, the features of a lunatic. Sometimes naive, peasant-like, boring, vulgar, easily amused, a man who slaps his thighs, a face like a thousand others. At times he would be all these in a single conversation. He would talk to himself for ten minutes, a quarter of an hour, three-quarters of an hour. After that he'd be exhausted. Then others could speak, and he was even able to smile. He was not a normal person, but a morbid, almost mad, Dostoevsky character, a person obsessed. He was an Austrian who passionately loved Germany, wildly romantic, full of half-baked ideas ... He wanted a new Germany that would take the place of the Holy Roman Empire, a pure race, an elite. He lived Wagner.'

Twenty-five years before, Hitler had learnt in the Vienna Men's Hostel how to combine day-dreaming with cold-blooded realism. The war in the trenches was his defining experience. Ruthless and extremist, he yet remained what he had been in his formative years before the First World War – a bohemian. A man of endless monologues, he was an actor who could talk himself into ecstasies; his time was the night, when he would talk and talk and talk; he saw himself as a lone wolf, he called his East Prussian headquarters the Wolf's Lair, and his armoury the Wolfsburg. On the Festival Hill in Bayreuth he allowed Winifred Wagner to worship him as 'Herr Wolf'. He kept his pack at a distance, and played with his followers, raising them sky-high or casting them into outer darkness.

Some historians have described his regime as chaos and himself as incapable of organized administrative work, as a weak leader – as if Auschwitz and Stalingrad had not been genuine expressions of his will. What he did do was encourage rivalry among his minions, giving them undefined powers, making them compete to follow his orders and even anticipate his every wish. There was a story going round in the 30s, half in jest, that Hitler desperately wanted a painting that had been put up for auction and had therefore dispatched two bidders, both with instructions to acquire the object of his desire, both without limit. When it

Nazi pageantry: *9 November 1936 and the cream of the Party re-enact their march through the streets of Munich thirteen years earlier, just before the ignominious end of the Beer Hall Putsch. It was a good year for Hitler: in March his troops reoccupied the demilitarized zone of the Rhineland without opposition from France or Britain, both soon distracted by the outbreak of the Spanish Civil War. The alliance with Italy was well advanced. The propaganda triumph of the Berlin Olympics in August was followed by the biggest Nuremberg Rally so far, lasting a week. And now the Führer could transform his humiliation in 1923 into yet another triumph choreographed by Alfred Speer, as he marched through the smoke given off by an avenue of beacons mounted on pylons. The only thing that defied Nazi presentational skills was Göring's girth.*

was pointed out to him that this was a contradiction, he is said to have replied curtly: 'The stronger man prevails.'

He was not given to paper work. The charismatic leader does not waste his time by being the chief servant of state and bureaucracy; he refuses to be fettered by business practices, cabinet meetings, minutes. If necessary he will cut through chains of command: the 'Führer's order' must be the law of the land. Arbitrariness becomes essential, otherwise the despot will himself have to submit to some kind of order or precedent. To explain to him the rules of conservative monetary policy, as Dr Hjalmar Schacht did, or to get past him a 'constitutional law of the Greater German Reich', as Professor Ernst Rudolf Huber did, was a waste of time. The misconception of the Reichsbank-president and the university professor was that of all those who believed politics could not be other than orderly, calculable and objective. Only this can explain why the German ruling class, the majority certainly not sinister figures, from senior civil servants to Reichswehr commanders, surrendered to an adventurer who knew no moral boundaries, no law, no rational aim other than totalitarian domination over Germany and Europe.

From start to finish Hitler saw himself as an artist called upon by providence to create the world anew. From his detention at Landsberg, which followed his botched Beer Hall Putsch of 9 November 1923, there is his design for a triumphal arch, compared to which the Brandenburg Gate looks like a mere matchbox. Later he made a present of it to Albert Speer in order to teach him the scale to which his drawings should aspire. His book *Mein Kampf*, 800 pages of bombast, hatred and semi-erudition, was a similarly maniacal design for Germany and the world, the past and the future.

He came from Braunau on the Inn, set in the idyllic landscape of the lower Salzach river between Salzburg and Passau. There he grew up, the son of a minor customs official; from there he went to Vienna to become an artist. But instead he, rejected by the Academy of Arts, learnt to hate the universe of the declining Hapsburg monarchy – its many languages, its supranationality, its Catholicism, its haute bourgeoisie, the Rothschilds and the Wittgensteins, its tall slim officers, its pluralism and its decadence.

The first day of the First World War was experienced by Hitler, amidst a cheering crowd in Munich, as a salvation; at the war's end, he had neither a physical home to return to, neither family or farmstead, nor a spiritual home. He believed in war as the ultimate truth about the lives of nations and people. In the big city jungle he had acquired his predatory instinct for survival; his time would come once the establishment that had rejected him had been reduced to the level of the Viennese hostel for the homeless where he had served his apprenticeship in murderous hatred.

In better days he would have found a living, somewhere on the lower edges of the bourgeoisie. But at a time when tradition was no longer valid, when there was no Kaiser, no God, no Fatherland, and no money – that was the hour of the Führer.

Yet there were plenty of Führers around (the Freikorps were full of them), and the libraries overflowed with global visions, cheap variations on Nietzsche and Spengler. But the world took no notice. So why did Hitler, member No.7 of a radical right-wing splinter group named the National Socialist German Workers' Party, NSDAP, stand out, become the curse of Germany and the whole of Europe?

The story of Hitler was one of underestimation, and it continued long after his death in the thesis of the 'weak leader' or in the equally mistaken assertion that he had merely been a tool in the hands of 'big business'. The Reichswehr officers who hired him as an agitator in 1919 treated him like a servant. The leader writers of the major liberal papers wrote him off as a has-been at the turn of 1932/33. Men like Papen and Hugenberg, when joining his cabinet in 1933, thought they had him pinned down, yet before long they counted themselves lucky to escape alive. Churchleaders and the Vatican hoped to manoeuvre him; foreign powers were charmed by his speeches about the blessings of peace, foreign statesmen signed treaties with him not worth the paper they were written on. Financiers believed accumulating state debt would crush him. Some old hands of Weimar party politics thought that the entire weird spectacle would be over in a few months. The Jews did not believe the evidence of what they saw every day. The Conservatives trusted in the ageing field marshal-president; the army relied on its strength, discipline and professionalism and on the ability, if need be, to take up arms and put an end to anything untoward. Never before have so many honest people allowed themselves to be so thoroughly deceived by their own wishful thinking and by their failure to realize that – to quote Hans-Bernd von Haeften, on trial a few weeks after the failed 1944 plot against Hitler – the Führer was 'a great executor of evil'.

Hitler's view of the world was fuelled by his hatred of life before 1914, by the trauma of the Bolshevik revolution, and by his revolt against modern civilization and everything that characterized the twentieth century – democracy, technology, the social sciences and history. Yet at the same time he made use of all these instruments – he let democracy carry him to the top, he made technology serve his propaganda machine and later carry out his murderous designs, while history to him was a way out of darkness into the light, from '14 years of shame and disgrace' to the 'Thousand-Year Reich'. He was first a demagogue who roused the masses to fury and then the redeemer who utilized the accumulated energy for his purposes.

However, the 'Third Reich' was not just the history of Hitler, nor did it suddenly start on 30 January 1933. The World War had destroyed the self-assurance of the old elite and the hopes

'Herr Wolf'. *Hitler poses in 1925 with props – pseudo-baroque chair, grand piano, noble hound – to improve on his recent image of agitator and street fighter.*

Goebbels recorded that the vegetarian Hitler 'has little regard for homo sapiens. Man should not feel so superior to the animals.'
[PHOTO: HEINRICH HOFFMANN]

of the middle classes. The Bolshevik revolution cast its shadow over Germany and created fears of Armageddon. Inflation undermined the well-to-do, and the Depression and mass unemployment pulled the rug from under the working classes. Not least, there was the national humiliation and the material hardship imposed by the Versailles Treaty: Paris in 1919 was not Vienna in 1815. The French Revolution and Napoleon's wars were followed by a Congress where the statesmen of Europe showed enough strength and wisdom to close the abyss, so their settlement held for a generation, perhaps two. But the age of ideologies, of mass democracy and of the nation state changed the rules. Even if politicians had shown more wisdom, the rage of nations would have rejected it.

Hitler himself, after a few months in power, was surprised to learn how quickly the institutions of the Weimar Republic, which he had once feared, collapsed. The hard-headed interest groups were eating out of his hand, the political parties dissolved more or less by themselves, as did the time-tested governments of the individual German Länder. What had become of the many-voiced press of Imperial Germany and the Weimar Republic? Where was the independent judiciary? Just as if they had only been waiting for a signal, they all conformed to 'Gleichschaltung'. That meant they were levelled down, brought into line, subject to disorientation and violence, resignation and fear.

The secret was that the 'Pgs', the 'Parteigenossen' or Party comrades, men and women, had long formed their political cells inside the police and the judiciary, in administrative offices, schools and universities. From the private bank of Sal. Oppenheim jr. & Cie. in Cologne, a bulwark of sound business, a medium-level employee rose to be the Chief Mayor of Cologne, soon driving Konrad Adenauer from office. Hermann Göring – the new top man in Prussia – raised the SA, the Nazi Brownshirt formations, to the rank of auxiliary police, and they began to arrest, beat up, torture, pillage and murder whomever happened to be in their way. Up and down the country camps – soon to become known under the short and sinister abbreviation KZ – were set up, the SA actually jumping the gun and opening them before specifically ordered to by Hitler. They were no secret, the facts were reported in the press, as the regime found it useful not only to keep the public in fear, but also to turn the Germans into accomplices.

One day during the Munich carnival a lady of doubtful virtue demanded admission to the renowned 'Vier Jahreszeiten' hotel and the head of reception turned her away; an hour later, her protector Reinhard Heydrich appeared in a black limousine and in SS uniform, and demanded to see the director of the

hotel, called Waltherspiel. Heydrich promised him a visit to Dachau if the lady were ever treated like this again. A few years later, when Hitler's right-hand-man Martin Bormann needed space for his residence on the Obersalzberg, he told the director of a sanatorium there, called Dr Seitz, to move out at once, along with the children, little tuberculosis patients. When the physician remonstrated, Bormann asked him: 'Does the name Dachau mean anything to you?'

Within a few days of moving into the Reich Chancellery, Hitler summoned the top military leaders. What the men in uniform heard was entirely to their liking – ancient virtues and Prussian tradition, rearmament and power politics. But then the man in brown party uniform informed the disbelieving generals that the overriding goal of German foreign policy must be the acquisition of 'living space in the east, in order ruthlessly to Germanize it'. What else did this mean other than war and mass murder? The comment of one of those present was unsuspecting and disdainful: 'New brooms sweep clean.' Just as he promised rearmament to the generals, so Hitler promised the industrialists the elimination of the trade unions and the end of political parties. The elections of 5 March 1933 would be the last for a long time to come.

A few days before, the Reichstag building had burned down. Was the fire the work of Göring, the Reichstag President, and his SS helpers? (On February 20 Count Harry Kessler reported in his diary a rumour of 'a fake attempt on Hitler's life which is to be the signal for a general massacre.') From the president's palace there was a subterranean passage to the Reichstag building. A mentally disturbed person called Marinus van der Lubbe, a former member of the Communist Party, was caught on the spot and charged. There is no final certainty in this matter, but there is no question of who benefited from it. The very next morning, 28 February 1933, the 'Decree for the Protection of Nation and State' was promulgated. It abolished civil rights and threw centuries of good government in Germany into the dustbin. And yet it only legitimized what for the past four weeks had become common practice in Germany – unfettered power. On February 17 Göring had told local police officers to cooperate with the SA and SS to combat the Left: 'Every bullet that now leaves the mouth of a police pistol is my bullet. If you call that murder, then I am the murderer, for I gave the order and I stand by it.' It is astonishing that, regardless of the ubiquitous SA storm troopers, surveillance and intimidation, the NSDAP and the German National People's Party only just achieved a bare majority in the Reichstag elections of 5 March.

This Parliament had but one final task – to lend Hitler the cloak of legality. This was done by the Empowering Law of 23 March 1933. The required two-thirds majority was achieved only by the annulment of the Communist deputies' mandates. The deputies themselves were already imprisoned or underground. Two days previously, in the Garrison Church in Potsdam, under the carillon which played the traditional

The Reichswehr stamps its approval on the new regime, as the crack Infanterieregiment Neun march past President Hindenburg in Potsdam during the parade on 21 March 1933 *that also included the SA and the Stahlhelm (ex-servicemen's association).*

[PHOTO: MARTIN MUNKACSI]

The demagogue and the condottiere *(opposite)*: *Hitler's ruthless and brilliant 'Minister of Public Enlightenment and Propaganda', Josef Goebbels, looking like a mannekin beside the bulk of Hermann Göring. Goebbels controlled the hearts and minds, Göring the economy, much of the police, and the Luftwaffe, as well as being 'Reichsjägermeister' – Chief Huntsman of the Reich. The event at which they were photographed was a vivid example of how truth was manipulated: Labour Day held on 1 May 1935, in spite of the fact that trade unions had effectively been abolished two years before.*

Outside the Feldherrnhalle, *(right) Munich. Another photo taken on the same day as that on pp148–149. This was close to the spot where the Beer Hall Putsch melted away once the Bavarian police opened fire on Hitler and his co-conspirators in 1923. The crowd waits for the re-enacted march to pass by.*

[PHOTOS: MAX EHLERT]

heard. The regime, based on a messianic promise of salvation, could not tolerate any independent force, but its anti-religious attitude became somewhat diluted during the war, when people, including many non-believers, were seeking solace amidst death and ruin. The SS, however, was set to make sure, after Germany's certain victory, that the matter would be cleaned up for good.

Goebbels, writing in his diary in December 1939, reported Hitler as saying, 'The best way to deal with the churches is to claim to be a positive Christian ... the technique must be to hold back for the present and coolly strangle any attempts at impudence or interference in the affairs of the state ... He [Hitler] views Christianity as a symptom of decay. Rightly so. It is a branch of the Jewish race ... The Führer is a convinced vegetarian, on principle ... He has little regard for homo sapiens. Man should not feel so superior to the animals.' Later, in 1941, Goebbels was to claim 'The Führer is a man totally attuned to antiquity ... what a difference between the benevolent smiling Zeus and the pain-wracked crucified Christ ... between a gloomy cathedral and a light, airy, ancient temple ... The Führer cannot relate to the Gothic mind.'

It has often been asked, accusingly or by way of excuse, how much did people know at the time? The concentration camps were an open secret from the start, reported on in the German and foreign press. On 1 April 1933, when intimidation, death threats and acts of violence against Jews began, everyone knew what was happening and who had organized it all. Those in power hardly bothered to hide anything. The whole world was in the know. The regime made a deliberate effort to make the entire nation an accomplice before itself and the world – repeating ancient rituals of collective responsibility for a dreadful deed. Whoever had ears to hear and eyes to see was able, at an early date, to realize that the regime was merciless and without any restraint. But in this kind of situation people

invariably reassure themselves with the argument that you can't make an omelette without breaking eggs. There was talk of growing pains and transitional phenomena. Besides, it soon became dangerous to pass on what one knew, let alone to criticize the regime. By mid-1934 the Gestapo's spider-web covered the entire nation, reinforced by an army of willing informers. The block warden system, copied from Soviet Russia, ensured that everyone lived under meticulous and constant surveillance. Those arrested were lucky if they were formally tried and went to a state prison, rather than being thrown straight into a concentration camp.

The regime, moreover, preserved a confusing double character, as an emigré trade union lawyer, Ernst Fraenkel, explained to the Americans in the Thirties in his book *The Dual State*. One part of the power apparatus operating in the twilight would threaten, impose 'protective custody', expropriate, torture and kill; the other, in the light, would function as before, often rather better. Turnover tax and income tax were collected, land registers and trade registers were kept – including details of the expropriation of Jewish property, the protection of its new owners and the 'Aryanization' of firms. Libel suits were conducted, divorce suits were heard, pensions claims adjudicated – including that of Dr Adenauer, the deposed Mayor of Cologne, who had retired into a kind of internal emigration among the hills of Rhöndorf on the right bank of the Rhine.

The brutality of the regime and its leader is exemplified in an account by Hermann Rauschning, the Nazi leader in Danzig, who defected in 1935. A revulsion against SS cruelty in Stettin was reported to Hitler in 1933 when Rauschning was present: 'He foamed at the mouth, panting and stammering in uncontrollable fury, "I won't have it! Get rid of all of them! Traitors! [after calming down] Haven't you ever seen a crowd collecting to watch a street brawl? Brutality is respected. Brutality and physical strength. The plain man in the street respects nothing but brutal strength and ruthlessness – women too for that matter, women and children. The people need wholesome fear. They want to fear something. They want someone to frighten them and make them shudderingly submissive ... Why babble about brutality and be indignant about tortures? The masses want that. They need something that will give them a thrill of horror ... I don't want concentration camps turned into penitentiary institutions. Terror is the most effective political instrument. I shall not permit myself to be robbed of it because a lot of stupid,

16. Juli 1933
10. Jahrgang / Nr. 28
Verlag Knorr & Hirth,
G. m. b. h., München

Preis: 20 Pfennig
Österr.: 40 Grosch. / Tschechosl.: 2 Kron.
Schweiz: 30 Rappen / Italien: 1,50 Lire
Frankreich: 1,50 Frs. / Elsaß-Loth-
ringen: 1,25 Frs. / Holland: 15 Cent
Jugoslawien: 5 Dinar / Estland: 25 Cent

Münchner Illustrierte Presse

Aufnahme: Bauer-München

Frühappell im Erziehungslager

Disziplin erzieht zu gemeinschaftlicher aufbauender Arbeit

bourgeois mollycoddles choose to be offended by it ... Anybody who is such a poltroon that he can't bear the thought of someone merely having to suffer pain had better join a sewing-circle, but not my party comrades!"'

Without any dramatic break the old welfare state became the new guardian state which, on the side, also allowed ten thousand eyes and ears to spy on the people. Who, in the face of the 'Winter Relief Scheme', or 'Strength through Joy', or the 'Mother and Child' programme, would think of evil? Were the new Labour Day, the office outing, the greenery in the factories, or the Sunday 'One-Pot Meal with the Führer' immediately seen as sops of dictatorship? Yet everybody knew that he was living under the controlling gaze of the 'block warden' and the local Party leader, and that behind it all stood the threat of the Secret State Police, the Gestapo. Würzburg is one of only three European towns whose Gestapo records were not destroyed by the Nazis at the end of the war. These reveal that there were only twenty-two Gestapo officials allocated to the town, of whom almost half were purely administrative. The system could only work with the support of the ordinary population.

After the first year the Reichswehr alone stood between Hitler and unrestricted power. But the generals were breathlessly busy transforming their cadre and élite troops into a mass army. The necessary financial means were provided by Dr Schacht, Hitler's arrogant and elusive president of the

Reichsbank, through special budgets concealing the mounting deficit of the regular national budget. Only when it was too late did the generals realize that Hitler wanted not great power status but war, not to play a part in world politics but world power, and that he was driving the country and the army into a gigantic adventure. The military leaders saw much more of a threat in the semi-revolutionary SA Brownshirts and their rowdy leaders, hating their indiscipline and beer-sodden vulgarity. Hitler also felt threatened by the SA Commander Ernst Röhm who now had more than a million men behind him. Röhm, in turn, knew that the ground was shifting under him, as he told Hermann Rauschning early 1934:

'Adolf is a swine. He will give us all away. He only associates with the reactionaries now ... Getting matey with the East Prussian Generals. They're his cronies now ... Adolf knows exactly what I want. I've told him often enough. Not a second edition of the old imperial army. Are we revolutionaries or aren't we? ... The generals are a lot of old fogeys. They never had a new idea ... I'm the nucleus of the new army, don't you see that? Don't you understand that what is coming must be new, fresh and unused? The basis must be revolutionary. You can't inflate it afterwards. You only get the opportunity once to make something new and big that'll help us lift the world off its hinges. But Hitler puts me off with fair words.'

The generals therefore were pleased when, on 30 June 1934,

Hitler sent out the SS to shoot the leaders of the SA summarily. The murdered men also included two Reichswehr generals, which made the military leaders realize their own precarious position, though not the need to oppose disaster there and then, while there was still time. But was there still time? Hitler never allowed any rival for power a chance to gather his forces. Heinrich Himmler, the son of a middle-class family from Munich-Schwabing and now the utterly loyal Chief of the SS, was given permission to raise armed formations up to a strength of 20,000 men – but who was to supervise or control him? When the Reich President died in the summer of 1934, the 'Führer and Reichskanzler' abolished the post and made the forces take their 'sacred oath before God' to his own person – the Führer in fact became the law of the land. The Reichswehr

The new salute *(opposite) is tentatively tried out by children as participants in the 1933 Nuremberg rally drive by. It is a fresh beginning and more children are conceived this year than for many years past.*

Spontaneous support *for the Party was much better organised by 1937, as this truckload of teenagers (right) on their way to that year's rally indicates. They are not in uniform and may be a delegation of enthusiasts from Austria.*

[PHOTOS: MAX EHLERT]

The guardian state *replaces the welfare state. A Hamburg Party chief appeals for donations (opposite) to the 'Winter Fund' in December 1933. It was better to give than to ask questions.* [PHOTO: JOHANNES SCHORER]

The face of hatred: *Josef Goebbels (right) in full flight in 1933. The Gauleiter of Berlin, wearing a three-piece suit, addresses a middle-class audience.*

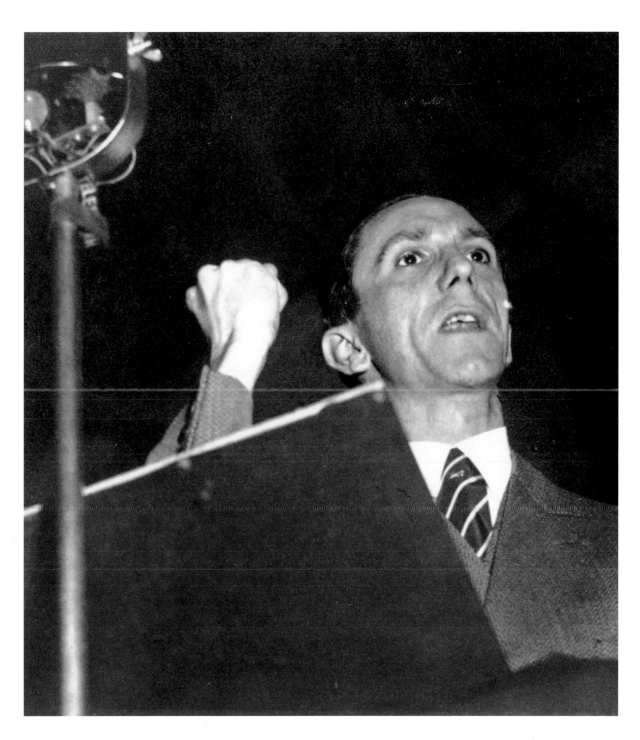

took this oath to Hitler man by man, and few realised that this proud 'state within the state' thus became the accomplice of tyranny. Many among the young officers were enthralled by a regime that promised rapid promotion, military glory and a return to power politics.

It remains one of the great questions of German and European history how a middle class educated in the humanities, powerful industrial leaders, churches rich in tradition, an army and a civil service of longstanding probity could have become prey to a vulgar mass movement, itself the tool of a ruthless preacher. The short answer is that they were willing victims or even executioners. The long answer lies in the combination of seduction and violence. Disorientation, demoralisation and fear of the abyss had undermined all tradition. How far the new beginning of 1933 went is shown by

the fact that soon there were more marriages, that more children were fathered – in and out of wedlock – than for many years. There was more at work than just coercion and propaganda, and even the new marriage allowances do not explain much. The economic revival was still a long way off. What did exist was the laying of foundations, speeches, banners and festivities. Determined gestures and national symbols gave rise to the hope that everything would turn for the better now. This was not a new political beginning of the familiar type, with a lot of words and little action, but rather a revolution and a pseudo-religious awakening.

Propaganda, nevertheless, filled the ears of the public and shut its eyes. Joseph Goebbels, a limping German studies PhD, a pupil of the Jesuits from the Cologne region, became 'Reich Minister of Public Enlightenment and Propaganda' – as his title

'UnGerman' books *are hurled into the flames (opposite) in Berlin's Opernplatz by students in May 1933. Erich Kästner, author of the children's classic* Emil and the Detectives, *stood watching, even though his works were burning. Above, smug*

Hamburg Party officials take away more fuel for the bonfires. A century before, Heinrich Heine had warned that where books were burned, humans would follow.

[PHOTO, ABOVE: JOHANNES SCHORER]

proclaimed with astonishing frankness. Goebbels fanned the flames of mistrust. In many university towns, especially in Berlin in the great square in front of the library of the Friedrich-Wilhelm's (now Humboldt) University, books were burned. Modern painting and sculpture was condemned, wholesale, as 'Weimar-suspicious' and 'depraved', including that of the Bauhaus. In November 1936 Goebbels banned all art criticism:

'I granted German critics four years after our assumption of power to adapt themselves to National Socialist principles … Since the year 1936 has passed without any satisfactory improvement in art criticism, I am herewith forbidding, from this day on, the conduct of art criticism as it has been practiced to date … The art critic will be replaced by the art editor … In the future only those art editors will be allowed to report on art who approach the task with an undefiled heart and National Socialist convictions.'

In 1937 key works of modern art were exhibited behind the columns of Munich's newly built, multi-pillared House of

National Socialist Art *in 1937. An exhibition (left) named after one of Hitler's slogans, 'Give me four years', shows what has been achieved. At Munich (right) a triptych of 'The Four Elements' is on view at the 'Day of German Art' in the 'House of German Art'.*
[PHOTO: MAX EHLERT]

The Nuremberg Rally, *1933 (overleaf). A sense of strength and unity was generated by these events, and all doubt and dissent banished. The British ambassador admitted, 'For grandiose beauty I have never seen a ballet to compare with it.' Hitler was as intoxicated by the mass emotion given off as anyone present.*
[PHOTO: MAX EHLERT]

German Art, works combed out from museums to be exposed to public revulsion as 'degenerate art' and subsequently sold at international art auctions. In their place, official art wished to present heroic men and child-bearing women in merciless naturalism.

The press was well advised to print what Dr Goebbels instructed editors to say, but right up to the start of the war, French, British and Swiss papers were available in Berlin and Munich. The regime did not use the press alone; its authentic instrument was the weekly newsreel and the radio. The 'people's receiver', covering medium and long waves, ensured

that the Führer was omnipresent in every home and every factory. During the war, nocturnal listening to 'enemy transmitters', especially the BBC and Swiss Radio Beromünster, would be punished by death. The cinema was used in two ways: first as a tranquilliser – it was the great period of slush and tear-jerkers – and secondly as an ideological stimulant. The weekly newsreel used a rabble-rousing tone to peddle political indoctrination; there were also feature films retelling German history the Nazi way.

Leni Riefenstahl's film about the 1934 Nuremberg Party Rally, *The Triumph of Will*, was a seductive work of art. The

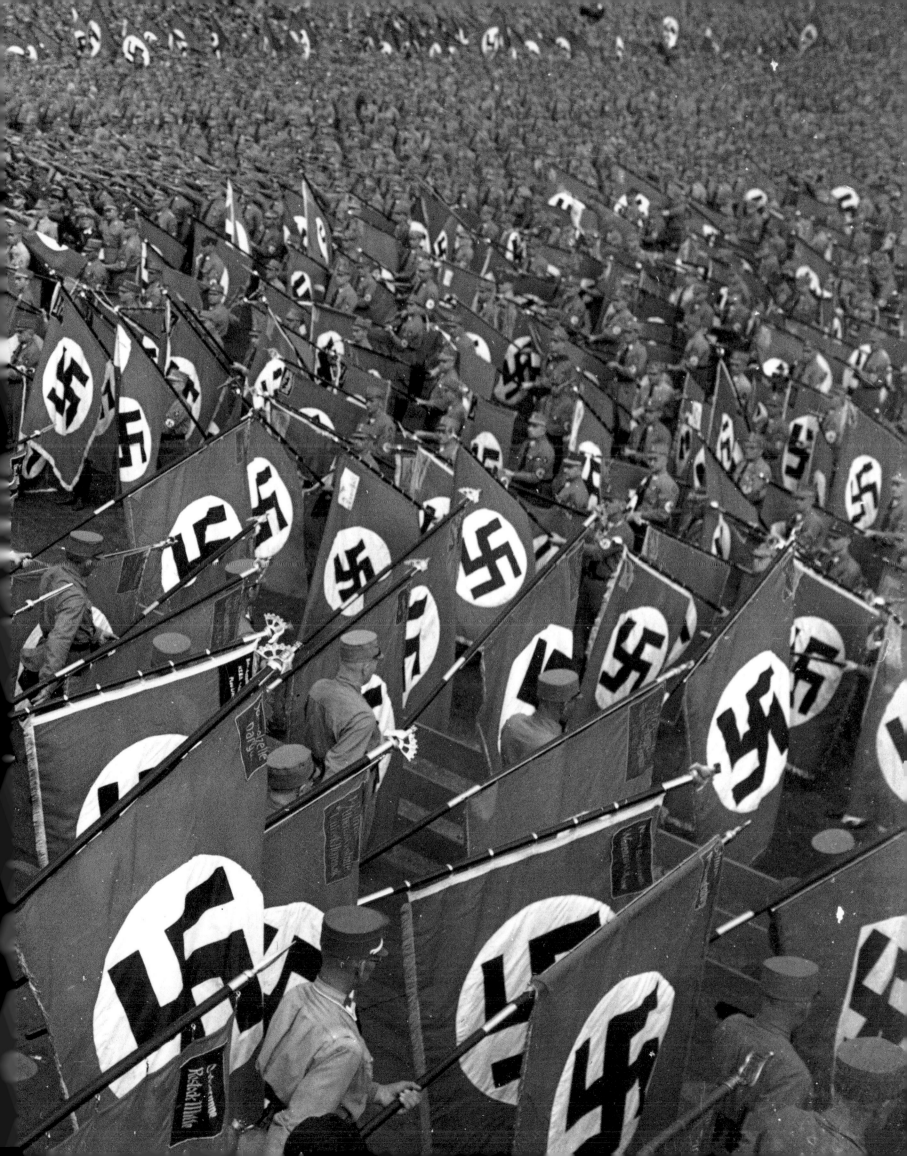

slow descent of Hitler's aircraft from heavy clouds made an inescapable symbol of political redemption. Then Albert Speer, Hitler's star architect and artistic right-hand man, used anti-aircraft searchlights to form domes of light in the night sky. The Nuremberg Party Rallies were structured from the outset to ensure that the avenues and rows of flags provided a *mise-en-scène* for the 'Führer'. The red standard bearers of the Nazi organisations contrasted with the surrounding brown mass, as they marched through the ranks. Each standard was topped with a gilded eagle that glittered in the searchlights. In Germany in 1935 during the Long Vacation from Oxford, undergraduate Denis Hills witnessed that year's Nuremberg Rally:

'The opening display was a parade of 54,000 Labour Corps youths shouldering burnished spades. Stripped to the waist, sunburnt and corded with muscle, they goose-stepped past Hitler, who took the salute standing in his car. The drill was perfect, their bodies toughened by months of Spartan diet,

road- and bridge-building, harvesting and reclaiming land. The cheering and march music was continuous, one military band relieving another every few minutes. For those who admired disciplined youth the spectacle must have been impressive as well as worrying. What was this ballet of muscular young robots leading to? ... The parade of the SS Leibstandarte (Hitler's personal bodyguard) through the Altstadt was in a different class. Every man was at least six feet tall. As they tramped in their black uniforms past the little houses familiar from Dürer's engravings they seemed to be moving slowly, with great strides, but it was not easy to keep up with them. Their wooden faces were half-hidden by black helmets and the sweat was running down their chins. As a piece of military ceremonial these giant Praetorian guards were magnificent. The end product of Kadavergehorsam (blind or corpse-like obedience), they looked almost inhuman.'

Speer was furnished with unlimited powers and resources. The central architectural showpiece was the 'New Reich

The people's car, *(above left) the Volkswagen, introduced by Hitler at the 1939 Berlin motor show. It was to go alongside the Volksempfänger, the new cheap radio.*

An Autobahn *in 1937 (above). By 1939 there were 3000 kilometres built and a huge kick-start given to the economy. The largely horse-drawn army would have preferred the money spent on railways.* [PHOTO: MAX EHLERT]

Chancellery' in Berlin with its gigantic reception rooms, designed, like the temple of some murderous deity, to make all visitors tremble. Large residential areas in the centre of Berlin were being cleared for the future Reich capital, 'Germania'; the inhabitants were assigned apartments formerly occupied by Jews, and the entire process was supervised by the Gestapo. It was only the demands of the war that caused the far-reaching plans for the 'world capital' to be postponed. There was a strange contrast between the Fascist-totalitarian style buildings

at the centre and the steep-gabled houses built for large families in Berlin's green belt.

This kind of contrast was created by the regime everywhere. Heinrich Himmler had a romantic enthusiasm for everything Germanic, but this met with little public echo. He felt himself to be a reincarnation of the early-medieval King Henry I, also known as Henry the Fowler, and therefore placed the cathedral of Quedlinburg, associated with him, under SS protection. The fact that Christmas became the 'Yule Feast' and Santa Claus turned into 'Knecht Ruprecht' – just as Stalin made him 'Father Frost' – was generally felt to be rather bizarre. But it was unwise to utter criticism in public.

The regime was intent on breaking through every barrier. Technological advance prompted it to think the unthinkable; lust for power fired technology. No matter whether the regime was building Autobahnen, motor highways – Speer's staff claimed these to be modelled on American 'parkways', sensitively adapted to the character of the landscape – or

Grass-roots Nazism *in Hildburghausen, about a hundred miles east of Frankfurt, in Thuringia. (Top) the local Party newspaper is sold on the streets in 1936. (Middle) the drums and trumpets of the Hitler Youth parade in front of the Town Hall on 1 May 1937. (Left) middle-aged members of the SA march by the old town wall in 1937. (Bottom) the war has come, and the potato ration is being distributed.*

[PHOTOS: RUDOLF MEFFERT]

Bund Deutscher Mädchen, *the German Maiden's League, camping in the woods (opposite) and singing round the fire at night (above), not just Nazi songs such as the Horst Wessel Lied, but also older, innocent ones from the Wandervogel era of their parents.*

Jumping across the fire *(left): one of the more harmless virility tests of Hitler Youth being performed to celebrate the summer solstice.*
[PHOTOS, OPPOSITE AND ABOVE: MAX EHLERT]

concentration camps, organizing the broadcasting service or the surveillance system of the Gestapo, with its countless eyes and ears, informers and listeners, developing the Luftwaffe – too hurriedly with disastrous consequences in the war – or erecting the 'Westwall' along the French frontier – everything had to be 'blow by blow', as the phrase went, with no expense spared. Usefulness was defined by power, and although wild plans came from power-obsessed adventurers and eccentrics, their implementation was in the hands of experienced technicians, administrators, lawyers, bankers and officers. They saw their opportunity to do great things, and they were fascinated, like Albert Speer, until they realized too late that they were trapped in a Faustian bargain. Few walked out in protest, like Dr Hjalmar Schacht in 1938 and several members of the Reich Bank Council, because they refused to continue to organise the financing of a war effort. Schacht was even thrown into a concentration camp, which later on was to save him a lot of embarrassment at the Nuremberg trials. Some resigned their posts, like Colonel-General Beck, the chief of the General Staff and subsequent leader of the officers' conspiracy of 24 July 1944. Others, like the poet Gottfried Benn, sought an internal

exile (in his case as an army doctor), or committed suicide, or sought exile proper – but the doors of foreign countries were mostly closed to Jews and non-Jews alike.

Many were attracted to National Socialism, not so much by its gigantic utopias, but because it linked everything, or nearly everything, together – the 'workers by brain and by hand' were no longer apart, employers and employees were no longer opponents, town and country were merged in the nation. Romantic talk of Blut und Boden, 'blood and soil' and the simple life of the farmer, his wife and their many children mixed with trumpetings about unleashed technology. Folk dancing and the residential settlement movement, the Mothers' Cross, the Winter Relief Scheme and 'Strength through Joy' allowed many to join in, gave them an identity. Within the labyrinth of modern society the Nazi dictatorship opened up spaces where no law applied, except the Führer's command. The past meant nothing; at best it was a dark period that had to be overcome – the Hitler Youth referred to old people as mere 'cemetery vegetables'. Breathlessness was the tenor of the times, the sky was the limit.

People were intoxicated to begin with, but substantial

successes soon followed, gaining support for the regime and stabilizing it. Nothing was more important than overcoming mass unemployment, no matter by what means. The numerous Party officials who gained posts in 1933, all the way through to concentration camp guards, were the first to get work. They were followed by hundreds of thousands in the Reich Labour Service (DAF) and, from 1936, in the Wehrmacht, the armed services. Rearmament intensified after 1934, as did expenditure on public works. Everything was accompanied by propaganda. Bread and circuses, the recipe of the Roman emperors, worked once more. Robert Ley, Leader of the German Labour Front said 'Nothing is more dangerous to a state than homeless men … even a bowling club or a skat club assumes a state-maintaining function … It was of tremendous value that the DAF put these twelve million people back in their place in the state.' The Nazi Women's Movement's slogan was: 'The German woman is knitting again.'

But how was growth created, considering that Germany was an exporting nation and the world economy was in a slump? Demand was generated by the state, beginning with a stepping-up of the Autobahn programme from the final years of the Weimar republic and with Party buildings, followed by armaments and further Party buildings. The statistics of the gross national product reveal a continuous shift from private to state consumption. By 1936 full employment was achieved. After that, skilled workers were desperately sought for the booming metal industries and wages kept rising despite government efforts to put the brakes on.

In 1938 the real level of wages in 1928 was attained again. The German Labour Front – created to avoid industrial conflict – wrested concessions from the employers, and this contributed to general satisfaction. A great deal of noise accompanied welfare programmes such as 'Beauty of Work' – strips of lawn outside factories and flowers and curtains to cheer up works canteens. The majority was soon learning to live with the regime, while a new fashionable class was emerging, noticeable

Two extremes *Lore Meyer from Frankfurt (far left), a member of Makkabi, the Jewish youth movement. A sun worshipper (left) at a 'brides' school' organised by the SS in Berlin as part of Himmler's 'Lebensborn' Aryan breeding establishment with which he attempted – and failed – to raise the SS birthrate.*
[PHOTO, FAR LEFT: ABRAHAM PISAREK]
[PHOTO, LEFT: HEDDA WALTHER]

Mud bathers *(right) at a beauty farm near Hamburg tone up their skin – perhaps not exactly what Himmler had in mind when he talked of 'blood and soil'.* [PHOTO: MAX EHLERT]

Nazi high society. *Robert Ley, (opposite) with his wife Lore and Himmler, attends Munich's 'Day of German Art' in 1939. His personal fiefdom was the Labour Front, which replaced the trade unions in 1934. Hitler (above) charming the ladies at the Munich opera in July 1937. (Left) Göring's second wife, Emmy, on the right, receives guests in 1935.*
[PHOTOS: MAX EHLERT]

first at the 1936 Olympic Games. Party bigwigs like Goebbels and Göring surrounded themselves with actors and sycophants; the Mounted SS, with a heavy concentration of aristocracy, participated in equestrian events, where – to the malicious delight of Wehrmacht cavalrymen – they were often outclassed by the horses of the Oppenheims, the Cologne banking dynasty. The boxer Schmeling, the motor-racer Rosemeier, the actor Gründgens – they all showed themselves and were shown.

The new 'Schickeria' lived in Grunewald and Schwanenwerder in Berlin or in Bogenhausen and Grünwald near Munich. Hitler moved to the Obersalzberg near Berchtesgaden and his paladins followed him. Town residences

For the generals, Hitler in power meant more rearmament than they could swallow, for aims which they regarded as daydreams. But the majority went along. For the industrialists there was a state-generated demand independent of the hopeless world market, driven from 1936 onward by Hermann Göring's Four-Year-Plan Ministry. All this gave to most people a sense that the country and every individual in it was moving upwards. Anyone failing to join in the feast would find himself hopelessly alone at a time when the regime was staging spectacular mass events and when there was no lack of applause from abroad, of generous treaties and new alliances. Concentration camps, Gestapo, block wardens and Party bigwigs all existed, of course, but it was better to look the other way. In 1935 came the Nuremberg Laws, formalizing past practice, which made German Jews into aliens with no rights. Dr. Hans Globke in the Reich Ministry of the Interior, a man from the Catholic Youth Movement, reassuringly commented as did others, that what had until then been happening arbitrarily was now being codified and brought under control. For many who might entertain doubts, there was a defensive mechanism in the phrase: 'If only the Führer knew …'. Or they reassured themselves that others in their place would behave much worse.

Much as the Germans had found it easy to succumb to the regime, the European powers found it easy to appease it. Rearmament, the overthrow of 'Versailles', had been Hitler's programme from the start. Mastery of Germany was to be followed by mastery of Europe, starting with the neighbouring regions, deep into the Soviet Union, and down the Danube, to the Mediterranean and North Africa. Hitler deceived and tricked the world and relied on his opponents' wishful thinking. His power base had been created through the method of brutal surprise attack and the same would also secure him the mastery of Europe. Speeches about peace meanwhile reassured the masses, the 'Volksgenossinnen und Volksgenossen' as Hitler addressed them at the opening of his speeches.

This sick procedure started in October 1933 when the German diplomats were given orders from Berlin to leave the League of Nations and to slam the door, and the Entente powers merely watched. Hitler ordered a plebiscite after the event to furnish himself with an endorsement by the people. Western governments chose to tolerate the farce. Each subsequent surprise act of violence took place at weekends, in order to gain time before foreign governments could react. Each action was followed by peace rhetoric, every demand presented as the last and final one.

Yet Hitler's first moves on the international chessboard seemed conciliatory. He was aware that he had to pass through a danger zone before he could realize his wilder plans. During the first few years, had it come to a military showdown, the Reichswehr could have defended Berlin for just about three weeks. There was also a pretence of continuity. The Concordat

whose owners had fled could be bought cheaply. Firms were 'Aryanized', with many a small employee becoming a big businessman. The old elites were rendered impotent, class distinctions counted for little, traditions for almost nothing, the churches largely conformed. What the Great War had failed to achieve and the Weimar Republic had scarcely attempted became part and parcel of a 'Brown Revolution'.

To many the regime brought hope, advantage and the chance to rise from nowhere. Was it reactionary? Was it progressive? Was it right-wing or left-wing? It burst all the categories of the nineteenth century and confused friend and foe alike – as it still does. From the legacy of socialism came a radical levelling instinct, the German comprehensive school, the anti-capitalist drive, the guardian state which supplies universal care but also intrusive supervision. The caps worn by schoolboys from the elite gymnasium schools, formerly symbols of class distinction, disappeared; competitive sport and football became obligatory for middle-class sons. 'National-political educational institutions' (Napola) and the 'Junker schools', the elite cadre schools of the SS, opened new roads to the top for social groups which had not known such opportunities before. The same was true of the Wehrmacht, whose rapid expansion gave chances for promotion, for the return of retired officers to active service, while for others it provided a place of internal exile.

A new generation *of Nazi leaders (opposite) is trained at elite 'Napola' institutions.*
[PHOTO: HANNS HUBMANN]

Pigtails and plaits *(right). Political supervision was normally omnipresent and invisible but here one of the enforcers sits in on a class at an East Pomeranian school.*
[PHOTO: MAX EHLERT]

with the Vatican seemed to expunge the godless tirades of the past, the friendship treaty with Warsaw – unthinkable for Stresemann ten years earlier – made people forget Hitler's old songs of hate against the Slav world. It was hard to imagine that a man was concluding treaties merely to lull his opponents into a sense of security, and that he would break them as soon as it pleased him. Ironically the only foreign leader to show Hitler his teeth was Mussolini, moving troops to the Brenner Pass in 1934 when the Austrian Nazis, massively supported from Berlin, tried to stage a coup-d'état in Vienna. Mussolini's 'Stresa Front' to contain Hitler with the help of Britain and France, however, did not last long.

By 1935 Hitler was ready to shake off the restraints of Versailles in a rapid succession of bold moves. He got off to a good start when, in a plebiscite on Sunday 15th January the coal-rich Saar territory voted overwhelmingly to return to the Reich. The League of Nations agreed to return it to Germany on March 1st, hoping that this concession would pacify the Germans. In a proclamation to the German people on Saturday 16th March Hitler announced the introduction of conscription and the building up of a peacetime army of 550,000 men. The next day, Heroes' Memorial Day (Heldengedenktag), a brilliant military ceremony in the State Opera House celebrated the rebirth of the German Army. The first open breach of the Versailles Treaty was met with solemn protest from Britain and France. In April the League of Nations passed a motion of censure against the Germans. However, diplomatic visits continued, and in June, a mere three months after the introduction of general conscription, Hitler signed the naval treaty with Britain – 'my most beautiful day' – which lifted the restrictions of Versailles. Admittedly, the Reich Navy was not to exceed 35 per cent of the tonnage of the Royal Navy's surface fleet, but for one thing the British ships were scattered over half the globe, and for another the treaty gave Germany the right to build up to the full submarine strength of the British Empire. This agreement also made the British contractual partners of the German dictatorship. France was furious at not being consulted and the united front against German rearmament was destroyed. Was it surprising that Hitler began to fantasize about a share-out of the world with the British? At any rate, he took the treaty with them as silent permission for German hegemony on the Continent.

On Saturday, 7th March 1936 – a year after the introduction of conscription – Wehrmacht troops, initially only light infantry, marched across the Rhine bridges into what, under the Versailles treaty, was the demilitarized zone of western Germany. London and Paris were paralyzed by pacifism and grave social conflicts, so nothing happened. But the system of the Paris peace treaties had been unhinged. It is known that, if the West had acted with any determination, Hitler would have given orders for a withdrawal and presented the whole thing as excessive zeal by subordinates.

One year after the Nuremberg laws had outlawed the Jews of Germany, the Olympic Games were held in Berlin and Garmisch Partenkirchen, a celebration to the greater glory of the regime. Hardly any of the foreign athletes, sports

functionaries or diplomats found it offensive to turn themselves, with arms raised, into the murderous regime's performing monkeys. The American-born Member of Parliament, Sir Henry 'Chips' Channon, enjoyed himself greatly as a privileged guest. In the Olympic stadium,

'German wins were frequent and then, not only "Deutschland über Alles" was bellowed, but also the Horst Wessel song, the Nazi anthem, which I thought had a rather good lilt. Thus an hour or so passed, and then, suddenly the audience was electrified. Hitler was coming and he looked exactly like his caricature – brown uniform, Charlie Chaplin moustache, square, stocky figure, and a determined but not grim look ... I was more excited than when I met Mussolini in 1926 in Perugia, and more stimulated, I am sorry to say, than when I was blessed by the Pope in 1920 ... The new régime, particularly Göring, are masters of the art of party giving. Tonight [a state banquet at Berlin Opera House] in a way, must have been a little like the fêtes given by the Directoire of the French Revolution, with the upstarts, tipsy with power and flattered by the proximity and ovations of the ex-grand, whom once they wished to destroy ... [at Göring's own party:] roundabouts, cafés with beer and champagne, peasants dancing, and 'schuhplattling', vast women carrying pretzels and beer, a ship, a beerhouse, crowds of gay, laughing people, animals, a mixture of Luna Park and White Horse Inn, Old Heidelberg and the Trianon. The music roared, the astonished guests wandered about. "There has never been anything like

this since the days of Louis Quatorze," someone remarked. "Not since Nero," I retorted, but actually it was more like the Fêtes of Claudius, but with the cruelty left out ... Goebbels, it appears, as well as Ribbentrop was in despair with jealousy.' Meanwhile the man in the street suspected, in some obscure way, that Hitler was out for war. Yet the 'Führer' was clever enough to conceal his specific aims behind much peace-and-reason rhetoric. The key memorandum on the Four-Year Plan

of 1936 organising the German economy for autonomy, remained secret because it demanded readiness for war by 1940. On 5 November 1937 Hitler explained to the top men of the Army, Luftwaffe and Navy that for 'solving the German question' there could 'only be the way of force'. Until 1944/45, he reckoned, the Wehrmacht would have a chance of victory, so delay would be a mistake: Germany's opponents were rearming and the burden of rearmament was becoming ever heavier for the Germans. Everything would have to be completed in his own lifetime.

Three months later, having ousted the top military leaders by intrigue and calumny, Hitler assumed supreme command of the Wehrmacht. For a major European war, however, there was a conspicuous lack of in-depth armament and raw materials, especially iron ore and oil. The only operations possible – as Hitler's first biographer, a journalist in exile by the name of Konrad Heiden, explained to a disbelieving international public in 1936/37 – were 'lightning strikes'. These attacks would aim to increase, step by step, the very limited military potential of Germany.

Why did Germany's neighbours not realize what the Nazi regime was scarcely concealing? The sight of the field-grey regiments, of the armoured columns and the dive-bombers displayed in military exercises – in the Spanish Civil War Hitler dispatched the Luftwaffe's 'Condor Legion' to support Franco – was worrying and, simultaneously, demoralizing. France's Third Republic, dug in behind the Maginot Line, badly shaken by scandal and serious strikes, watched mesmerised as the security system of 1919 collapsed. Britain was stuck deep in economic depression and had to hold an overstretched Empire together – larger than ever but also weaker than ever. While the Tories believed that Germany provided a protective dam against Bolshevism, the Left, almost unconditionally, demanded 'No more wars'.

Meanwhile in Moscow, Stalin, having had *Mein Kampf* presented to him in Russian translation, refurbished his armoured forces – whose value the Red Army had learned from its Reichswehr instructors ten years earlier – and prophesied the final struggle of the capitalist states against each other. At its 1936 Party rally he promised the Communist Party of the Soviet Union that the Red Army would enter the world stage as an arbiter, at the very end, and decisively.

Hitler realized that war on two fronts had been the fatal mistake of imperial Germany and must therefore be avoided at all costs. In his stage-by-stage plan he aimed at expanding his continental base, if possible avoiding war with France and Britain. He was prepared to conclude a compromise with the British Empire – the land for Greater Germany and the sea for Great Britain. He calculated France, if abandoned by Britain, would hardly dare fight.

Regardless of all tactical moves, war and conquest in the East, undoing the Bolshevik revolution and winning 'Lebensraum', remained Hitler's ultimate objective. For that he

needed more of Central Europe – for raw materials, as a source of armaments and as a deployment area. The attempt to incorporate Austria had been unsuccessful in 1934, but the Anschluss in 1938 was Hitler's first conquest of foreign soil, without a single shot being fired. The Vienna government had prepared for a referendum to demonstrate that the great majority of Austrians did not want to join Nazi Germany. But, abandoned internationally and domestically paralyzed by a conflict bordering on civil war on two fronts, against Socialists and National Socialists, it was presented with a German ultimatum. German newsreels showed the Wehrmacht rapidly advancing through cheering crowds. What it did not show were the long lines of broken-down Wehrmacht vehicles which alarmed the German high command, or the ruthless settling of accounts with their fellow-countrymen of different political views by Austrian Nazis, or the sweeping operations of the Gestapo. Henceforth there was no longer any Austria, only the 'Greater German Reich'. SS and Gestapo could hardly cope with the number of applicants from the 'Ostmark'. Gitta Sereny remembers, two days after the Anschluss:

'Elfie [her best friend] and I walked around Vienna all day. On the Graben, one of Vienna's loveliest streets, near my home, we came upon a scene of fear. Guarded by men in brown uniform with swastika armbands – with a large group of Viennese citizens watching, many of them laughing – a dozen middle-aged people, men and women, were on their knees scrubbing the pavement with toothbrushes. In horror, I recognized one of the cleaners as Dr Berggrün, our paediatrician, who had saved my life when I had diptheria as a four-year-old. He saw me start towards one of the men in brown; he shook his head and mouthed, "No," while continuing to work his toothbrush. I asked the soldier what

they were doing; were they mad? "How dare you," he shouted. "Are you a Jew?" "No, and how dare you?" I said, and told him that one of the men they were humiliating was a great doctor, a saver of lives. "Is this what you call our liberation?" Elfie called out to all of them. She was a stunningly beautiful child, but her voice was already trained for singing, as clear as a bell. Within two minutes, the crowd had dispersed, the guards had gone, the "street cleaner" had got up and gone away. "Never do that again," Dr Berggrün said to us sternly. "It is very dangerous for you." They gassed him in Sobibor in 1943.'

Six months later Hitler demanded the German-speaking frontier regions of the Czechoslovak Republic, the lands under the Sudeten mountains. Army and Luftwaffe moved into deployment areas. Göring was anxious to preserve his sybaritic life as a latter-day renaissance prince and urged the Duce to mediate in order to avoid war. Mussolini in fact brought about a conference of Western statesmen in Munich. Meanwhile leaders of the opposition within the German army, notably General Höppner, made final preparations to have Hitler arrested and placed before a court. Wehrmacht forces were on the alert in Thuringia; major SS units, as if they suspected something, were on the alert at the Grafenwöhr training ground in Franconia half way between Höppner's divisions and Munich. Emissaries of the opposition implored the British government to stand firm this time. Ernst von Weizsäcker, Secretary of State in the Foreign Office, yet opposed to Hitler, expressed his fears that the British Prime Minister was no match for him: 'Chamberlain is too good for these people, they ought to send some forceful soldier who can also scream and beat the table with his riding crop when he needs to, preferably a Field Marshal with a whole string of decorations and war-wounds, a man without too much consideration ... It is only reasonable transactions and at the same time strength of character that he [Hitler] is able to foil, outwardly you must play the same dangerous game that he has applied inwardly with so much success.' Sure enough, in Munich on 29 and 30 September the Great Four agreed to the incorporation of the Sudetenland into Germany. This was not only the end of France's 'petite entente' with Czechoslovakia, Yugoslavia and Romania; it was also, before the shattering defeats of 1943, the last chance for the German military opposition. To overthrow Hitler the warmonger was one thing, to take out a triumphant Führer quite another.

The Soviet leader had been the great non-participant in Munich. He came to the conclusion, when France and Britain ignored him while doing their deal with Hitler, that he should soon do his own. In March 1939, Hitler moved into Prague after the Slovaks had split from the Czechs; the façade of the German 'national revision policy' crumbled and the 'living space' strategy began openly. Was Poland to be the next prey to fall to Hitler? Britain announced a guarantee for Poland – not so much an open encouragement for Warsaw to stand firm,

come what may, but the final stern warning to Berlin. The British government acted with more firmness now that new interceptor fighters were becoming available to the Royal Air Force. Britain, traditionally a naval power, unequivocally put its faith in air power.

A compromise at Poland's expense was still possible; the policy of 'peace and settlement' was not yet exhausted. But Hitler regarded the British deterrent as empty in military terms and hence a bluff. Meanwhile, like Paris and London, Warsaw was convinced that the two dictators, who had only just been waging war by proxy in the Spanish Civil War, could not possibly make common cause. But since the spring of 1939, as a fall-out from 'Munich', secret negotiations had been conducted between Berlin and Moscow. Hitler feared an alliance between Stalin and the West. Stalin's moves were governed by ideology, i.e. the theory of a worldwide imperialist conspiracy, as much as by his interest in restoring the Tsarist empire and reconquering the Baltic states and parts of Poland. The signing ceremony between Molotov and Ribbentrop took place on 23 August 1939 in Moscow. While on the face of it the treaty was nothing but a non-aggression pact, the secret protocols provided for the delineation of spheres of influence right across Poland. This meant war.

Vienna, 1938 *(opposite). Through the portals of the Hapsburgs' huge former palace, the Hofburg, a trite Nazi slogan can be seen: 'The same blood belongs to the same Reich'.*

Sudeten Germans *(right), one decorating a motor-bike with flowers, welcome German*

troops in October 1938. Their path into this border area of Czechoslovakia had been made smooth by the British prime minister, Neville Chamberlain, and the French the month before, who thought they had bought 'peace for our time' by this appeasement of Hitler.

[PHOTO, RIGHT: MAX EHLERT]

CHAPTER SIX

HITLER'S WAR

Oᴺ 1 Sᴇᴘᴛᴇᴍʙᴇʀ 1939 Gᴇʀᴍᴀɴ ʀᴀᴅɪᴏ ᴀɴɴᴏᴜɴᴄᴇᴅ with fanfares that fire had been returned at Polish positions since 4.45 that same morning. At that time the German attack had long been in progress. It had opened with a naval bombardment of the Westerplatte near Danzig. Polish infantry and cavalry fought tenaciously, but nowhere did the front hold for more than a few days. On 17 September the Red Army began to attack from the east to make sure of its share of the spoils. Behind the German front 'Einsatzkommandos' – special squads – of the SS and the SD, the 'Security Service', were driving Jewish men, women and children to the edge of mass graves and then machine-gunning them. By the end of the first week of the war SS commanders were boasting of 200 shootings a day, including many from Poland's educated classes and aristocrats. Behind the Soviet front in the forest of Katyn near Smolensk the Soviet NKVD shot dead the flower of the Polish officer corps. The Wehrmacht and the Red Army fraternized with schnaps from Westphalia and vodka from Mother Russia. By the end of September Warsaw surrendered.

Hitler had promised a 'new order' for the East: it was Lebensraum for the master race, a model SS state, a racial experiment, a vast colony divided into three parts, ruled by three pro-consuls. The Warthegau under Arthur Greiser and Danzig in West Prussia under Albert Forster were to be 'Germanized', and to be the home for the many ethnic Germans (Volksdeutsche) returning home to the Reich (Heim ins Reich) from the Baltic States, allocated to the Russians by the Nazi-Soviet Pact of August 1939. Germans were encouraged to settle the new lands. Jews were moved into the ghetto at first to make room for incoming Germans, who took over their homes and businesses. The 'General-Gouvernement' under Hans Frank became the dumping ground for 'undesirables', who were resettled from the other districts. This was where, later, the extermination camps were to be: among them Treblinka, Sobibor, Majdanek, Belzec and Auschwitz-Birkenau. The SS wanted to reduce the Poles to slaves, hence their targeting of the intelligentsia. In November 1939 the professors at the Jagellonian University in Krakow were called to a meeting. They expected discussion but found they were met by German soldiers who beat them with rifle butts, arrested them and took them off to concentration camps. Poland suffered more than any other occupied country. Six million Poles were to die during the war – almost one out of five citizens of pre-war Poland. About this time Goebbels reported in his diary:

'The Führer's verdict on the Poles is damning. More like animals than human beings, completely primitive, stupid and

'Not a justifiable act of war' was the verdict of an English bishop on the area bombing of German cities carried out by the RAF. The most notorious example was Dresden, flattened on 13th and 14th February 1945 by 1000 bombers with the loss of between 60,000 and 120,000 lives, and many beautiful 18th-century buildings. The view here is from the tower of the town hall. Germany's 'Florence on the Elbe' was full of refugees fleeing from the advancing Russians. It has been strongly argued that the whole Allied air offensive was a disastrous mistake, failing either to cripple production or sap civilian morale in Germany, absorbing more than one-third of British war production at the expense of tank and landing craft construction, keeping aircraft away from more important tasks such as hunting the U-boats over the Atlantic, or supporting ground forces in the Middle and Far East.

[PHOTO: RICHARD PETER SENIOR]

Ghetto children, Warsaw 1941 *(opposite). This and other ghettos had been sealed in 1940 and over 2,000,000 Polish Jews were then murdered in the years that followed, though the Warsaw Jews fought back in 1943.*

Hans Frank, *Chief of the General-Gouvernement in Poland, formerly that contradiction in terms, the Nazi Minister of Justice, greets church dignitaries (above). Many Polish priests were killed under his regime.*

amorphous. And a ruling class that is an unsatisfactory result of a mingling between the lower orders and an Aryan master-race. The Poles' dirtiness is unimaginable. Their capacity for intelligent judgement is absolutely nil. The Führer has no intention of assimilating the Poles. They are to be forced into their truncated state and left entirely to their own devices. If Henry the Lion [Duke of Bavaria 1129-1195] had conquered the East, a task for which he possessed the power at that time, the result would certainly have been a strongly slavicised race of German mongrels. Better the present situation: now we know the laws of racial heredity and can handle things accordingly.'

Some ranks of the Wehrmacht were upset at what was going on. Colonel-General Johannes Blaskowitz sent memorandums:

'It is misguided to slaughter tens of thousands of Jews and Poles as is happening at present...The acts of violence against

Jews which occur in full view of the public inspire among the religious Poles not only deep disgust but also great pity...The attitude of the troops to the SS and police alternates between abhorrence and hatred. Every soldier feels repelled and revolted by these crimes which are being perpetrated in Poland by nationals of the Reich and representatives of State authority.' This complaint dates from February 1940. Hitler had responded to an earlier memorandum by saying 'One can't fight a war with Salvation Army methods.'

Hitler had started the war against Poland on the assumption that Britain would remain a spectator. This proved only half correct. On 3 September 1939 Paris and London declared war on Germany. After that, however, nothing much happened. Where was the offensive of the Western powers that the Wehrmacht high command had been so afraid of? After the four-week Polish campaign German troops were running out of equipment and supplies. The campaign had been no blitzkrieg, using concentrated armour backed up by attacks from the air. It had relied to a great extent on the railways and on horses. Why did the West waste precious time? The military opposition at that point tried once more, in vain, to get Hitler to negotiate or to overthrow him. Even 'Reichsmarschall' Hermann Göring, Hitler's successor-designate, sent out peace feelers to Roosevelt.

To secure supplies of iron ore from Sweden and to be able to

Vision and reality. *A beautiful composition (opposite), all the more effective for avoiding crude propaganda, summons up the German dreamland, though boys are having to do the work of the men away at the front, around 1940. The Nazis wanted to extend this dream into Poland, killing millions of Poles, Catholics and Jews, in the process, uprooting countless others, and replacing them with Volksdeutsche, Germans from the Baltic states and Russia, like these peasants (right) from Wolhynia in the 'before' and 'after' shots. Arthur Greiser (bottom), Gauleiter of the Warthegau (Poznan), one of the areas of resettlement, has a picnic at harvest time in 1942. It was his request the year before for help in eliminating the 100,000 Jews still in his area that ushered in the era of murder by gas rather than by bullet.*

[PHOTO, OPPOSITE: MAX EHLERT]

thrust out into the Atlantic from Norwegian ports, in April 1940 Hitler ordered the Wehrmacht to invade Norway. This forestalled a matching British operation by a matter of hours. Denmark was occupied at the same time; only Sweden was spared, though at the price of far–reaching cooperation with the German war industry. The German sphere of control now extended from the North Cape to Sicily.

On 10 May 1940 the attack in the West began, many times postponed both because of the weather and in the hope of British appeasement. The war machine rolled through Holland and Belgium. Avoiding towns and bypassing strong points, armoured divisions used as blitzkrieg wedges in open terrain and backed by air attacks smashed the French army. This success came despite the fact that Germany had fewer tanks than the French and fewer planes than the British. The Wehrmacht's secret lay, according to Britain's leading military historian Sir Michael Howard, in its generals and in the dedication and professionalism of its men, which made its army the finest the world had ever seen. The British Expeditionary Force was hemmed in on the beaches of Dunkirk. Unexpectedly, because of a holding order by Hitler, some

200,000 British and 100,000 French troops managed to escape by sea, leaving all heavy equipment behind. On 10 July 1940 there followed a victory parade in Berlin, the crowds delirious with joy. In Paris the Wehrmacht marched down the Champs Elysées from Napoleon's Arc de Triomphe to the Louvre of Louis XIV. Hitler arrived by air with Speer and entourage to view the buildings of Paris in the early hours. Göring had antiques and works of art confiscated or, in some cases, bought up for him. He even placed a few Jewish art dealers under his protection. Hitler had bestowed on Göring the title *Grösster Feldherr aller Zeiten*, Greatest War Lord of All Times. To which the public ironically responded by terming Göring *Gröfaz*.

In June 1940 Soviet troops, conforming to the Hitler-Stalin pact, swiftly occupied the Baltic states and began their rule of terror by deportations and executions. On the Black Sea Bessarabia was annexed — a move which brought Stalin closer to the Romanian oilfields. Sooner or later Soviet expansionism and German economic interests were bound to clash.

When Molotov came to Berlin in November 1940 he demanded, in return for continued Soviet compliance, Romania, Bulgaria and control of the Turkish straits.

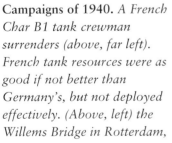

Campaigns of 1940. *A French Char B1 tank crewman surrenders (above, far left). French tank resources were as good if not better than Germany's, but not deployed effectively. (Above, left) the Willems Bridge in Rotterdam,* *seized by seaplanes landing on the river and by paratroopers. (Above) Norway's Narvik harbour cost the German navy most of its destroyers, sunk in two attacks by the Royal Navy. (Above right) Blitzkrieg in France.*

Romanian oil would then have flowed only at the pleasure of the Soviet Union. Moreover, Moscow wanted a free hand against Finland and some kind of arrangement regarding access to the Baltic, controlled, ever since Germany's occupation of Norway and Denmark, by the German navy. It was during this visit that Ribbentrop repeatedly had to ask his Soviet visitor to accompany him to the air raid shelter because of British bombers. 'Is that really necessary?', Molotov asked maliciously, 'given that the war, as you are telling us, is already won?' In the skies above Britain Hurricanes and Spitfires, guided by early radar, were more than a match for the German Luftwaffe. By the turn of 1940/41 the Battle of Britain had been won by the

young fighter pilots of the RAF, though Hitler controlled the Continent except for Sweden, Switzerland and the Soviet lands. In this constricted situation, Sweden supplied iron ore without too many scruples as to its use, while Switzerland allowed Reichsbahn trains to roll through the Gotthard Tunnel without being too curious about what they carried. Both countries were paid in gold and foreign currency, clearly of sinister origin, and again no questions were asked. Switzerland, in need of foodstuffs and coal from Germany, also acted as a banker – admittedly when the country was encircled by the Axis powers and a military invasion seemed possible at any moment, perhaps up to 1944. As time went on, there could be less and less doubt that some of the payment in gold and currency was coming from the safes, bank accounts, jewellery boxes – and teeth – of concentration camp victims.

Stalin was supplying raw materials and called on French Communists to work in German arms factories. He was also bidding in the great geopolitical auction and wanted to secure some lots for himself. To Hitler Russia was the 'opposite principle', the totalitarian counterpart. Oil, strategy, living space – all these were subsidiary arguments, lending rationality

Mud then Snow, *Stalin's most loyal allies, brought the German advance to a halt in the winter of 1941. 'Corduroy' roads of birch trees, sometimes even of frozen bodies, had to be built. German jack boots were the worst footwear if frostbite was* *to be avoided. Women's fur coats had to be collected at home to supplement the troops' inadequate clothing (right), but many still died a quiet death in the snow. The lorry above is a Citroen, war booty from France.* [PHOTO, ABOVE: HANNS HUBMANN]

to primeval hatred. If Hitler had been a classical power politician, he could have been content in the spring of 1941, when he had brought Yugoslavia and Greece, including the island of Crete half–way between continental Europe and the Suez Canal, under German control. He could have established a German–dominated 'Fortress Europe'. Ernst von Weizsäcker, Secretary of State in the Foreign Ministry, stated in 1940 that even to hold on to what had been conquered so far dangerously exceeded Germany's strength. However, the demons of hate and power were driving Hitler further along the road he had chosen, towards the end of history.

In 'Operation Barbarossa', feverishly planned by the Wehrmacht high command as another blitzkrieg since the

summer of 1940, illusion and reality finally became inseparable. The attack on the Soviet Union was delayed by the need to complete the occupation of Yugoslavia begun by the Italians, and by the fighting in first Greece then Crete, until there were only a few months left before winter. Stalin might have shot most of his best generals and the Red Army might have proved a failure against the Finns in Karelia, but oil industry and rail transport experts in Berlin uttered warnings. Senior military figures feared the infinite expanses of Russia, the winter and the mud.

Hitler behaved as if he came from another planet or as if this was a game of poker in a night shelter, declaring with utter coldness that if the Germans did not know how to be victorious, then they deserved their ruin. Many suspected, when the Wehrmacht was unleashed on 22 June 1941, that this was the beginning of the end. Grey fear descended like a lead weight and enveloped the silent populace. The special radio announcements no longer triggered triumphant frenzies. Those listening attentively were able to detect that the slogans were changing, becoming more dramatic. Goebbels gave instructions that reference was now to be made to a 'life-or-death struggle', and to the 'salvation of the West from the Bolshevik hordes'.

Summertime on the Steppe, 1942. *The third act of Barbarossa and the German army is advancing once more, the horrors of the Russian winter forgotten. 'It was almost as if we had two parts in our head,' said Count Clemens von Kageneck of the third Panzer Division. 'We were charging ahead exultantly and yet we knew that the enemy would attack again in the winter.' In fact much of the infantry had to foot-slog along at the 'ten-kilometre tempo', and most artillery was horse-drawn. Their target was the southern Caucasus and the oil wells of the Caspian Sea, but Stalingrad stood in the way.*

[PHOTO: GERHARD GRONEFELD]

did, and our commanding officer accepted my report without comment. As far as I know, no "commissars" were shot by our regiment to the end of the war, though many other Wehrmacht units appeared to have no hesitation to carry out the Kommissar Befehl.'

There are instances of senior front commanders reporting to Hitler, presenting the situation to him unvarnished, and subsequently returning to their headquarters reassured that the Führer would make everything come right. In fact, it was dangerous to utter doubts, because these revealed faint–heartedness and bordered on treason. The war, Hitler demanded, was to be concluded before the winter, a line beyond Moscow was to be reached and held. The Red Army would go to pieces under the hammer–blows of the Wehrmacht and the road to the oil wells of the Caspian Sea, Iraq and Iran would be open.

The German offensive aimed in three different directions — to Leningrad, to Moscow, and later to Stalingrad on the Volga. At first the Wehrmacht succeeded in encircling hundreds of thousands of Red Army troops, cutting off entire armies by outflanking moves by armoured divisions. But Leningrad, though mercilessly besieged for more than two years, half–starved and desperate, did not surrender. By the beginning of December 1941 the German advance had got stuck twenty kilometres from Moscow near today's Sheremetjevo airport when fresh Soviet forces from Siberia were thrown into the battle. The icy cold of the winter and unimaginable quantities of snow paralyzed the German war machine. Albert Speer, Hitler's rising architect and armaments minister, later remembered in Spandau jail where he was imprisoned after the war: 'Our new wool production process which produced a fabric easier to work with and less bulky to wear, had not taken account of the fact that it is precisely the grease that was removed to reduce weight that provides protection from humidity.' In the spring of 1942, when the mud ended, the German offensive regained momentum, reaching the Caucasus and the Black Sea — but the Red Army's backbone was not broken. The Soviet T–34 tank proved superior, as did the Russian submachine–gun. The vastness of the East devoured the German armies and, even more so, their poorly equipped Hungarian, Romanian, Italian and Spanish allies.

Klaus von Bismarck, a distinguished figure in post-war Germany, remembered the Kommissar Befehl being issued to all German units on June 21. The young officer was on the staff of the Ninth Infantry Regiment when he learned that all political commissars, who accompanied each Soviet unit, were to be shot forthwith.

'Before passing the order on to my superiors, I assembled a group of my friends and told them that I was determined to refuse to carry out this order. All of them, joining me in rejection of this order, agreed to have me report our refusal to our commanding officer, with a list of our names. This is what I

Rassenkampf, race war, in the East. Behind the front line the SS and the special police squads set about exterminating commissars, partisans, above all Jews. Some wretched Pole in the camp at Chelm, strapped to the perimeter wire, waits to be shot in 1941.

[PHOTO: KARL-ARTHUR PETRASCHEK]

Stalin realized the deadly danger in which the Soviet regime would immediately find itself if the German command succeeded in mobilizing the oppressed nations against Soviet domination. But the barbaric method of German warfare, the mass executions of the SS and the treatment of the Ukrainian peasants as 'subhumans', drove the population into the forests to join the partisans. Stalin proclaimed the 'Great Patriotic War', restored some rights to the Church, granted more responsibility to senior military leaders, and – good old 'Uncle Joe' – received oil and war material in ever-increasing quantities from the UK and US via Murmansk.

On 30 March 1941 Hitler had addressed two hundred commanding officers of the Wehrmacht on the impending great war in the East, telling them bluntly what would happen: 'Clash of two ideologies. Crushing verdict on Bolshevism as antisocial criminality. Communism an enormous danger for the future. This will be a war of annihilation, very different from the war in the West. In the East harshness is too gentle for the future.'

Thus, the war in the East had been intended to be a war of annihilation from the start, with Poland being the horrendous overture. The shrill propaganda songs predicting death to Jews and Bolsheviks had not been empty talk. At home fear of cruel punishment was designed to chain the population to the regime in one great criminal community. In terms of international diplomacy these murderous actions blocked any road to a negotiated peace, and this was what Hitler intended. No one was to jump off the speeding train or force the engine driver to apply the brakes. The dilemma for the Wehrmacht and for the military opposition was that anyone fighting for the fatherland was also serving Hitler and his criminal regime; anyone standing up against the wrecker of the Reich conspired in his own country's defeat, with all its horrendous consequences.

On 7 December 1941, when the Kremlin was within sight of the German infantry spearheads, the Japanese navy attacked Pearl Harbor. A few days later Hitler declared war on the United States. Was this an act of despair and delusion? Or was it calculated to get the Japanese to wage a parallel war against the Soviet Union? This was neither in Japan's interest nor within its power. When General Jodl rang General Warlimont, chief of the Plans Section of the operation staff, for an appreciation of American intentions, the latter replied: 'So far we have never considered a war against the United States...We can hardly undertake this job just like that.' Jodl answered, 'Well, see what you can do.'

When, at the turn of 1941/42, the European war became a world war, the Nazi regime cast all caution to the wind. Shortly after the attack on the Soviet Union the Jews throughout the German sphere of power were made to wear a yellow Star of David sewn onto their clothes. It was to set them apart, to mark them as untouchables. All those who saw the yellow star became silent accomplices of the Nazi regime, even though they could not be quite sure to what. But their conscience would tell them unremittingly that it was something terrible. More and more frightening reports found their way back from the East, whispered stories of mass executions, death marches and horrendous ghettos. But the mass murder of the Jews surpassed all belief. In 1942, when the Cologne Oppenheims secretly passed on the shocking reports to London, they were told not to engage in atrocity propaganda, as had happened in 1914.

Initially the murders were committed by shooting, next by fumes from trucks and, finally, on a systematic industrial basis, with the poison gas Zyklon B. On 20 January 1942, orders were given in a villa on the Wannsee near Berlin for the 'final solution of the Jewish question'. But the death machines had long been working. A perfected extermination apparatus, in varying degrees supported in the occupied countries by local police and administrators, rounded up and transported the victims to their squalid death in Auschwitz, Bergen–Belsen, Belzec, Sobibor and other places of hell. As many as six million Jews were murdered, as well as countless gypsies, mentally deficient men, women and children, homosexuals, prisoners of

This sequence shows some moments from the mass execution of 2800 Jews among the dunes near the beach at Liepaja in Latvia in December 1941, carried out by the SS with the help of local police. The final indignity for these women was to be forced to strip to their underwear.
[PHOTOS: CARL STROTT]

Contemplating the future, *or the lack of it. A young soldier (left) in the Caucasus, summer 1942.*
[PHOTO: HILMAR PABEL]

Stalingrad aftermath. *Survivors of the 6th army wait to march off to captivity. Its commander,* *Paulus, had been made a Field Marshal days before by Hitler, but he did not take the hint and commit suicide. Instead he turned pro-communist in prison and served the East German regime after the war.*
[PHOTO: GEORGJI ZELMA]

war and all those who aroused the suspicions of the regime.

Admittedly, there was the odd Wehrmacht commander who opposed the massacre — until he was replaced. There were individuals like the Shell manager Berthold Beitz in Galicia, who protected the Jews who trusted him. There were entrepreneurs like Oskar Schindler, who time and again protected the people working for him. And there was the astonishing coexistence in Riga, principal supply port for the eastern front, between the Wehrmacht and several thousand Jews who worked for the Germans, making themselves indispensable. But these were exceptional circumstances: normally there was no stopping the murderous bureaucrats of the SS. In October 1943 at Posen in Poland, Himmler addressed a group of high-ranking SS: 'We had a moral duty towards our people, the duty to exterminate this people which wanted to exterminate us... Most of you know what it means to see a pile of 100 corpses, or of 500, or of 1,000. To have gone through that, and still – with a few exceptions – to have remained decent people, that is what has toughened us. It is a glorious page of our history, which has never been written and never will be...'

The summer of 1942 was the turning point of the war, in North Africa and in Russia. The German Afrika Corps under Rommel had advanced via Tobruk to El Alamein, close to Cairo. But supply lines were overextended, the Luftwaffe failed to give air cover and the British counter-offensive threw the German and Italian troops back. American forces landed in Morocco. The remnants of the Afrika Corps were taken into captivity. Even more catastrophic was the military disaster which befell the 300,000 men of the Sixth Army at Stalingrad.

Encircled, tied down by senseless 'Hold on' orders from Hitler, starved and frozen, the survivors, some 90,000 men, staggered into Soviet captivity in the last days of January, 1943; scarcely more than 5,000 saw their homeland again. 'Stalingrad mass grave', Soviet propaganda ceaselessly repeated over loudspeakers. After this blood-letting the military collapse of the Axis powers was but a matter of time.

Night after night, and soon also in daylight, Germany's cities were pounded by British and American bombers, often in formations of several hundred aircraft. Operation 'Gomorrah' against Hamburg began with massive high-explosive bombs which blew out doors and windows. They were followed by phosphorus incendiaries, and the firestorm swirled those who had not yet been asphyxiated or incinerated in their cellars like sparks before it. The more the war progressed the more systematic was the bombing, directed against the civilian population rather than against industrial targets. But the daylight raids on Schweinfurt, centre of Germany's ball-bearing industry, cost the lives of so many American crews that they were not repeated until the Mustang escort fighter was fitted with long-range fuel tanks. Shortly before the end of the war Germany's most beautiful old towns, from Würzburg to Potsdam, were systematically destroyed by air raids.

The Allied landing in Sicily had been followed by an advance up mainland Italy with further landings at Salerno and Anzio. Decision in the West came with D-Day, 6 June 1944. The British and Americans disembarked on the Normandy coast, along with their French, Canadian and Polish allies. Two German armoured divisions had been kept back on Hitler's direct orders because he expected another landing in the Pas de Calais, misled by bogus Allied radio signals that German monitors were meant to overhear. When orders to move eventually came through, these troops were annihilated from the air. At this point it was obvious that the war was lost for Germany, yet Hitler, in a frenzy of destruction, rejected any idea of ending hostilities: 'The Germany of the past laid down its arms before the clock struck twelve. I make it my principle not to stop until the clock strikes thirteen.' Any expression of doubt concerning 'final victory' was punished by death. A Berlin joke of the time ran: 'I'd rather believe in final victory than run around without my head.' For their part, in Casablanca in 1943, the Allies proclaimed their war aim to be 'unconditional surrender'. This formula was to stop any one member of the alliance making a separate peace, and so to hold the fragile anti-Hitler coalition together. But

The Home Front. *The first 1000-bomber raid was on Cologne in May 1942. In 1943 the Ruhr was attacked from March to June, then Hamburg, until Berlin became the main target in November. From then until March 1944 German night fighters destroyed more than the equivalent of the whole front line of RAF Bomber Command, but the deaths caused by the bombing were horrific, reaching a climax of 40,000 on one night. Fires sucked in air, creating winds of 150 mph, and temperatures reached 1000 degrees centigrade.*

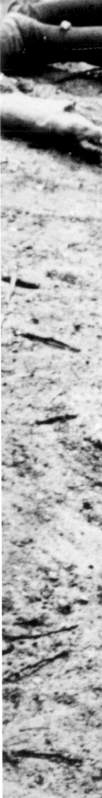

A soldier on special leave *(below) in Hamburg in 1943 finds his home a ruin and chalks a message asking where some members of his family might be.*

[PHOTO: ERICH ANDRES]

Rescued from the rubble. *A boy is led away by two youths (above) not much older than him (all grown men had been called up some time ago) after a raid on Remagen, on the Rhine, 2 January 1945.*

[PHOTO: HILMAR PABEL]

Among the victims *(above) on 23 July 1943, a man and the small boy he was trying to rescue.*
[PHOTO: ERICH ANDRES]

beyond this overriding war aim there was a blatant failure to agree on any common idea on the future order of Europe and the fate of European nations.

Hitler had bound the masses to his regime first by hope, then by making them criminal accomplices, and finally by fear. To dissolve this bond required the experience of armies destroyed, of cities burning and of approaching revenge. Putting an end to a messianic tyranny demands not only control of the state machinery but also the ability to win over hearts and minds. This applies even more in total war, when elementary feelings of fear and hope are projected onto the Leader. The only point from which Hitler's dictatorship could effectively be challenged was at the centre of the armed forces. Soon after the mass killings began in Poland, Colonel von Stauffenberg, at the head of a growing conspiracy, had recruited a young captain from the 9th Infantry Regiment, Axel Freiherr von dem Bussche, who had been shocked by mass-killings he had seen. But his suicide mission to take Hitler's life, wearing an explosive belt, was

frustrated, as were other attempts by Lieutenant von Kleist and Captain von Breitenbuch, as if some demonic angel protected the dictator. On this occasion, in Autumn 1943, the new winter uniforms to be modelled in front of the Führer by von dem Bussche, a blue-eyed blond-haired war hero, were destroyed on their way to Berlin by RAF bombs. Captain von dem Bussche went back to the Eastern front, where he won the highest decorations and had one leg shot off.

The network from Colonel Stauffenberg, General Beck and several hundred senior officers reached far into the Churches, the former labour movement and the senior civil service. The idea that united it sprang from raison–d'état and from Christian conscience. The principal motives of the German resistance were not just to regain freedom lost or to avoid military catastrophe, but to revive the country's legal system extinguished by Hitler's murderous excesses and the SS. But was there any prospect of success? Was it not much too late? The answer to these doubts was given by one of the leaders of

Normandy. *There were 59 German divisions manning the Atlantic Wall, but many were below strength, or of doubtful military value, or in the wrong place when the Allies landed on 6 June 1944. Still, the Wehrmacht was able to contain them in their beachhead until the end of July. By late August 50,000 Germans had been trapped in the 'Falaise Pocket' and De Gaulle had entered Paris. A cageful of captured Germans (left) awaits shipment to England in that month.*

US paratroopers *land (right) near Wesel on the Rhine, 26 March 1945. Robert Capa, the famous photographer, was able to take this picture because he had been the second man to jump out of the lead plane a minute or two before. Hitler never used paratroopers again as such after the mauling they received taking Crete in 1941.*
[PHOTO: ROBERT CAPA]

the conspiracy, Major-General Hans-Henning von Tresckow, chief of staff of Army Group Centre which was bleeding to death in the defensive fighting in the East. In a letter to Stauffenberg immediately before the often–planned and often–postponed attempt, Tresckow wrote:

'The attempt on his life must be made, *coûte que coûte*. If it were not to succeed, action is nevertheless necessary in Berlin.It is no longer the practical purpose that matters but the fact that the German resistance movement should be seen by the world and by history to have risked the decisive stroke. Compared to this everything else is immaterial.'

Stauffenberg was the key figure in the conspiracy. A dashing cavalry and tank officer who had lost an eye and a hand in Northern Africa, he was now chief of staff of the Home Army and was ordered from time to time to report Hitler. The bomb placed by him on 20 July 1944 at Hitler's 'Wolfsschanze' headquarters exploded during the daily briefing.   Back in Berlin, the 'Valkyrie' order – for mobilizing troops against an

unspecified uprising – was given by Stauffenberg, declaring the SS to be the enemy in question. When the alarm-order from Berlin reached the soldiers of the 9th Infantry Regiment in Potsdam, live ammunition was handed out, together with the explanation that the SS had staged a coup. This had to be put down immediately, without compromise, and strategic positions had to be taken up in the middle of Berlin. 'An order is an order', was the only comment from the soldiers, sometimes accompanied by a furtive grin, since now the hated SS would be on the receiving end.   But, since Hitler had survived, many troops were half–hearted, counter–orders arrived and the action stalled. That same evening, 20 July, Stauffenberg and his ADC, First Lieutenant Werner von Haeften, were shot by men of the Guards Regiment in the inner courtyard of the Bendler block. In Paris, SS and Gestapo, who had immediately been arrested by Wehrmacht troops, had to be released the next morning. In France and Germany the Gestapo set about squaring accounts with a wide circle of

The White Rose: *Sophie Scholl (top left), a member of this resistance group, threw leaflets condemning the Nazis and their crimes into the great hall of Munich University, where she was a student. The* group were rounded up and executed.
July plotters: *(top right) Julius and Annedore Leber. He had been a trade unionist and socialist member of the Reichstag. Executed. Adam von Trott zu Solz (on right in picture* above) and his family. After failing to enlist British support for the German resistance, this senior diplomat joined the conspiracy. Executed. Claus Schenk Graf von Stauffenberg (above). Executed.

suspects. The 'People's Court' in Berlin completed the retribution – hundreds of death sentences were passed, families were torn apart, property was confiscated. Torture was followed by brutal execution, filmed so Hitler could enjoy the horrid sight.

The German resistance saw Hitler as the monstrous product of unleashed modernism. After their experience with the failed first German Republic the men of the resistance lacked enthusiasm for liberal democracy. Pluralist industrial society, regarded as the seedbed for Nazism, was likewise suspect. Thus the moral strength of the resistance was greater than its political foresight. The test of reality was denied to the men of 20 July. But the courage and martyrdom of the conspirators were a reminder that there had been another Germany – and perhaps there would be again some time. That, in spite of their failure, was the legacy of the dead. They enabled the Germans later to look back to the horrors of their most recent past with feelings other than incomprehension and revulsion alone.

At the turn of 1944/45 the Russians arrived in East Prussia, the Americans in Aachen. A gunner from a self-propelled gun detachment which surrendered in Königsberg remembered:

'The Ivans were out of the control of their officers and the things they did were ghastly – just blood-lust. But there was also brutality at Command level. I was told that most of the Königsberg Volkssturm [home guard] men were shot by the Reds as partisans. In some cases tanks were deliberately run over wounded soldiers. The sickening thing was that the Reds had made our men lay the wounded on the roadway, very carefully lined up. Soldiers and civilians were tied together and set alight. There was nothing, no crime, no bestial act that they did not commit.'

The fact that Hitler employed the last battle–worthy troops in the West against the Americans in his Ardennes offensive, instead of in the East, was final evidence of the silent collusion of the dictators. Hitler would rather the Soviet armies arrived first in Berlin, in order to complete the ruin of the Germans after they had failed to carry him to final triumph. As he put it, 'Someone who has no heir for his house would do best to have himself burned with everything that is in it – as if on a magnificent pyre.' In early 1945 several Soviet armies mounted an attack against the Seelow Hills on the western bank of the Oder. In the last great battle of the Second World War, after sustaining vast losses, they achieved the break–through to Berlin.

With the sounds of the guns in the distance, the Berlin Philharmonic gave their last concert under Furtwängler on April 12: Beethoven's Violin Concerto, the finale from *Götterdämmerung* and Bruckner's Romantic Symphony. Speer, who had circumvented Goebbel's instruction to draft all the musicians into the Volkssturm, had warned the conductor that when he asked for the Bruckner piece, 'it would mean the end was near and they should get ready to leave Berlin.' At the close of the concert the audience were offered cyanide capsules from baskets proffered by Hitler Youth, children in uniform. Speer was horrified and never found out who organized this. Before he shot himself and Eva Braun in the bunker under the ruins of Berlin on 30 April 1945, Hitler could have noted with satisfaction that the victors shared his intoxication with destruction.

It was, of all people, Speer who made an all-out effort at the end to quash Hitler's 'scorched earth' orders. After deposing

Göring because of his attempts to open negotiations with the West, Hitler had appointed Grand Admiral Dönitz, commander of the U-boats and a devoted follower, to be his successor. At this time, Soviet troops at Torgau on the Elbe joined hands with US troops, as they had done five years earlier with Wehrmacht soldiers in eastern Poland. This time the toasts were drunk in vodka and bourbon. The Wehrmacht surrendered to the West in Rheims on 7 May 1945, and once more on the following day in the officers' mess of the former army engineering school in Karlshorst, a Berlin suburb. After that there was no German government and no German army, except for trivial remains of local tax departments and fire brigades.

But this ending was also a beginning. Only three days later Churchill sent a cable to Harry S. Truman, the new US President, warning him not to trust the Russians, who had dropped an 'iron curtain' in front of their troops. This made the London Protocol of September 1944, dividing Germany, and Berlin at the centre, into three zones of occupation, all the more important. The West's mistrust of Stalin was so strong that it had to ensure its share in the occupation of Berlin by treaty. In return, early in July 1945, the British withdrew from Mecklenburg and the Americans from Thuringia and Saxony, abandoning the hapless inhabitants to Soviet detention squads and to Communist revolution, in progress wherever Soviet forces reached. In so far as the delirium of victory and war propaganda were not paralyzing all serious reflection, the West was beginning to ask whether this had been the goal for which all the sacrifices had been made.

'Exposed on the shores of nothingness' is how Wolfgang Borchert, terminally sick poet and ex–soldier, described German existence in 1945. In the new world system Europe, ruined and burnt out, counted only in so far as it was important to Stalin's Eurasian empire and to America's Atlantic alliance. Anticipating Churchill, Goebbels had forecast in February 1945

The road home. *Humiliation and pain as German troops pull a wounded or exhausted comrade in a cart towards captivity or worse in Russia.*
[PHOTO: YU CHERNISNEV]

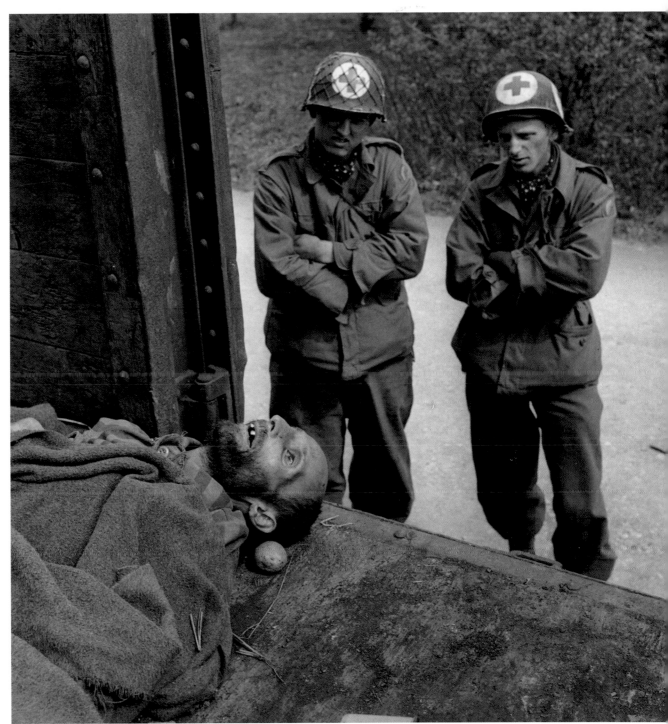

that an iron curtain would fall across Europe, and Hitler concurred. On April 2, 1945, in the last of his monologues recorded by Martin Bormann, he said: 'With defeat of the Reich...there will remain in the world only two Great Powers capable of confronting each other – the United States and Soviet Russia. The laws of both history and geography will compel these two powers to a trial of strength, either military or in the fields of economics and ideology. These same laws make it inevitable that both powers should become enemies of Europe. And it is equally certain that both these powers will sooner or later find it desirable to seek the support of the sole surviving great nation in Europe, the German people.' However, Hitler also said that as the Germans had not been able to succeed in their mission they deserved to be destroyed.

Overcome with horror *at the reality of death in the local concentration camp (left), a woman walks past corpses. She in turn is watched by the G.Is. forcing her and other civilians to confront the truth.*

Too late. *US paramedics (above) contemplate the corpse of a camp victim in a railway truck, probably one of the many thousands being moved aimlessly round Germany by their guards as the Russians advanced.* [PHOTO, ABOVE: LEE MILLER]

CHAPTER SEVEN

DIVIDED COUNTRY

Fratting: *US soldiers take out German girls in 1946, in spite of regulations forbidding fraternisation with the vanquished. From the girls' point of view, there were few young German men left around to escort them, while Allied troops were the source of cigarettes, chocolate, nylons – the new currency which could make the difference between freezing starvation and a tolerable existence.*

[PHOTO: HANNS HUBMANN]

O N 8 MAY AN UNCANNY SILENCE DESCENDED ON Germany. The noises of war had stopped: no more bone-piercing sirens, no roaring bomber fleets overhead, no barking of anti-aircraft guns, no artillery fire, no rumbling tank tracks. The Soldatensender Calais, a clandestine British-operated transmitter broadcasting to German troops in France, was silent and Goebbels' 'Twilight of the Gods' bombast was ended; but also there was no more 'Lily Marlene', the sentimental song of soldiers' love and death, sung by Lale Andersen and listened to by friend and foe. The clip-clop of the wooden clogs worn by prisoners being marched from the concentration camps south to the elusive mountain fortress, the Alpenfestung, suddenly stopped when American troops arrived on the scene. In the East, Russian words of command were heard: 'Davay, davay' to the soldiers taken prisoner, a menacing 'Come, woman', preceding gang rape.

In the West, there was weary relief among the population that the Americans had arrived first. For those who came out of prisons, torture chambers and concentration camps an ecstasy of joy ensued. Many were reduced to living skeletons with large, staring, half-dead eyes which had seen too much. Some died of the first real meal given them by Allied soldiers. On the roads, where black GIs were driving US Army trucks with their five-pointed white star at a dizzy pace, crowds of children soon collected, shouting 'chocolate, chocolate', and mostly getting some. Otherwise the rule was 'No fraternization' for the victors and 'Off Limits' for the vanquished. Among Germans there were mixed feelings of liberation and defeat, but certainly considerable relief that they had got away by the skin of their teeth.

Along the seam of the American and Soviet occupation zones all those who were able to do so made for the west, because the Americans' reputation was infinitely better than the Russians'. One of the last battles of the Second World War took place in the extensive pine forests south of Berlin, near the village of Halbe, where an army of mostly very young soldiers, encircled by two Soviet fronts, desperately tried to escape Siberia and the Gulags, in the direction of the Elbe and the Americans. Those who made it left 60,000 dead behind. Anyone falling into the hands of the Russians could expect long years of captivity somewhere in the vastness of Russia, perhaps forced labour in Vorkuta on the Arctic Ocean, perhaps work in the mines at Magnitogorsk, perhaps construction work in the Ukraine. Soon after unconditional surrender an endless column of German prisoners was driven in triumph through Moscow towards a gloomy fate, some to war crime trials, often on invented charges, resulting in no less than 25 years' forced labour, and

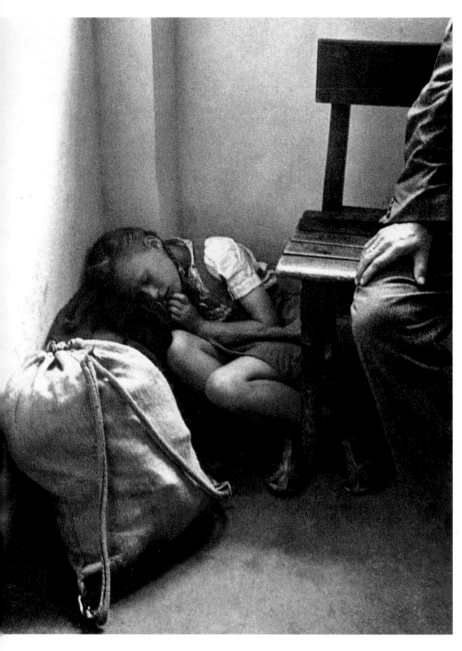

Refugees: *a child sleeps (left), exhausted, in the corner of a station waiting room, her rucksack of worldly possessions almost as big as her body. (Right) Trainloads near Dresden flee from the Russians east of the Oder or from Czechoslovakia. There were 16 million Germans among the hordes of DPs (displaced persons), prisoners of war and slave labourers trying to reach safety or get home.*
[PHOTO, LEFT: HILMAR PABEL]
[PHOTO, RIGHT: HÖHNE/POHL]

often in execution by public hanging.

The hundreds of thousands of Vlasov's anti-communist troops and Cossacks who had fought alongside the Wehrmacht were now handed over to their merciless masters who either liquidated them or sent them to Siberia for a slower death. The Americans set up huge camps in the open, where many of the inmates froze and starved; the British kept some of the Wehrmacht formations together until, in the summer of 1945, Stalin protested. He was afraid of collusion. The few who had survived in the U-boats – less than one man in ten – returned home. In the Baltic the remnants of the German navy were busy, in a last all-out effort, saving hundreds of thousands of refugees from the Russians. The 'Strength through Joy' cruise ship *Wilhelm Gustloff* was torpedoed by a Soviet submarine on the way from East Prussia to the British zone of occupation and sank in the icy Baltic with many thousands of refugees, and perhaps the amber panelling looted from one of Catherine the Great's palaces.

An unending stream of refugees was flooding westward along all highways and roads: women, children, old people, lugging heavy rucksacks or pushing bicycles and perambulators, or walking behind overloaded carts. This river of fear and misery had begun when the Red Army reached East Prussia in October 1944. The atrocities – such as multiple rape followed by crucifixion – perpetrated by Russian troops in Nemmersdorf were revealed when the village was retaken in a Wehrmacht counter-attack. The reports, given ample publicity by Goebbels, made the blood freeze. At first Nazi officials had forbidden westward flight on pain of death; then they saved themselves, and after that there was no holding anyone back. The Germans who stayed behind were subsequently systematically expelled from their farms and villages. Of 16 million driven out or taking flight some 12.5 million reached the West. The rest became victims of rape, shootings, hunger and epidemics. After 8 May systematic expulsion of Germans from the border regions of Czechoslovakia followed, especially from the Sudetenland. Two years after the end of the war the population of the three western zones of occupation, where some 38 million had lived before the war, totalled 50 million. Horror stories emerged from internment camps set up by the Czechs to house Sudeten Germans: babies drowned in latrines while their mothers were forced to look on; German doctors forced to crawl and eat human excrement; legs and arms systematically broken. In Camp Lamsdorf in Poland 6488 inmates died in the year after the war. A British colonel witnessed a refugee train arriving in Berlin from the East, its occupants expecting the capital to be a comfortable haven:

'The train was a mixture of cattle and goods trucks, all of which were so packed that people lay on the tops, clung to the sides or hung on the bumpers. Children were tied by ropes to ventilation cocks, heating pipes, and iron fittings. The train stopped and a great long groan rose from the length and breadth of it. For a full minute no one moved a limb. Eyes that were full of anguish examined the people on the platform. Then people began to move, but everyone seemed crippled with cold and cramp. Children seemed dead, purplish-blue in the face; those who had clung to doors and fittings could not use their hands or arms, but went about, arms raised or outstretched, hands clenched. They hobbled, legs numbed, to fall on the platform. The people who had arrived days before pressed back to make room, and looked on in silence. Soon the platform was

filled with cries of disillusionment as the newcomers learned how they had been deceived.'

Long before 8 May a tentative return to normal life had begun in the West, where Allied troops had been in control for some time. The British, Americans and French were seeking Germans with a clean record. This was the time of good-conduct certificates, known as Persilscheine, 'Persil White vouchers', which were a passport to the future. Urban and district administrations were re-established in order to kick-start normal life, and so were the fire service, tax offices, housing offices and ration-card centres. Life went on, in a banal manner or otherwise. In the East the 'Ulbricht group' was flown in from Moscow – German Communists with orders from Stalin to reawaken party-political life on the Weimar model and to place Communists in key positions. As their chief, Walter Ulbricht, soon to be Secretary-General of the Communist party, put it, everything had to look democratic, but Communists were to be in control.

Russians, Britons and Frenchmen began to dismantle whatever German industry could still be moved. Large areas of the Harz and the Black Forest were cut down. The most far-reaching measures were taken in the Soviet zone between the Elbe and the Oder, where entrepreneurs were shot or expelled, and in all cases expropriated. Particular hatred was focused on 'Junkers and war criminals', which were just convenient labels for the owners of large estates, even if they had been persecuted, hanged or robbed by the Nazis for involvement in the assassination attempt of 20 July 1944. Many families which had once owned property were happy to get away with their bare lives. In Buchenwald and Sachsenhausen, where the SS had ruled until now, the Soviet NKVD took control, supported by willing German helpers. Railway tracks were dismantled in the East and the rails transported to the Soviet Union. But at Aue uranium mining continued at full speed. Prisoners were employed there regardless of radiation danger. Stalin wanted the raw material of the bomb, no matter how many lives it cost.

The question facing the Germans was not so much what to do but how to survive. Food rations were reduced to 1,500

Trümmerfrauen, *rubble ladies clearing up wartime damage on the banks of the Elbe, with the remains of the old city of Dresden in the background, 1947 (below).*
[PHOTO: HÖHNE/POHL]

calories – not enough to live on and too much to die on; civilians in Britain were getting 2800 calories while American GIs got 4200. Hardly anything was on sale for grubby Reichsmark notes. Whatever anyone had to sell was offered on the black market, where nylon stockings, Camel and Lucky Strike cigarettes, and anything available in the American PX or the British NAAFI soon became common currency.

The Germans had scarcely anything left to offer, except their bodies. 'Veronika Dankeschön' was the American code for venereal disease, VD. One alternative was to join the 'rubble ladies' who cleared up the burnt-out ruins, cleared the roads, made the trams run again, found half-decomposed corpses in the basements. War widows had to earn a living for their children, from sewing to letter-writing, from translating to puppetry – anything that secured survival. At the same time, the 'Fräuleinwunder' took place, when strictly brought-up German Gretchens attempted to look like their new Hollywood idols. At the end of 1945 a German police official said 'It is impossible to distinguish between good girls and bad girls in Germany. Even nice girls of good families, good education and fine background have discovered their bodies afford the only real living. Moral standards have crashed to a new low level. At the present rate, in two months I wonder if there will be a decent moral woman left.' By December 1946 the number of girls selling sex for western goods in Berlin was getting on for half a

The shell of the Reichstag *(above) in what Malcolm Muggeridge called 'the drama's centrepiece, blitzed Berlin'. It is the backdrop for potato gatherers in the Tiergarten, in 1946. The white structure is the war memorial erected by the Russians as soon as the fighting stopped, using materials salvaged from Hitler's 'New Reich Chancellery'. Soviet victories in the 'Great Patriotic War' are inscribed on it and T34 tanks stand on pedestals in front of it.*

million. In the British Zone alone there were 100,000 orphaned youngsters and 80 per cent of the girls suffered from VD. Overall, as a result of war deaths, there were nearly three women to every man. The Russians had brought a nasty variant of syphilis with them which made joints, limbs and face swell up. There was a thriving black market in contraceptives. A British official's wife was puzzled by a game she saw Berlin children playing. The boys would seize the girls and try to pull their clothes off while shouting 'Komm, Frau'. Then a German mother pointed out they were merely re-enacting what they had seen happen to their own mothers and sisters during the Russian sack of Berlin.

The writer Heinrich Böll recalled how 'The thought of freshly baked bread tumbled through my head, and often I

would walk the streets in the evenings and think of nothing but bread. My eyes were burning, my knees weak, and I felt some wolfish instincts grow inside. Bread. I was bread-thirsty like others are drug-addicted. Even now, the wolfish angst of those days comes back from time to time, and I buy bread as it is displayed in shop windows.' To hunger was added cold. The first two postwar winters were the harshest of the century, when most of the buildings in the big cities were still in ruins, glass was replaced by cardboard, there was no coal, and the cold crept through the cracks. The few who had contacts among occupation authorities, those who had hoarded Wehrmacht stocks, or who had access to timber, foodstuffs or clothing, were better off. The rest just struggled through. In Cologne Cardinal Frings stated in a sermon that God would look mercifully on a mother who picked up coal which had accidentally dropped from the trains of the occupying power. "To fringsen" became a current term. In the schools, which

reopened in the summer of 1945, there was food from American Quakers to be carried home in old army tins. Soon the first CARE parcels arrived containing the wonders of America, filling not only empty bellies but reassuring souls in need of consolation.

The Nuremberg Trials began on 20 November 1945, in the Palace of Justice, miraculously preserved there through the firestorms and carpet bombing that had reduced the place to a giant heap of rubble. Its aim was to set new standards of international and humanitarian law. What followed were summary proceedings against the Reich-Government, the top political functionaries of the NSDAP including the SA, SS, Gestapo, but also against the Wehrmacht High Command (OKW). Heinrich Brüning, former chancellor and now Harvard professor, was asked what to do. His answer: 'I would prefer Streicher to be tried by a German court... Robert Ley would be sentenced to death, and most likely also Ribbentrop...' But in

1945 there was no German authority, and no inclination among the Allies to allow any German settling of scores.

Hermann Wilhelm Göring, and 21 other 'main war criminals' were accused and the main charge was 'conspiracy against peace'. It was a grim fact that the Soviets were now called upon to sit in judgement on their one-time allies. After more than ten months, on 1st October 1946, sentences were pronounced. In the early hours of 16th October ten Nazi leaders were hanged; Hitler, Goebbels, Himmler, Göring had comitted suicide, Hess was sentenced to life imprisonment; Baldur von Schirach, the 'devil's youthleader' and Albert Speer, the 'devil's architect', were sentenced to twenty years in the ancient fortress of Spandau in four-power custody. Von Papen,

Hitler's one-time foreign minister and Dr Hjalmar Schacht, his one-time Reichsbank-Präsident, were acquitted, in spite of protests from the Soviet judge.

A British official's impression in 1946 was that most Germans seemed to be hurrying around trying to find something, and that they all pulled small wooden handcarts behind them, 'sometimes even two, the Germans having a passion for trailers'. They were to carry anything that could be found, bought or 'acquired'. If you didn't have a cart, you had a rucksack. In 1947 he met a family off on holiday. 'They had to travel with their two children in appallingly overcrowded trains, yet they were taking with them luggage which contained all their rations for two weeks, a suitcase full of potatoes which

Adaptation. *An open-air notice board (right) works as a primitive labour exchange advertising jobs in various sectors of industry – textiles on the left. An open-air concert (top right) takes place by the famous grotto in the badly bombed Residenz, the royal palace in Munich, in August 1945. Corks and wooden cylinders (above) are substituted for rubber bicycle tyres in Dresden, 1946.* [PHOTO, ABOVE: RICHARD PETER JUNIOR]

Lost and found. *(Opposite) A mother shares the joy of reunion with her daughter from whom she had become separated earlier in the war. This scene is in 1946 while the other (right) dates from the 1950s. A father, just released from a Soviet camp, sees his daughter, perhaps for the first time, and it is all too much for the little girl. She cries because her father cries, or because the effects of the camp are all too evident on the face of this strange man.*

[PHOTO, OPPOSITE: HILMAR PABEL]

they hoped to be able to use for barter, some eggs intended for the same purpose and a large box filled with coal which the boarding house proprietor would demand before he would serve any hot meals.' His evenings out were often ruined for him by the pervading smell of unwashed Germans in old clothes smoking poor tobacco.

In the East, anyone chancing a remark that Hitler and Stalin had been allies for a long time would have regretted it in Bautzen – one of the notorious jails for political prisoners, which soon had the name of 'yellow misery'. Many were taken there, but few came out again. Matters were easier in the West, clearer and more hopeful. Hardly anyone mourned the passing of the 'Führer'. If, for a while, people were saying that things had not all been bad, if they remembered 'Strength through Joy' and the 'People's Community', the construction of the Autobahnen and full employment, this was probably more an attempt to explain to themselves how everything came to happen and why they had allowed themselves to be seduced, than any mourning over the passing of the deadly dance of

National Socialism. When people were summoned before the tribunal, to be granted 'clearance' or to be classified somewhere amongst categories of the principal culprits, fellow-travellers and 'not concerned', or if they completed the American 'Questionnaire', they were reluctant to accept what had actually been a complex reality. Of the intoxication nothing was left but ashes. Hans Rothfels, a volunteer soldier in 1914, an emigré since 1935 and now an American historian about to return to Tübingen, pointed out a 'profound paradox': 'Those were German patriots who prayed for the day of surrender, even though they had no illusions about what would follow.' On 15 October 1945, when the Council of the Evangelical Church in Germany met with the Ecumenical Council of the Churches, it formulated a self-indictment: 'We accuse ourselves of not having made our avowal more courageously, not having prayed more faithfully, not having believed more joyfully and not having loved more ardently.'

Friedrich Meinecke, one of the intellectual leaders of the democratic cause during the Weimar period, wrote a book in

A new start. *Students at the Technische Hochschule in Darmstadt (left) living in an air-raid shelter in 1948, when many of those at university were war-wounded or had just been released from prisoner-of-war camps. To qualify for admission students had first to help clear rubble. Tuition fees were paid in part in the form of coal briquettes.*
[PHOTO: HANNS HUBMANN]

Wolfgang Borchert, the writer, *(right) who died aged just 26 in 1947, part of a generation wiped out by the war.*

which he summed up the German past. The title sounded like a cry of despair *The German Catastrophe* (1946). The book went into many editions. He was the first Rector of the Free University in Berlin-Dahlem, founded by students who wished to escape Communist indoctrination at the ancient Friedrich-Wilhelm University in the centre of Berlin. Ludwig Dehio, marked by internal exile, could find no reassurance in history: 'Where we are seeking a firm place we find that the ground is swaying, shaken far back into the centuries by the same disaster that is shaking us at present. Our history is ambiguous, more ambiguous than any other – but the interpretation entrusted to us and familiar to us has collapsed.'

Universities and technical colleges opened up as best they could for the winter semester of 1945/46. Half-starved figures in worn Wehrmacht uniforms without insignia brought briquettes of lignite coal for the stoves in the icy lecture theatres, happy to have been admitted, men without an arm or a leg in reserved seats in the front rows, the rest standing, tightly packed, listening to lectures on law, history, philosophy, given by old men who had become wise. Emigrés returned, and were respectfully appointed to university chairs; puppetry and theatre flourished; the visual arts experienced a frantic boom. People were eager for messages offering meaning and direction. Tennessee Williams' *The Glass Menagerie* was staged, so was *By the Skin of Our Teeth* by Thornton Wilder, *Antigone* by Jean Anouilh, *Mourning Becomes Electra* by Eugene O'Neill. Wolfgang Borchert's radio play *Draussen vor der Tür* [Outside the House] hit the mood of the period, chiefly in the consolation offered to a dead man's little brother who cannot

Gruppe 47 *(left)*, *the most influential group of post-war German writers, meets with some British friends in Berlin in 1955. (Sitting, l to r) Heinrich Böll, Hans Werner Richter, Wolfgang Hildesheimer, Martin Walser, Milo Dor; (standing) Ingeborg Bachmann, Ilse Aichinger, Christopher Holme, Christopher Sykes.* [PHOTO: H. KÖSTER]

Des Teufels General, *a scene (below right) from Carl Zuckmayer's play, 1947.* [PHOTO: HANNS HUBMANN]

Axel Springer *(far right) built up the largest newspaper group in post-war Europe. When he sensed the impact of TV he created the magazine* Bild, *which featured a semi-nude girl on the cover and many pictures inside, while its limited amount of text always expressed a solid working-class conservative outlook.* [PHOTO: MAX EHLERT]

sleep because he has to keep a vigil for him: 'Rats sleep at night.'

Whoever had a radio receiver and electricity listened to AFN, the American Forces Network – 'Begin the Beguine', or 'Sentimental Journey', and 'How High the Moon' by Glenn Miller. Body language changed, voices became softer, less strident. Men adopted a new ideal of relaxed cool, while women attempted a Hollywood look with scant means. The mass-produced novels of the Rowohlt publishing house in Hamburg, printed on newspaper, opened to German readers the world of the American novelists – Faulkner, Wolfe and Hemingway – and with them a different, non-bombastic, terse and laconic style. *Neue Zeitung* appeared, sensibly subsidized by the American occupation authorities. In Hamburg *Stern*, *Der Spiegel*, *Die Zeit* and *Die Welt* were granted licences. Their owners became influential and prosperous, each in their own way, with a calling not from God but from the occupying power to go forth and teach the people. While books and newspapers imported the American way of life, love and death to post-war Germany, the most important films were coming from France: *Orphée*, *Les enfants du paradis*, *Sous les toits de Paris*. The reason was that in the ambivalence of France after collaboration and resistance the Germans would more easily recognize their own painful experience and come to grips with it. *Casablanca* never became the success it was in the Anglo-Saxon world. *Entscheidung um Mitternacht* (Midnight Decision) was the first German film with Hildegard Knef, *Berliner Ballade* featured Rudolf Platte in the role of Otto Normalverbraucher, the average little guy. There was remarkably little self-pity, while Carl Zuckmayer's play *Des Teufels General*, showing an impressive Luftwaffe commander fighting his own struggle against the Nazis, women and death, brought home the moral dilemmas of the past. Another of the early films from a German studio was *Meines Vaters Pferde*, the story of a Panzer-commander saved from his physical and mental agonies by a beautiful young nurse who gives him his memory and identity back by telling him the story of his father's horses – and women. Germans, on the whole, looked for reassurance that there was life after the nightmare. *Wir Kellerkinder* was about life among the ruins, *Rosen für den Staatsanwalt* about the shocking amorality of the legal profession.

It was unwise to criticize the US policy of re-educating the Germans. When the editors of *Der Ruf*, an intellectual journal under US tutelage, bit the hand that was feeding them, they were fired. Hans Werner Richter and Alfred Andersch planned an alternative called *Skorpion* in Autumn 1947, but a publishing licence was withheld. Instead, an informal group was formed named 'Gruppe 47', which for two decades determined very largely the development of German post-war literature. Quality counted, but right-wingers were excluded. The overall aim was that of a rebirth of intellectual and social life in Germany: even if reality could not be readily changed, at least alternatives could be aired.

In the East there was sovietization pure and simple with the German Communists often surpassing their Soviet masters. In the West the Americans practised 're-education'; the British half-reconstructed and half-dismantled the German past, with some British occupation officers believing that they could build up in Germany, from scratch, that Labour state that British tradition was denying them. The French were preaching western values, if anything. For them, memories of collaboration and treason and cowardice were still too vivid.

Germans soon discovered, albeit with mixed feelings, that there was a rift between the victors. If they stuck together Germany would, for a long time, perhaps for a century, remain a pariah state. If, however, they split up, then Germany's social and political unity would become untenable. On both sides of the 'Iron Curtain' the Germans, from being simply the vanquished remnants of the 'Greater German Reich', were turning into inhabitants of a country which had strategic importance in the mounting global conflict between the American way of life and Leninist dictatorship.

The Potsdam conference of 16 July to 2 August 1945 had the impossible task of preserving the Allies' unity beyond military victory. Ever since the summer of 1944 British and American

diplomats in Moscow had ceaselessly sent alarming messages to London and Washington, warning that peace with Stalin was not to be had. On the eve of the conference a flash of light lit up the desert of New Mexico and a shining cloud assumed the shape of a gigantic mushroom rising towards the skies. The USA had tested the super weapon, the atom bomb. Stalin congratulated Truman casually, as though the world was unchanged, but the cunning Georgian knew what was at stake. His physicists had long been instructed to develop the bomb by every means, including espionage. Truman for his part realized that the time for compromise was running out. The Potsdam conference took place at the Cecilienhof, a country residence in the English Tudor style set in a spacious, lake-studded park, completed in 1916. Until the final assault of the Red Army it had been the home of the former German Crown Prince and his family. A gigantic round table arrived from the GUM department store in Moscow, and in the inner courtyard Red Army men planted a floral red star of busy lizzies, to demonstrate who was the master of this piece of real estate. Averell Harriman, US ambassador to Moscow, congratulated Stalin on standing as a victor in the capital of Germany. After a moment's reflection Stalin tersely replied: 'Tsar Alexander got to Paris.'

Poland had already been abandoned by the West, and so had the countries down the Danube. Stalin declared that Germany

Long live Stalin! *East German 'Young Pioneers' (left) in Hildburghausen sing for joy and State. Village photographer Rudolf Meffert captured them as he had the Hildburghausen Hitler Youth band ten years earlier (see p. 172).* [PHOTO: RUDOLF MEFFERT]

Walter Ulbricht *(above) ruled East Germany until 1971: 'While everything should look democratic, we must be in control'.* [PHOTO: ROLF GILLHAUSEN]

was 'nothing but a geographical concept'. Churchill wanted to keep France in play and divide Germany, but on a north-south basis, not on the Soviet-proposed east-west basis. The descendant of the Duke of Marlborough was thinking of Hanover and Prussia in the north, and the Austrian lands from the Rhine to the Hungarian plain in the south. This was not to be, though the maps showing the proposed divide still adorn the walls of the Cecilienhof as museum pieces. Truman and Stalin tried to avoid open conflict. Germany was to remain together, but only west of the Oder and the Neisse. The population east of this line was to be expelled 'in an orderly and humane manner' – though everybody must have been aware by then that the process had long been concluded, in a disorderly and inhumane fashion. Central authorities were to be established in Berlin, but these never met. The country was

to be denazified, demilitarized and democratized. Anyone could make of these concepts whatever they pleased. The Americans had 'free enterprise' in mind – the Soviets the opposite. Each victor was to take reparations from his zone; the Soviets were to be recompensed by industrial goods from the West in exchange for foodstuffs from the East.

At the time of the Potsdam conference a man of seventy was awaiting his moment at Rhöndorf on the right bank of the Rhine – Dr jur Konrad Adenauer, a pensioner and rose grower during the Third Reich. Immediately after the entry of the Americans into Cologne, on 9 March 1945, he had once more been appointed Oberbürgermeister, or Chief Mayor. But the British who followed the Americans kicked him out of office – he was accused of spending too much effort on politics and too little on clearing up. He was familiar with the Gestapo cellars;

although an 'anti', he had kept aloof from the Resistance because he did not think generals capable of successful conspiracy. The Swiss Consul-General von Weiss had, throughout all the Nazi years, passed on to him his copies of the *Neue Zürcher Zeitung*, so that Adenauer was used to seeing Germany from the outside and well informed on what was going on in the world. At the time when the 'Great Three' disposed of Germany at Potsdam he wrote, not unlike Churchill a few months earlier: 'Russia is letting down an Iron Curtain. I do not believe that, in the administration of the half of Germany entrusted to it, it will allow itself to be influenced in any way by the Control Commission.'

More clearly than anyone Adenauer perceived the opportunities which the discord between the victors was offering to Germany. For that he was prepared to accept the division of the country, not forever but for whatever time the West needed to put the Second World War behind it and to create a counterpoise to the Soviet Union. Adenauer came from the Rhineland. To him, a close link with the West, or indeed integration, had nothing to do with giving up on German unity – which was how his great opponent, the Social Democrat leader Schumacher, viewed it. Adenauer understood association with the West, especially with France, as the fulfilment of Germany's destiny. He realized that the more the Soviets oppressed the East and threatened the West, the faster the Germans under Western occupation would become allies in the inevitable 'Cold War'.

Much as Bismarck in 1866 had prepared for the eventual unification of Germany by separation from Austria, Adenauer very soon saw the actual division of Germany as the undesirable precondition for two desirable objectives. The first was West Germany playing a key role as a bulwark against the Soviet threat, and the second was her integration with France, Italy and Benelux in a new European equilibrium. This, however, was based on the assumption that the Americans would understand their European role as guardians of peace and opponents of the Soviet Union. He wanted a Germany that, while divided, was indispensable to the West, just as the West would be indispensable to that future West German state. He was convinced that no one but himself knew how to realize this grand design. About that time he received a visit from a young British historian and intelligence officer, Noel Annan. Annan was charged with the task of informing Adenauer that, as far as the British occupation authorities were concerned, there was nothing against him, and of apologizing for his earlier dismissal. Before they parted Adenauer asked his guest what he thought had been the greatest mistake of British diplomacy. Annan mentioned Munich. But Adenauer went back to 1815: 'It was at the Congress of Vienna. All that Prussia wanted was Saxony, but the British brought Prussia into the Rhineland, against France, and that was the beginning of the misfortune.'

Adenauer had influential friends in Cologne, such as the banker Robert Pferdmenges who had steered the Oppenheim

bank through all the perils of recent years and who was preaching the resurgence of the Bürgertum – the middle classes – and civil society. By founding the Christian-Democratic Union (CDU) Adenauer succeeded in overcoming the old religious split within those middle classes. He became party leader in the British occupied zone. He did not have great trust in the Germans, and his experience of democracy was, at best, ambiguous. But he seized the opportunity – as de Gaulle once formulated it in a similar situation – of doing the work of a psychiatrist. West Germany was not an entity with which to be satisfied, but for the foreseeable future it had to suffice, and it gave the chance for the Germans to prove themselves.

Adenauer was a penetrating judge of human character, which allowed him to adopt an attitude bordering on contempt. His utterances were as sparse as his vision of his objective was clear. After the bombast of imperial Germany, after the violent expressionism of Weimar and after the sound and fury of the Third Reich German politics were in need of sobriety and realism. In this regard Adenauer was more in tune with the desperately exhausted nation than Dr Schumacher, who tried to combine national grandiloquence with the language of the class struggle. Adenauer, like many in Cologne, was a liberal Catholic. People, he said, had to be 'taken as they are; there are no other ones.' In the right place at the right time, he was untainted politically and commanded natural authority because of his advanced age and vast experience. He accepted that, for an unspecified period, freedom was attainable only at the price of unity. His long-term press-spokesman Felix von Eckard remembers 'his upright composure which made him look much younger than his age...The first characteristic that I noted was his extraordinary politeness, including to his subordinates. In political or official exchanges, he could, on occasion, be very outspoken, but he would never be impolite. During those ten years, I must have entered his study a thousand times or more. Always he would rise to greet me and always, at the end of every converation, he would rise again and accompany me all the way to the door to say goodbye. I am convinced he did the same to every visitor.' Eckard also described Adenauer's political instinct, his gut feeling for the balance of power at any given moment, at a conference or a party meeting. He was a good listener, but his patience could wear thin, if his counterpart was pompous or did not know his brief. Foreign correspondents who were granted an interview would often find themselves being asked about political details at home. Brief meetings of about ten to fifteen minutes he would refuse, saying that if the person was important, then it would take more time; if unimportant, it would be a waste of time.

Chancellor Adenauer, *on the left, holds a reception for Sir Winston Churchill in 1956, shortly after the retirement of the British Prime Minister.*

Without Hitler's war neither would have moved from the fringes of power to centre-stage.
[PHOTO: ROBERT LEBECK]

A 'Superworker', *modelled on Stalin's Stakhanovites of the 1930s. East German coal miner Wolf Hennecke (opposite) fills in his bogus production records which will then be held up by the regime as the 'norm' for all miners to reach.*

An expropriated estate. *Buildings are demolished (above) and the materials carted away to be used on the new collective (but unmechanised) farm.*
[PHOTOS: HERBERT HENSKY]

Adenauer showed not the faintest trace, when in the United States or the Soviet Union, of an inferiority complex. It became a legend, how, on assuming office and making a formal visit to the Allied High Comissioners on the Petersberg, overlooking the Rhine valley and Bonn, he had been warned not step on the carpet reserved for them. Adenauer however, made a point of doing precisely that, and made sure that photos were taken.

The Soviet Union probably had not one plan but two as far as Germany was concerned, and these were mutually incompatible. Forty per cent of the industrial capacity of the Soviet zone was being removed. At the same time, however, a kind of Soviet Germany was being established. If the Soviets meant to make the land between the Elbe and the Oder a bastion and deployment area against the West, they surely had to try and win over the population. Yet the opposite happened. At Easter 1946 the KPD, the Communist Party of Germany, encouraged by the Soviets, absorbed the SPD, the Social Democrats, to form the SED, the Socialist Unity Party of Germany. Anyone protesting was arrested by the NKVD. The mass flight increased: entrepreneurs, craftsmen, physicians and professors all went to the West or at least sent their children. Although the 1300 kilometres of border were closely guarded, the sector crossings from East to West in Berlin remained open due to the complexities of the city's four-power status.

After 1945 there existed in what was left of Germany two sharply contrasting societies. In the East there were the party

Sunday Morning Miracle, *21 June 1948, the day when a new Germany really emerged, as each citizen was issued with forty marks of the new currency. Munich citizens (left) queue to receive theirs. The notes looked very like US dollar bills, underlining the source of their validity.*

Sale time in Cologne, 1950s. *Housewives (opposite) enjoy the blessings of capitalism and growing prosperity, rummaging in the shoe department of a large store.*
[PHOTO: CHARGESHEIMER]

Byrnes made a speech in the patched-up Stuttgart Staatstheater to smartly turned out US officers and shabby-suited German politicians. He tried to reassure the Germans that this time they had not backed the wrong horse. American troops would remain as long as they were needed. This was a promise, scarcely veiled, that the Germans would be protected against the Soviets and also against counter-productive measures by the occupation authorities, including the de-industrialization proposed by Morgenthau. Slowly, slowly a US strategy emerged, centered around what was left of Germany, after the trials and tribulations.

In 12 March 1947 President Truman proclaimed the Truman doctrine in a message to both Senate and Congress. The Soviet Union had become the enemy of the 'free world' which comprised the Atlantic nations. George F. Kennan's subsequent 'Containment' strategy, but for Germany's involvement, would have lacked depth. Without the territory between the Elbe and the Werra, as President Truman stated a little later, the defence of Western Europe would be nothing but a rearguard action on the beaches of the Atlantic Ocean.

As a first step towards the establishment of a West German state the British and Americans combined their zones into the Bi-Zone. Soon afterwards, when the French merged their zone too, the new country was nicknamed 'Trizonesia' by the Germans. The crucial issue, however, was the creation of a credible currency. On 25 March 1948 the Bank Deutscher Länder was set up, the first central institution of the three Western zones. It was to be independent of instructions from state bodies and mandated to ensure stability. While the new currency was expected any day, everyone hurried to pay their bills and settle their debts with old money. People made as many railway journeys or telephone calls as they could; they consulted lawyers about hypothetical legal cases, and paid for the advice in cash.

The new currency was prepared in close co-operation between the US Federal Reserve and the Economic Director of the trizonal administration, Professor Ludwig Erhard. On 21 June, a sunny Sunday, West Germans received 40 marks, children under 18 half this amount. The bills showed a close similarity to American greenbacks and their tie-up with the dollar lent them validity. Elaborate devaluation systems cushioned hardships. On Monday morning, as if by magic, desirable goods, hitherto available only by shady barter, appeared in the shop windows –

cadres of the totalitarian system with no more than remnants of the older class structure and with a little freedom given to the churches – balanced by Stasi control – and an ever-increasing pressure on farmers and small businesses to conform to the collectivist party line. In the West a tentative reconstruction took place based on older élites, without the military and without large estates, but with a high percentage of exiles from East Germany, anxious to start a new life. While the East was bleeding to death, the West was soon suffering from high blood pressure.

American policy was at first driven by revenge – US Secretary of the Treasury Henry Morgenthau's Plan aimed at the de-industrialization of Germany, and would have resulted in mass unemployment, hunger, desperation and probably a surge of communism. On 6 September 1946 the US Secretary of State

bicycles and sewing machines, light bulbs and zip fasteners, cigarettes and nylon stockings. Ludwig Erhard soon went all the way. General Lucius D. Clay accused him of having changed the rationing regulations of the occupation authority. Erhard replied: 'I did not change them, Herr General. I scrapped them.'

The Western powers had decided that the new West German mark, should be valid in the Western sectors of Berlin, though with an overprint B, to signify the city's special status. Stalin nevertheless understood this as a Western claim to cement the West's position in Berlin. The Russians thereupon severed rail, road and canal links to Berlin with the intention of starving the city. The Americans had a mere 50,000 men left in the whole of Europe, hardly enough for a trial of strength with the Red Army. Instead General Clay devised the 'air bridge' and planes flew in everything the Berliners needed, from coal to bricks, from vegetables to coffee and chocolate.

The fact that the Russians continued to participate in the Allied air traffic control centre offered a modicum of insurance against war. But there was some anxiety nevertheless, and the Americans stationed two squadrons of heavy B-29 bombers, potential atom-bomb carriers, on British air bases. Two aircraft of the same type were dispatched with considerable publicity on a round-the-world flight. The man in the Kremlin understood the signal. In May 1949 an agreement was reached which safeguarded future access rights for the Western occupation powers to Berlin. Admittedly, the rights of Germans to travel into and out of Berlin were tenuous. The airlines of the three Allies were the only way of getting to Berlin without Soviet or East German inspection. This first east-west crisis in Berlin earned its inhabitants the respect of the West and put the West Germans into a more favourable light. They had stood up to the totalitarian threat, this time alongside the Western victors. America was delighted.

While the 'cookie bombers' were still flying through the skies of East Germany, eventually with one landing every forty-eight seconds at the three airports of West Berlin, a convention of eminent jurists coming together in the arcadian landscape of Lake Chiemsee was working out a draft for a West German constitutional arrangement. Most of the Länder had been put back on the map in 1945 or 1946 in an attempt to recreate political life from the grassroots. The Parliamentary Council, consisting of representatives of the Parliaments of the West German Länder, then met in Bonn, largely undamaged and pleasantly situated on the left bank of the Rhine, as far away from Soviet tanks as could possibly be, so predetermining the future capital. Debates were chaired by Konrad Adenauer.

The Berlin Airlift. *An American plane comes in to land in July 1948 at Tempelhof, one of the city's three airports, while German children wave at the 'cookie bomber'. The original idea for the airlift came from an RAF officer and many British planes participated alongside the American ones.*
[PHOTO: HENRY RIES]

On the face of it the Basic Law emerging from these deliberations resembled the constitutions of Germany's western neighbours, but in substance it was a constitution reacting against Weimar and the Third Reich: no referendum, no directly elected Reich president, many checks and balances. It had little scope for encouraging leadership and less for change. Instead it embodied unchangeable basic values, out of the reach of parliament. Later a clause was added, also with silent reference to Weimar, saying no party attaining less than five per cent of the total vote would get a seat in parliament. The parties, once established, were highly privileged, more powerful than ever before. The constitutional court in Karlsruhe and the Bundesbank in Frankfurt, however, were to provide the most important checks and balances.

Just as currency reform had been seen through by the Allies,

so political power continued to be controlled by them – sovereignty, external security, emergency powers, and the future of 'Germany as a whole', the formula agreed at Potsdam in 1945. The Social Democrats, hoping for support from the British Labour Government, wished to keep economic and social issues open for revision at a later date, as did the Liberals and Christian Democrats, looking towards the American way of life. The former believed in a planned, collective economy and expected mass suffering to sweep Erhard's 'social market economy' away. The latter believed in the Dollar, the Market, cheap oil and German efficiency. After two or three years it was the social market economy which won and became the common ground as it developed over the decades, supported by the boom of the 1950s. Both the balance of power within the country and the threat of Soviet

Stalin Allee, *East Berlin 1954. Hitler might have approved of the totalitarian grandiosity of this overblown triumphal way, with hardly a car to distract the eye from its concrete expression of the cult of personality. The workers constructing it in the previous year went on strike, in protest at the excessive 'norms' imposed on them, and triggered an uprising throughout East Germany.*
[PHOTO: MAX EHLERT]

frontier, rearmament, and emergency powers.

On 14 August 1949 elections were held in the West for the first German Bundestag. The people in the Western sectors of Berlin did not take part; their representatives in the Bonn parliament were appointed by the West Berlin assembly rather than elected. The centre-right parties, to their own surprise, achieved a narrow majority. The CDU formed a parliamentary association with its Bavarian sister party, the Christian Social Union (CSU) and Adenauer, as a matter of course, claimed the post of federal chancellor. Against all expectations, especially those of the Social Democrats, the centre-right camp was to form the faith and face of the Federal Republic during its first decades. Not until 1968 did the student scions of the bourgeoisie, among them not a few children of Nazi leaders, channel this development in a different direction.

When it convened in Bonn, the German Parliament met in a building the style and size of which suited the conspicuous modesty and sobriety of postwar Germany. Erected on the banks of the Rhine, and owing its inspiration to the Bauhaus, it had been finished in 1933. Now the architect Hans Schnippert added, in equally parsimonious style, an assembly hall, finished within five months. On the front wall, a symbol was fastened, an eagle with spread wings, less reminiscent of imperial glory than of Churchill's wartime dictum that he wished the future Germany to be like a turkey, fat and impotent. Later on, the entire edifice was declared a listed building. But when it was discovered that there were serious cracks, it was cheerfully pulled down and, in its place, a playful glass construction put up, reminiscent of an oversized kindergarten and lacking the dignity parliamentary buildings in London, Paris or Washington tend to display. It was still unfinished in 1991 when, after a passionate debate, a slim majority decided that United Germany's capital should be Berlin.

'Man benimmt sich wieder' (We are behaving again) was the title of a successful book by the lady in charge of protocol at the emerging Bonn ministry of foreign affairs. Students addressed one another with the polite 'Sie' to distance themselves from the embarrassing familiarity of the Reich Labour Service, the SA and the Wehrmacht. Dancing classes lent some style to gawky secondary schoolboys, girls wore petticoats and waited to be asked. People acted in an emphatically relaxed and civilian manner. No one wished to hear wartime recollections, except perhaps exciting revelations about top Nazis. Protestant, Catholic and political clubs and forums were flourishing, just as if this part-nation in the West needed a continuous discourse with itself and others as a form of psychotherapy. Grammar schools, Waldorf (Montessori) schools, private schools and church schools flourished again, more so in the CDU-governed Länder, less so in those run by the Social Democrats, who never gave up the idea of a standard comprehensive school system for all.

Statesmen and industrialists again wore black Homburgs. On the members of Adenauer's first cabinet – all of them gentlemen

Communism helped Adenauer as he carefully manufactured consensus and equilibrium. He provided reassurance to a deeply troubled nation, and never were there more fitting slogans than his vote-winning 'Keine Experimente' – no experiments – and Erhard's 'Wohlstand für alle' - wealth for all.

Adenauer from the start had wanted a Constitution, not a Basic Law which would always have a provisional air. But a definite framework was unfeasible, given the continuing pain over the division of the country and its unsettled international status felt within the CDU/CSU, among the Liberals and the Social Democrats. There was a problem in accepting the West German state while preserving the goal of German unity. But for the time being the constitutional compromise of Bonn had the advantage that insoluble questions did not have to be solved, most importantly, those of Germany's future eastern

Ludwig Erhard *(above), the new prosperity personified, champion of the social market economy* *('capitalism with a heart'), armed not with a lance but a glowing cigar, in 1958.*

the concept of a nation either and tended rather to define themselves as Bavarians, Hanseatics or Badeners, or alternatively as Europeans.

Simultaneously with the Federal Republic of Germany — and as a framework for its role in Europe – the North Atlantic Alliance was created. Both were part of the same American grand design. On the eve of the signing ceremony in Washington D.C. President Truman invited the foreign ministers of the future NATO states to the White House to explain to them that American protection came with one vital condition – Germany had to be made part of the club. The British objected that Germany would have to become socialist, the French wanted a neutral Germany. Truman and Secretary of State Dean Acheson – *Present at the Creation* was the title of his memoirs – brusquely swept any objections aside. The West was confronted, Truman said, by a worldwide Soviet Communist offensive. Germany and Japan were defeated, but not removed from the map. Sooner or later the Kremlin would make them an offer impossible to refuse. That would safeguard Soviet power to the end of time. Against this threat, the free world must put up a positive design. Thus the Federal Republic of Germany came into being, not a state in search of a foreign policy but the product of American foreign policy in search of a state.

In June 1950 North Korean troops attacked the south of the divided peninsula, and overnight German rearmament became a serious prospect, since this Communist regime had the backing of Stalin and Mao while South Korea was under US protection. In 1952 the draft of a European Defence Community was put forward jointly by Adenauer and his French counterpart Schuman, by means of which France hoped to bring Germany's future military potential – if that was inevitable – under its own control. Two years later it failed in the French National Assembly, removed from the agenda by a majority of Gaullists and Communists – it was too much too soon. But France also proposed the European Coal and Steel Community in 1952, in order to merge forever the hard core of Germany's and France's industrial potential. This provided the basis for the system of the Treaties of Rome in 1957 setting up the European Economic Community (EEC) and Euratom.

'Wirtschaftswunder' was the term applied to the outburst of energy directed at reconstructing not only the Western wastelands left behind by World War Two but also the lives of many millions of individuals. The term miracle, however, should not obscure the fact that the 1950s saw a unique combination of favourable economic and political factors: from the Marshall plan, to the advantageous dollar/D-mark exchange rate; from cheap oil and then nuclear energy, to wide-open world markets; from low wages, to favourable tax conditions encouraging rapid investment in ever more modern machinery. Professor Ludwig Erhard the Finance Minister, was a staunch believer in market forces. By contrast Great Britain kept economic controls much longer than Germany, expanded the welfare state before the economy could sustain it, and

of mature age – the black suits still hung loose as on scarecrows. Ludwig Erhard alone, always with a cigar, a gift to cartoonists, and with his chubby face, radiated confidence and a promise of plenty. After prolonged consideration there was a national anthem again, or strictly speaking, two – in the West the third verse of 'Deutschland, Deutschland über alles' innocently enough praising 'unity and law and freedom'; in the East, by the gifted party poet Johannes R. Becher, 'Auferstanden aus Ruinen Deutschland einig Vaterland' (Risen from ruins, Germany the united fatherland). Later, when the Communists of the SED no longer wished to be reminded of Germany and unity and when, in all seriousness, the 'socialist nation' was proclaimed, the tune was only hummed, just as the party daily *Neues Deutschland* was only referred to as ND. Admittedly, West Germans were not quite at ease with struggled with the burden of empire. For the Germans the past had been closed so brutally that privilege and delusion were replaced by realism and resolve.

Their economic expansion was based on mature technologies which Germans were used to, and in fact had developed during the war, notwithstanding carpet bombing. The post-war dismantling of factories by the occupying powers was often a blessing in disguise because it meant production lines had to be built from scratch and could incorporate all the latest advances.

A gastarbeiter *(below), one of the countless 'guest workers' who helped Germany to perform its economic miracle. In this case it is an Italian working on the Volkswagen production line in 1962, though many came from Yugoslavia and Turkey, particularly when the supply of East German refugee labour was cut off by the Wall.*

Glare of publicity. *(below right) A trio look out of the rear window of an early 'Beetle' in 1953 giving the impression of much more room inside than there is. It's from Lower Saxony in the British Zone.*

From machine tools to consumer goods, from toy model railways to giant steel bridges, the Germans were able to offer what the world market would buy, with very little competition coming from the Far East. While the supply side was rapidly reconstructed the demand side also expanded, not only through the need to rebuild devastated cities and to furnish new homes, but also to accommodate the hundreds of thousands fleeing from East to West, until 1961. An 'eat well' drive was followed by an 'embellish your home' fixation. After that, mass travel became the craze, to Rimini and the Costa Brava, with travel agencies soon becoming giant enterprises.

Professor Erhard's 'Wohlstand für alle', 'wealth for all', was expressed in its most obvious form by the rise and rise of the motorcar as the Germans' favourite status symbol. The German car industry was reconstructed, not withstanding the vast advantages of Detroit or Coventry. The Volkswagen Beetle, initially costing a little under DM 2000, soon dominated the rapidly expanding network of autobahns. BMW rose from the ashes under the guidance of Herbert Quandt, the half-blind entrepreneur who believed in sportscars and motor travel. Friedrich Carl von Oppenheim, the Cologne banker, brought together engineers, designers, and managers at Ingoldstadt in

Fashion and fast cars. *Two illustrations from the magazine* Film und Frau *(Film and Woman). One shows the actress Ruth Leuwerik (opposite) posing on the magazine's seamstresses' table. Her films brought the German dream of* the 1950s to the screen. *The other is a fashion shot at the AVUS test track in Berlin (above) with the Mercedes star in the ascendant, not only over its own latest model, but also over the Jaguar sports car on the left.* [PHOTOS: F. C. GUNDLACH]

Bavaria, all from the former Audi works in Saxony, now reduced to rubble, to build on the Audi tradition of creating high-class cars for the world market. Daimler Benz in Stuttgart, used to producing great cars for every régime, provided Konrad Adenauer with his legendary black limousine, a Mercedes 300S,

an immediate symbol of power and export-driven prowess. Ford in Cologne and General Motors' Opel factory in Rüsselsheim soon provided for a mass market as never before. Rising wages encouraged demand, spurred production, and then increasing production enabled wages to rise again, in a virtuous circle. In 1959, the deutschmark became a freely convertible currency still at DM 4.20 to the US dollar and DM 12 for the pound sterling. Two years later a five percent revaluation took place, to the chagrin of German industry. But when the Swiss political commentator Fritz René Allemann published his book *Bonn ist nicht Weimar* (Bonn is not Weimar), it met with approval and self-congratulation. While Adenauer never forgot that he was the 'chancellor of the vanquished', as he said, Ludwig Erhard was soon credited with the cheerful remark 'Once again, we are somebody'– 'Wir sind wieder wer'.

The Democratic Republic. *A family (left) flees the socialist paradise through the woods to the West, carrying what it can of its possessions. In June 1953, the East Germans mounted the first rebellion against Soviet hegemony in Eastern Europe, even though most realised how hopeless it was. The scene of desperate civilians throwing stones (opposite) at Russian tanks on Berlin's Potsdamer Platz was to be repeated in Budapest in 1956 and Prague in 1968.*

[PHOTO, LEFT: HILMAR PABEL]

In the East, things were dramatically different. On 17 June 1953 it became obvious that the 'German Democratic Republic' was nothing but a Soviet garrison state, propped up by Soviet tanks. After the SED régime had put up work norms, the workers went on strike in more than two hundred towns large and small throughout the 'GDR'. The vast majority of the population was united in a public uprising. For half a day there was feverish hope encouraged by Western radio stations; then Soviet troops moved in, firing into the crowds as they came. Despair, trials, death sentences or long imprisonment in Bautzen were the outcome. Some Soviet soldiers who had refused orders to shoot were court-martialled and were shot themselves.

In the West there was embarrassment and helpless fury, but also dramatic confirmation of the fact that there was no substitute for American protection. Adenauer's electoral support was consolidated in the autumn 1953 elections, and rearmament became acceptable to broad parts of the population. In October 1956, the bloody crushing of the Hungarian uprising by Soviet tanks merely underlined the lesson learnt in June 1953. A year later, when Adenauer won an absolute majority, an election poster abhorred by the Left showed a Red Army soldier with bared teeth and greedy eyes over the slogan 'All Marxist roads lead to Moscow'. The message was not lost on the electorate.

In 1957 the Russians sent the first satellite into space, the Sputnik. The strategic community in the US was worried; if the Soviets could master the technology of intercontinental ballistic missiles, the US was no longer invulnerable. At the same time, the Soviets wanted to use nuclear muscle to draw a new map of Europe. In November 1958, Nikita Khrushchev demanded the whole of Berlin for the GDR and thus for the Soviet empire. His ultimatum had been preceded by massive troop deployments by the 'Group of USSR forces temporarily stationed in Germany', clearly designed to frighten the West.

Near Berlin there were exercise grounds which lacked nothing in realism – copies of actual Berlin Metro stations were constructed for close-combat training. Soviet military planners expected to seize Berlin by a surprise coup between dawn and mid-morning coffee. However, behind the 6,000 Americans, the 3,000 French and the 3,000 British in the Western sectors of divided Berlin there was still the Bomb.

Meanwhile the SED régime in its blindness was doing all it could to turn up the pressure on the people in its hands. While every day hundreds were crossing the sector boundary in the centre of Berlin towards the West, farms were forcibly collectivized. There were to be no more farmers in Eastern Germany, only rural workers in agrarian complexes. The middle classes were systematically wiped out. Pupils and students had to learn Russian and testify to the purity of their ideological indoctrination by voluntary activity and conspicuous enthusiasm. A whole generation considered leaving, and nearly half of it did, abandoning families, homes, familiar dialects. How long could this process continue without the whole East-West structure breaking down? The current joke was that the last East German to leave must remember to switch out the light.

There seemed to be no answer. The Social Democrats presented a plan which proposed the removal of nuclear weapons and 'foreign troops' from Central Europe; this would not only deprive West Germany of its crucial anchoring in NATO, but would also pull the rug from under the feet of the Americans in Europe. A multi-stage plan for bringing the two German states together – sometime, somehow – was to resolve the Berlin problem. The key was to be the eventual neutralization of Germany when reunited – just what Austria had undergone in 1955. But Germany was the keystone of the European system, not a peripheral Alpine republic. When Willy Brandt, youthful Mayor of West Berlin, presented these ideas to the US Secretary of State John Foster Dulles, the American's cold

answer was as condescending as it was frank: 'We may disagree with the Russians on a thousand things. But on one point there are no differences between us – we will not permit a reunited armed Germany in the no-man's-land between East and West.'

The young President John F Kennedy, with slight experience in office, returning from the Vienna summit with Khruschchev in the summer of 1961, observed that he had had 'most sombre talks', adding: 'It is going to be a cold winter.' West Germans were torn between fear of war and anxiety that the great powers would reach agreement over their heads. Never since the Berlin blockade twelve years previously were villas in prime situations in the divided city, such as Dahlem and Grunewald, offered so cheaply. On 13 August 1961, on a fine Sunday morning, what had long been whispered about in the GDR but invariably denied by its rulers actually happened – construction workers, guarded by frontier troops with steel helmets and sub-machine guns, set up barbed wire a few steps behind the border. A few days later a breeze-block wall was constructed. That was the end of mass escape. But was it also the end of military confrontation?

In the West, outrage and relief were evenly matched: outrage at the sealing-off of the East, relief over a solution without war. The US government had formulated three 'essentials', outlining an eventual compromise: presence of the Western powers in Berlin, with their own troops; free access for them by land and air; self-determination for the inhabitants of Berlin's western sectors. Nothing much was left of the four-power status – just about enough to make Germans realize that, whatever divided East and West, no one intended to demand a settlement of the German question, let alone leave it to the Germans. The spheres of influence were painstakingly respected. Soviet soldiers guarded the memorial west of the Brandenburg Gate, where they had set up their victorious World War II weaponry on a high pedestal; they also made their contribution to the guarding of the Spandau prison for war criminals where Albert Speer was held for twenty years and Rudolf Hess, Hitler's deputy, until his death. From time to time Western patrols drove into the Eastern sector or across the 'Bridge of Peace' into Potsdam to demonstrate their right to do so, and to conduct a little espionage.

With the stalemate some of the gloss disappeared from the image of the USA during those years, much as the self-confidence of the West Germans was deflated. With the Berlin wall the end of the Adenauer era was made visible, especially as in the election campaign of 1961 the old gentleman failed to address the angst of the nation. Willy Brandt, the Socialist candidate for the Chancellorship, expressed vast disillusionment with the West when he observed: 'The curtain went up, and the stage was empty.' The limits of American power were the limits of German hope.

Life in the East. *Two moments captured in Leipzig in 1956. A bride and groom (opposite) outside a tenement block, which has not seen painter or plasterer since before the war. An old lady, dignified in her long summer dress and hat (right), comes out in the sun to shop. The traffic policeman behind her does not look overworked.*
[PHOTOS: URSULA ARNOLD]

246

CHAPTER EIGHT

EITHER SIDE OF
THE WALL

Leap for freedom: *a 19-year-old East German border guard called Conrad Schumann seizes his chance to escape into West Berlin, 15 August 1961. Two days before, barbed wire had been unrolled along the divide through the city, but he must have known it was soon to be replaced by a breeze-block wall. If he wanted to join the rest of his family which had already fled, now was the moment. The West Berlin police had tipped off some of the media that a border guard might be making a break for it, here in Bernauer Strasse so, while he escaped, his coolness was captured for all time. No shots were fired and he was quickly carried off in a waiting police van. In spite of the Wall, 50,000 were able to escape from East Germany in the first year after it went up, but gradually the flow was reduced to a trickle as it was 'improved' with mines, dogs trained to attack, and guards with orders to shoot to kill.*

[PHOTO: PETER LEIBING]

SOCIETY AND POLITICS IN GERMANY WERE PROFOUNDLY changed by the building of the Berlin Wall, which made the Iron Curtain brutally visible. But how the moral and political forces would realign themselves was not at all certain. The Adenauer era was visibly coming to an end. In the last few years everyone, except the octogenarian chancellor himself, had been expecting his departure. When he was forced out of office in 1963, he took on a pater patriae role, beyond time and politics. His successor was a man who seemed to come from a different world, one generation his junior, the personification of the economic miracle and of recovery – Professor Ludwig Erhard, the man whose cigar would never cease to send out confident smoke signals.

Until the Wall the Germans were said, rightly, to have been living in two waiting rooms. Now the eastern waiting room was locked up, and the western one had to force itself into accepting that the German Democratic Republic was a fact of political life. Previously unity was to come, somehow, or other, through the attraction and the weight of the West, through American power and European economic clout. This was called the 'policy of strength'.

To go from west to east in Berlin was very difficult, except for individual members of Allied forces who could cross at Checkpoint Charlie. Germans had to apply a long time in advance, and Berliners were treated in a markedly different way from West Germans in order to accentuate the Soviet theory that West Berlin did not belong to West Germany. Even so, coming in and going out involved waiting in line for a long time, undergoing humiliating searches and questioning, and having to account for every contact made or money spent. But it was not lethal. Going from east to west, by comparison, involved a much higher risk except for 'travelling cadres', mostly Stasi or old-age pensioners, whom the East German authorities were happy to get rid of. The odd dissenter like Wolf Biermann, the singer, was regarded as a nuisance and let out. Otherwise Republikflucht – fleeing the state – was a crime that would ensure the perpetrator many years in which to repent at leisure in prison. Some tried to cross the wall or the border fence; few succeeded, many were shot. Others chose the indirect approach, via Romania and the Black Sea resorts and forged passports. Others, again, found helpers who out of idealism – but also for money – would risk their lives or at least their freedom.

One young Protestant cantor by the name of Georg Gafron took a chance in 1973. He was told by his contacts – who might have been double agents or incompetent amateurs for all

stationing highly accurate medium-range missiles aimed at decoupling Germany from the West and at trimming back American 'extended deterrence'.

While this brutal bargaining was taking place between the superpowers, changes were also occurring within the Federal German body politic. In 1959 the Social Democrats had consigned Marxist revivalism to the archives and accepted private ownership and the market economy – admittedly with social correctives added in. A year later the Social Democrat chief whip in the Bundestag, Herbert Wehner – a Communist in the Weimar era, a survivor of Stalin's terror, a sullen figure though a man of power and energy – declared the SPD's support for Adenauer's Western policy. Wehner was trying to make his party, after its long wanderings in the ideological desert, capable of government. As a result it found itself increasingly in conflict with the left-wing intellectuals, the party's youth organization and the student activists. Some of them were relegated to the playgrounds of educational and school policy, where in the long run, they would change the republic to a greater extent than anything brought about by the trivial circumstance that the SPD had now forced itself to accept established facts as established facts.

Adenauer in his day had never forgotten that he was the 'Chancellor of the vanquished'. Foreign Minister Gerhard Schröder, on the other hand, began to speak of 'German interests' and Chancellor Ludwig Erhard of the 'end of the postwar period'. Both the Chancellor and the Foreign Minister meant the same: the Bonn Republic was about to become an economic giant and so did not wish to remain a political dwarf forever. Adenauer's heroic pessimism gave way to a more jovial political style as Ludwig Erhard looked to America instead of to France. He was united with President de Gaulle only by mutual incomprehension. He loved modern architecture and had a light glass pavilion built as his residence in the park of the Chancellery – though he was to enjoy it only for a short time. The reason for his downfall was a slight rise in unemployment, a minor recession and a modest rise in federal debts in 1965 and 1966. That was enough of a pretext for the party oligarchs in the Bundestag, who wanted a Grand Coalition, to overthrow him. As the 1960s continued, it became increasingly accepted that the foundations of German statehood – keeping open the issue of national unity, integration in the West and a line through to Moscow – were not to be sacrificed to the desire of the Western Allies for détente. These ideas were eventually given particular prominence in 1969 in Willy Brandt's Neue Ostpolitik.

he knew – the hour and the minute at which to be in a Transit-Autobahn parking lot somewhere in East Germany. Small and slightly built, he was bundled into the boot of a French car with a West German registration number. It was so small that the border police did not suspect a person could be crammed in there. Once across the other side, he went to the reception centre, joined the RIAS – Rundfunk im Amerikanischen Sektor – and became a successful publisher.

In 1961 the Soviet Union had proved strong enough to tighten its grip and to consolidate its sphere of power. Nuclear weapons, for more than a decade the symbol of America's strength, now that the Russians possessed them as well, became a symbol of America's frustration. Khrushchev, toning down the doctrine of class struggle and the final battle, talked of 'coexistence' with the West, and the West soon began to talk of the two sides of security policy – deterrence and détente. That was the lasting lesson of the dual crisis of Berlin and Cuba, symbolized not only by the retreat of both sides – Soviet missiles did not remain in Cuba and American ones left Turkey – but even more by the 'hotline' that from then on linked the situation rooms in Washington and Moscow in order to avoid strategic misunderstandings over Berlin and the Fulda Gap, over Vietnam or the Middle East. Mutual assured destruction, its acronym most appropriately MAD, became the foundation of the long nuclear peace that ensued. These new rules of the game among other things conceded to the Soviets that they would maintain order within their own empire. They made full use of their power, abruptly putting a stop to the 'Prague Spring' of the reformist Czech Communists in 1968. But in the following decade, they also challenged the 'rough balance' by

Flower Children: *Rainer Langhans and Uschi Obermaier (left), a famously anarchic couple who called themselves 'Commune No.1'. These 'beautiful people' became role models for many student revolutionaries.*
[PHOTO: WERNER BOKELBERG]

Party time, *East Germany 1965. Wolf Biermann the singer entertains friends in his flat (above), including the poet Sarah Kirsch and writer Fritz-Rudolph Fries standing behind him. A decade on, and the socialist dream having finally faded, both Biermann and Kirsch had left for the West.* [PHOTO: ROGER MELIS]

'Lappes and Evi spot Will'. *It's 1959 and Jazz has not given way to Pop and Rock at this 'Riverboat Shuffle' party (above right). Will McBride, the American photographer at whom they point and wave as he snaps them, founded the ground-breaking magazine TWEN in the 1960s, famous for its novel approach to layout, typography and illustration.* [PHOTO: WILL MCBRIDE]

Erhard's successor was the Minister-President of the Land of Baden-Württemberg in south-western Germany, a man who because of his upper-class Swabian accent and his eloquence was dubbed 'King Silvertongue' – Kurt Georg Kiesinger. Unlike Erhard, who had risked his neck by planning for a post-war and post-Nazi future, Kiesinger had been a lukewarm Nazi party member before 1945 – and left wingers saw the country heading backwards, impelled by sinister conspiracies of capitalists, Americans and neo-Nazis. These apocalyptic fireworks, springing from an unhealthy mix of utopia and paranoia, so heated the atmosphere that in 1968 when the Bundestag came to debate the transfer to the German government of the emergency powers, left with the Allies when the Basic Law had been approved in 1949, this was seen as proof positive of an imminent fascist seizure of power. It was characteristic of the Germans' habitual fear of themselves that the rebellious students would rather leave emergency powers in the hands of the Allies than give them into German hands. There were hysterical calls for 'resistance', just as if one was facing the execution chambers of the Nazi dictatorship and not, at worst, water cannons and television cameras. In the name of democracy political commonsense went through a severe crisis.

The faraway war in Vietnam became the catalyst of hate-inspired anti-Americanism. The notion of the 'end of ideology', that had accompanied Adenauer's later years and announced boredom among the intellectuals, proved premature. The later Sixties experienced a high tide of ideology, nowhere more violently than on the Left. This upheaval was reflected and

magnified by television, by now the most powerful medium. It coincided with the transformation of everyday life among Germans, old or young, men or women, of ideas governing politics and of deep instincts and gut feelings.

In the early Sixties statistics began to indicate that the aged were living longer, that fewer young people were getting married and that fewer children were being born, while the number of divorces was going up. Initially it was assumed that women were no longer satisfied with their traditional role between kitchen and kids, that domestic appliances were making life easier and that they, too, thought more in terms of a career than of family life. Later the contraceptive pill was used as a convenient explanation. Probably the causes lay deeper than in biochemistry – in the eternal generation conflict, in the rejection of old role models for marriage and family, of male domination and female submission, in the erosion of authority, of father figures and mother figures – and above all in new models for childhood. The absurd promotion of 'anti-authoritarian education' went the rounds on television and in the universities and undermined whatever standards of public or private decency had survived the Nazi period. Everyone believed himself entitled to infringe his neighbour's privacy, the more rudely the better, and the very civility that had been an object of hate to the SA was once again despised by the children of the Brown Shirts.

If explanations are to be looked for, then the Sixties generation had been moulded by contradictory experiences like no other before. Role models had been revealed as monsters, a

fatherland emerged without fathers, the menfolk long buried in some mass grave, or surviving as shattered shells with guilty consciences in need of laborious repair. Banal lives were lived at the centre of a nuclear confrontation which had the intensity of a religious war. The acceptance of the possibility of Armageddon was the precondition of peace. For good measure all of this happened in the middle of the Affluent Society, and exposure to the thousand temptations of freedom.

It seemed the end of the economic miracle might also mean the end of democratic stability. On the Right, there was some neo-Nazi revival, and on the Left there were furious protests – Rudi Dutschke and his APO, the extra-parliamentary opposition, always prominent. In 1967 the Shah of Iran paid a visit: mass demonstrations turned violent. In April 1968, when a socialist student leader was shot and killed by the police, protest exploded. Similar scenes were taking place in France, though

Rudi Dutschke *(above), on the right, whipping up his student followers during the heady days of early 1968, shortly before he was seriously wounded by a would-be assassin in April. Originally from East Germany, his suspicion of the consumer society, hostility towards America's Vietnam entanglement, and fears of neo-Nazism were shared by young would-be revolutionaries in the backward-looking universities. His creed of extra-parliamentary opposition reached eager ears.*
[PHOTO: SEELIGER]

focused more sharply against the Gaullist establishment. De Gaulle took the danger seriously – too seriously by all accounts – and went by helicopter to see his paratroop general Massu, chief of the French forces in Germany, to make sure of a solid base and of being able, if necessary, to intervene from outside. The elections which followed shortly afterwards showed that bourgeois France, and even the France of the Left, remained unimpressed by the revolt of the young. Much as in Germany, they were given a few universities as adventure playgrounds.

Pretty young girls and intelligent young men dedicated themselves, like monastic novices, to the study of writings whose authors simply could not have known much about the problems of the late twentieth century, wasting their youth on grey theory. An insecure older generation stood by, bewildered in the face of so much ingratitude and aggression. It had laboriously collected some ideas of state, justice, society, family and education from the ruins of the German past and slightly Americanized them. Now the students, with the rabid innocence of youth, attacked their fathers' most vulnerable spot – the past. It was ironic and revealing that the student spokesmen all too often bore names which had shone in the Nazi era. But that did not seem to worry anyone. That they

Neue Ostpolitik: *Chancellor Willi Brandt converses with the Soviet leader Leonid Brezhnev (left) in Bonn, 1973. Soviet Foreign Minister Andrei Gromyko, 'Grim Grom', sits on the left, with Egon Bahr, Brandt's special envoy, while Germany's Foreign Minister (and future President) Walter Scheel is bottom right.*
[PHOTO: BARBARA KLEMM]

Sunday motoring banned *(below right) after the price of oil was raised by more than four times in the aftermath of the Yom Kippur War in 1973. The energy crisis brought a change in the political, economic and moral climates and forced big government spending to maintain the social fabric.*

called not for atonement but for a radical departure in the name of the social sciences and socialism – who cared about such detail? 'The challenge of democracy', the slogan from Willi Brandt's inaugural speech after he had become Chancellor thanks to Social Democrat electoral victories in 1969, did not imply anything specific, it set no goals or boundaries, but its visionary rhetoric hit the nerve of the times: life as a playground, departure for departure's sake, the sky the limit, man the master of his fate.

After the excesses of 1968, sometimes playful, sometimes violent, left-wing intellectuals used the media to pour oil onto the smouldering ashes by denouncing not only West Germany's mild-mannered market economy as 'Capitalist repression' but also its democratic endeavours as 'hiding the fascist beast'. This was enough to bring an outbreak of virulent political terrorism in the mid-1970s, combining a hardcore of a few dozen activists with a wider layer of sympathisers who provided ideology, legal advice, infrastructure and even an occasional hide-out. Some near-Eastern countries provided training and cash, and even the East German Stasi, not normally prone to adventurism, gave shelter to some activists needing a respite.

The full harvest of terrorism was reaped in 1977. On 7 April the General Prosecutor, his driver and guard, were shot in Karlsruhe. On 30 July the chairman of the Dresdner Bank Jürgen Ponto, was killed, his godchild, a young girl student, having led the way. The Employers' Union President, Hans

Martin Schleyer, chief of Daimler Benz, drove into an ambush in the middle of Cologne. A child's pram was pushed into the path of his car to slow it, his driver and bodyguards were gunned down, and he was abducted in order to blackmail Chancellor Schmidt into trading some other imprisoned terrorists for Schleyer's life. From time to time desolate photos of him were sent to the media. After five weeks of nervous stand-off, four Palestinians captured a Lufthansa jet with 87 people on board, ordering it from one airport to another and finally to Mogadishu, where they shot the captain. In the early hours of 18 October, German Commandos stormed the plane and killed three of the terrorists, the local dictator having being promised generous compensation. In faraway Stammheim Prison, near Stuttgart, this triggered the suicide of the three imprisoned terrorists of the Rote Armee Fraktion (R.A.F.); it also triggered the death of Schleyer at the hands of his kidnappers, who dumped his body in the boot of a car near Mulhouse in France.

The terrorists, through their gruesome actions, cut themselves off from their intellectual supporters, who saw that they did not merely play with words but meant what they said. Germany's left-wing protest movements, not unlike the anarchists of a century before, slowly became converts to the rules of a more civilised political game, and went back to what they had promised themselves in 1968, 'a long march through the institutions'. Gerhard Schröder, who became Chancellor in

1998, and Otto Schily, his Minister of the Interior, were once lawyers in cases brought against terrorists, so they at least have confronted the phenomenon close up.

On the broader stage, Willi Brandt's Neue Ostpolitik merely implemented what followed from the general direction of western strategy – settlement by treaty of Germany's dangerous open conflicts with its eastern neighbours. That was what the Western Allies were urging. The Germans fell into line, albeit insisting that the real Germany was western Germany and that German unity remained a legitimate goal, for themselves and for Germany's allies. Despite all détente rhetoric and policy, the Soviets failed to get the West, and more especially the Germans, to recognize fully all Soviet wartime and postwar conquests. In order to achieve an overall European settlement freezing the status quo once and for all, the Soviets suggested a conference for harmony and cooperation in Europe, playing to French and German 'Europe for the Europeans' sentiments. In return they had to accept a political process in which the US and the Canadians played important roles, while the N plus N-states (neutral and non-aligned) became the catalysts of compromise. In 1975 the Helsinki Final Act comprised three 'baskets': one on the inviolability of borders, one on human rights, and one on trade; environmental cooperation was envisaged, and also arms control. But instead of cementing the status quo, 'Helsinki' turned out to be a force for change.

Adenauer's chancellorship had begun among stuffed animals in the 'Museum König', a natural history museum on Bonner Hauptstrasse. Then the Chancellor had moved into the neo-classical Schaumburg Palace. Under Willy Brandt the extensive park on the left bank of the Rhine was half consumed by a new rust-coloured chancellery, a two-floor, three-winged building, half fortress and half insurance company headquarters. Its interior, in the taste of the time, left a lot of free space for 'communication', but no one has since been seen communicating there, unless he has some time to waste. This was a suitable setting for the modern spirit of technocracy; the only concession to art was Henry Moore's 'Two Large Forms' in golden bronze on a raised piece of lawn which covered nuclear shelters or garages. At the same time in East Berlin, on the Spree embankment where until 1952 the impressive baroque residence of the Hohenzollerns had stood, the 'Palace of the Republic' was cast in concrete, with gilded window-panes and – as emerged later – infested by asbestos.

In the East the Communist regime suppressed any allusion to Germany as a whole, whether in its new anthem, or in the passports of its subjects, or in its Constitution. In the West, by contrast, the excessive zeal of the Neue Ostpolitik as pursued by the left wing, was slowed down by the Constitutional Court's ruling and at the insistence of Franz Joseph Strauss from Bavaria that in all treaties the substance of the nation and the claim to the national state must be beyond discussion: one nation in two states.

In 1973 the energy crisis caused by the rise of oil prices after the Yom Kippur war forced a new austerity on a nation used to affluence. Everything changed: interest rates went up, company profits down, labour markets shrank, investments nose-dived, money flows were reversed, and last but not least attitudes were transformed. For the past fifteen years the Allensbach Institute for Public Opinion Research had asked people whether they believed in progress. In 1967 more than half had said yes; in 1972 under Willi Brandt nearly two-thirds were positive; the grim autumn of 1973 changed things and the majority swung towards no. In 1982 the mood was particularly gloomy: a mere 28 per cent of Germans still believed in progress, half of those questioned said no, and the rest were undecided. 'Turning the Tide' became the code words for a cautious slowing-down, in fact a return to older standards of common sense and good government. Domestically the new and easier lifestyle had been linked to the name of Willi Brandt. In terms of practical politics there was more welfare policy and more administrative

Non-speaks. *Chancellor Willi Brandt sits beside his Defence Minister Helmut Schmidt in 1973. A year later and Schmidt was to be in his place as Chancellor. A deep split then grew between Brandt as party chairman and Schmidt as political manager which, in turn, was to cost Schmidt the Chancellorship in 1982.*
[PHOTO: BARBARA KLEMM]

intervention, and altogether a greater belief in the state, in planning, in technocracy, but without revolution. In 1974 Willi Brandt was to come to grief through the boundless demands of the Public Service, Transport and Communications Union, through his own diffuse style of leadership and thanks to an East German spy who was unmasked in his immediate entourage.

A crisis manager was called for, a can-do type, someone with economic credentials. Helmut Schmidt had risen as a Deputy and Home Affairs Senator in his native Hamburg. Later, in the

Bundestag, 'Loose-tongued Schmidt' was notorious for his sharp rhetoric when Defence Minister, in which office he displayed a profound understanding of nuclear strategy as seen from Germany. When he succeeded Brandt as Chancellor in 1974, he laconically described the situation as 'the end of the flagstaff'. This applied not only to the extensive welfare spending of previous years, which had expanded as if to test the capacity of industry to pay for it. It applied also to the more reckless educational reform policies in the German Länder run by the socialist left wing. The energy crisis had administered a salutary shock.

The total number of unemployed kept rising in spite of vast government deficit spending. At the end of Schmidt's chancellorship in 1982 the figure was two million. Admittedly the energy shock was mitigated by the oil states' petrodollars recycled to Europe in search of investment opportunities, just as it was by the development of environment-enhancing technologies. At the same time computerization and robots transformed much, in fact nearly all, work in the industrial and service sectors. Hundreds of thousands of jobs were vanishing every year, the more so as rapidly rising wages, negotiated cartel-like between employers' associations and trade unions, ensured that employers never missed a chance to cut jobs or relocate abroad. The more rigid and protectionist German labour laws became through trade union pressure, parliamentary legislation and court rulings, the more did enterprises avoid filling expendable vacancies. Instead they preferred to let overtime increase. The inflexibility of the legal framework was exacerbated by the growing burden of social costs imposed on wages.

After the visionary dream of a new Germany, Helmut Schmidt's idea of Modell Deutschland was more down to earth. Willi Brandt remained the great communicator of the Left, a medium for ideas rather than a leader of men, putting his hope in Left majorities – with the Greens who had been born of the energy crisis, with protesters and peace marchers. However, in doing so he omitted to keep Schmidt's flanks protected in the party. Schmidt bought trade union support with ever more welfare benefits – this also mollified the wage earners of the Christian-Social wing of the CDU. Yet he kept the coalition on course with the help of the Free Democrats, led by the twin-harness team of Count Lambsdorf and Hans-Dietrich Genscher, the one speaking the language of big business, the other appealing to the left-wing radicals. However, this uneasy alliance between the NATO-minded Chancellor and a fragmented SPD would not work for long. During Schmidt's

eight years at the helm (1974-1982) interest rates rose to delirious heights and there was a flight of capital into North American real estate and Swiss bank accounts. The European Community was put to the test shielding its welfare states against the ups and downs of the dollar, and the wild dance of oil prices. The cult of opting out, smart for individuals, fashionable with the Greens and on the left wing of the SPD when done collectively, suggested something of a hangover following the 'progress' binge. The label Toskana-Fraktion, the Tuscany Party, became common, referring to the preferred radical-chic retreat.

The Greens *get into parliament, 1983, in open-necked shirts and knitted socks, with a pot of forsythia on the desk in front of them. There were 28 members then; in 1990 they* *failed to get the five per cent of votes needed for a presence, but were instrumental in the Socialists forming a government in 1998.*

[PHOTO: J.H.DARCHINGER]

Herbert von Karajan *(above)
passes on the flame to the new
generation – violinist Anne-
Sophie Mutter – watched by
Beate Burchard, co-ordinator
of the Salzburg Easter Festival.
A darling of the Nazi art
establishment, and Party
member, he was too talented to
be denied work for long after*
*the war. The British record
company EMI sought him out,
eager for someone to lead their
assault on the huge new market
opened up by the long-playing
record and stereo sound. In the
1950s he was conducting the
Berlin Philharmonic; in the
1960s he became director of the
Salzburg Festival and in the*
*1970s of the Vienna State
Opera. When he died in 1989,
his estate was worth over £160
million. He was dictatorial in
the extreme, and of consuming
vanity – as can be seen by his
taut skin resulting from various
face-lifts – yet his artistry was
colossal.*

[PHOTO: TIMM RAUTERT]

Joseph Beuys (*right*), *Germany's greatest post-war artist, in his trade-mark hat and fishing jacket. Visionary, intuitive, with an almost shamanistic reverence for the animal and vegetable, politically involved, with a great gift for publicity and for engaging younger people, he invigorated the art scene with his 'happenings', his performance art. He also pioneered installation art and video art. Dismissed from the Düsseldorf Academy of Art in 1972 when he tried to introduce the principle of unrestricted admission, he established a 'free international university' there instead.*
[PHOTO: NOMI BAUMGARTI]

Günter Grass *(right), Germany's best-known living novelist, but also a playwright, poet, artist, sculptor, jazz musician and cook. His is the divided, guilt-racked Germany of post-1945, inspiring books like* The Tin Drum *and* Cat and Mouse. *Indeed he opposed reunification after 1989. Behind him is the Jewish writer Jurek Becker.*
[PHOTO: RUDI MEISEL]

Helmut Kohl, *just after he became Chancellor in 1982 (left). Ambitious, and with an apparently unfailing political instinct, he had formerly been Minister-President of the Rhineland-Palatinate – what he called God's own country – whose wine and rich home cooking contributed to his size. He oversaw the reunification of his country and a great acceleration in the drive for a united Europe, with the demise of the deutsch mark as a first step.* [PHOTO: BARBARA KLEMM]

Germany's intellectual foundations were beginning to work loose. Added to this the Soviets were deploying new medium-range missiles targeted at Germany, which may not have added much to the total apocalyptic arsenal, but represented a new political threat. The new Carter administration in the USA did not wish to include the new Soviet systems – their range limited to Europe – in the arms control agreements. Chancellor Schmidt, who saw the strategic danger more clearly, compelled them to do so. After the Berlin blockade and the building of the Wall, the third great East-West confrontation was arising, with Germany once more at centre-stage. In 1979 the Atlantic alliance responded with the 'double track decision': if the Soviets were to withdraw their SS 20 missiles, the USA would not station Cruise missiles – low-flying target-seeking air-breaking bombs against which there was virtually no defence – and the new Pershing II missiles in Germany. Protest exploded throughout Western Germany, tearing apart not only the Social-Democrats, but – along with worries about vast deficits – the Schmidt-Genscher coalition as well, in the autumn of 1982. In came the most underestimated figure ever to set foot in the Chancellor's office, Helmut Kohl, a tall, black-haired man from the Rhineland-Palatinate, at fifty a seasoned practitioner of party politics.

The Christian-Democratic Union had not been a conservative movement even under Adenauer. Under Helmut Kohl, leader of the party since 1973, it had been kept in a balance between European integration, Atlantic security and German nostalgia, between Catholic social doctrine and middle-class interests, between believers and non-believers, between North and South. In 1982 worries over the economy and the missiles put a premium on stability and predictability. That was where Helmut Kohl came in.

In European affairs economic integration was making progress; political unification, on the other hand, remained undefined and nebulous. The French, that is France's political class, saw the European dimension as a way of strengthening national independence; the Germans saw in it an exit from history and nationhood. Kohl found it prudent, therefore, to accept such contradictions rather than try to resolve them and so cause the whole edifice to collapse.

Meanwhile the Communist empire was showing serious cracks, resulting from external overstretch and internal rigidity. So long as the Soviets were able to cover their economic and technical shortcomings by oil and gas profits this remained unnoticed. But when, in the early eighties, oil prices dramatically slumped – some Arab oil states flooded the market in order to make life difficult for Iran – the process was accelerated. At the same time the oil slump gave the West a new freedom of economic manoeuvre. While on the face of it the Soviet empire was still at the peak of its strength, with more troops, more nuclear weapons, more tanks than ever before, deployed from the Brandenburg Gate to the Khyber Pass and beyond, its economy went downhill. In the air war over Lebanon's Bekaa Valley in the summer of 1982 the Syrian's Soviet Migs were shot down by Israeli American F-16s like clay pigeons. The war in Afghanistan could not be won. In Poland the Solidarity trade union could not be suppressed. The economies of the Comecon states of central Europe were in trouble. If it was not to collapse soon, the empire needed radical reform even sooner.

Mikhail Gorbachev soon taught the world two new words, Perestroyka and Glasnost, reconstruction and transparency. It all began with the withdrawal of the chastened Red Army from the blood-soaked valleys of Afghanistan. Next came arms control, and after fifteen years of unsuccessful negotiation a first agreement was reached to reduce conventional weapons between the Atlantic and the Urals within a short time. In parallel with this the nuclear medium-range missiles, which had been at the centre of the last great East-West confrontation, were reduced to zero, dismantled and destroyed. Then there were unilateral demobilization measures by the Red Army. Hovering far overhead was the threat of the USA's 'Star Wars'

technology which the Soviets were in no position to match. In 1988 the Kremlin chief announced that the countries of the Soviet camp were free to choose their alliances and their way of life. If this was not just rhetoric it meant a graceful farewell to the 'evil empire'. It seemed that people in Warsaw, Prague and Budapest were holding their breath and tiptoeing to the door, with much the same happening in the Baltic states. Among young East Germans soon no-one was more popular than Mikhail Gorbachev.

In the eighties the economics of the West and the Pacific Rim financial markets, weapons and lifestyles were revolutionized by the microprocessor just as the Eastern bloc split asunder. In Poland Solidarity continued to defy the regime. The Red Army moved up to the frontier, supported by the National People's Army of the German Democratic Republic, but it was too late for steamrollering the Poles: the strength was lacking, so was the resolve. Moreover the political price in terms of arms control and international trade and credit was too high. Ronald Reagan enjoyed the reputation of a tough guy. In Hungary everyone, including the Communist leaders, was thoroughly sick of Soviet mentorship. Seeking manoeuvring space beyond the Bloc, the Hungarian foreign minister signed the Human Rights Charter of the European Council in Strasbourg. For year after year the Hungarians had had hundreds of thousands of East Germans in their country, enjoying cheap holidays on Lake Balaton, with their weak currency and their Trabant cars. If the

Oskar Lafontaine, *then mayor of Saarbrücken, at a peace camp in 1983 (right), linking hands in an anti-nuclear demonstration. The mock-gravestone records the 'death' of NATO's 1979 'double track decision' not to station Cruise and Pershing missiles in Germany if the Russians agreed to withdraw their SS-20s. This leader of the left wing within the Social Democrat party, a regular official visitor to East Germany before 1989, was able to demand a big role in Gerhard Schröder's government for the first few months, until he overreached himself and resigned early in 1999.*

In the dunes, *(above) on the island of Sylt, a nude sunbather provides a startling rear view.*
[PHOTO: ERWITT ELLIOTT]

On the beach. *A confirmation that national character comes out when on holiday. Each shelter has been dug into the sand at this German resort and a smooth rampart built round it to deflect the wind. All is neat, orderly, keeping nature firmly in hand.*

[PHOTO: DOROTHEA SCHMID]

Life in the East. *Two boys (left) in summertime Berlin wait for something to happen in 1981. The nearest thing to a bit of action is a solitary Trabant passing behind them. A few years later, 1984/85, and it's an outdoor summer party (right), pretzels and beer. Given that about one in eight of the DDR population is an occasional informer, will this get-together find its way onto the Stasi secret police files?*
[PHOTO, LEFT: URSULA ARNOLD]
[PHOTO, RIGHT: GERHARD WEBER]

Hungarian border with Austria, and thus with the West, one day soon was opened to them, the GDR was bound to collapse, provided the Soviets refrained from intervention.

The regime in East Berlin had never had many friends – not in Budapest, not in Warsaw, and least of all in the Kremlin. It was too arrogant, hectoring even the Russians, while no longer delivering superior products. Gorbachev and the reformists around him were sick and tired of listening to homilies on Communism and on the wisdom of shunning reform from Erich Honecker and his sour-faced Politbureau. In May 1989 the Hungarian government instructed its frontier guards to cut the border fence with Austria in front of the TV cameras of the world. The Hungarian rulers did not forget to look towards Moscow, but when no countermanding orders came, the wire-cutting continued. The East Germans, not believing their luck, crossed the frontier, drove through Austria, and at Passau received West German passports and a small sum in cash. Suddenly they found themselves in a different world, previously known only through the prism of television.

Once the holiday season began, the early-summer trickle soon turned into a stream. The East German regime thereupon prohibited travel to Hungary. But there was something in the air that made young East Germans defy their police state, so couples with their children climbed over the fence of the Lobkowitz Palace in Prague in Czechoslovakia, which housed the West German embassy. Czech police were soon instructed to look the other way. It was a clear sign that Bonn and

Frankfurt were more important for Prague than the rulers in East Berlin. Negotiations soon began between Bonn and East Berlin. Trains brought the 'embassy refugees' via Dresden to the West. The Communists were helpless, the General Secretary gravely ill, and the Party obliged to be on its best behaviour if it wished the fortieth anniversary of the German Democratic Republic to pass off without protest demonstrations or bloodshed, or both.

The East German state was always based on three premises and all three had long worn thin. The first was the guarantee of its existence by the Soviet Union, yet now the reformers in the Kremlin and the Stalinists in East Berlin were sending each other to the devil. The second premise was the mutual understanding that 'we pretend to work and you pretend to pay us'. But there was less and less substance in this. The third anchor, finally, was support from within the West. When the GDR People's Chamber unanimously applauded the Chinese army's massacre of the rebellious students in Beijing's Tiananmen Square, this was too much even for the GDR's old friends and fellow-travellers in the West. The international media, including Moscow television, night by night carried pictures from a country whose inhabitants were running away. Frozen solid in the Cold War for the past forty years, the German question suddenly reappeared: the crucial issue between East and West. Alarm bells rang in every chancellery in Europe.

In early October 1989 the dreaded fortieth anniversary of the

GDR had to be celebrated with much fanfare, mass rallies and self-congratulation. The byzantine protocol of the Eastern Bloc demanded that the General Secretary of the CPSU, the Communist Party of the Soviet Union, should hear the cheering of the East German masses and exchange fraternal kisses with their leaders. Instead the GDR experienced the most passionate demonstrations since June 1953, this time with no Soviet troops intervening. Strong security forces separated the leaders from the people, but no one could fail to see that, in East Berlin, Dresden, Leipzig and other cities, the fate of the hated state was on a knife's edge. In front of television cameras in East Berlin, Gorbachev turned to the crowds and said: 'He who comes too late is punished by life.'

What soon became a favourite slogan was an almost uncoded message that the fate of the East Berlin regime was sealed. The masses sensed that this time the Soviet tanks would stay in their depots. When Gorbachev drove back to Schönefeld airport in the south of Berlin, none of the SED leaders accompanied him, a grave slight by any standard. The following day the Stasi and the Party intended to restore order, but the Soviet liaison officers with the National People's Army and the frontier guards advised against it, and without Soviet support the outcome would be uncertain. On 4 November

1989 more than half a million people stood in protest in Alexanderplatz, the symbolic centre of the SED state in the eastern part of a divided Berlin. Their silent presence, not far from the Wall, announced the beginning of the end of the Communist dictatorship. Everything, as though by a miracle, remained peaceful. A fortnight previously the ruling oligarchy had rid itself of the perpetually smiling Honecker, its leader for almost twenty years. His successor Egon Krenz was merely driven, then overtaken, by events. Posters, alluding to Krenz's striking facial features, asked like Little Red Riding Hood: 'Grandmother, why have you got such a big mouth?' At first the ironic chanting was 'We are the people.' But soon one could hear: 'We are one people.' The Wall had been symbolically removed while it was still standing.

A few days on, the rank and file of the SED made bitter critical remarks about their superiors on the GDR television, unhindered and unrefuted. Late in the evening of 9 November, a few contorted foreign travel regulations were being read to the press by the Politbureau spokesman Günther Schabowski, but he did not even finish. Events overtook words. People were streaming to the Wall and no frontier guards dared open fire. Within hours the same was happening along the entire border, from Lübeck on the shores of the Baltic Sea to Hof in Bavaria.

A DIFFERENT GERMANY

THE STATUS OF BERLIN AND 'GERMANY AS A WHOLE' in the Potsdam formula of 1945 was, strictly speaking, in the hands of the Four Powers. In reality it was in the hands of the crowds now streaming from East to West. International law, and even more so the interests of all concerned, demanded that the shaping of the future must not be left to the Germans – not to the government in Bonn and certainly not to the hapless Politbureau trying to save a German Democratic Republic that was so visibly beyond salvation. On the other hand the victors of the Second World War could no longer, as at Yalta or Potsdam in 1945, make decisions over the heads of 80 million Germans. What mattered was to keep down the demons of the past and to forestall the dangers of a major East-West confrontation. Around Berlin over 400,000 crack Soviet troops were deployed with full equipment, including tactical nuclear weapons. These were forces that for decades had practised nothing but attack. Would they give up the linchpin of the Soviet Empire?

While enterprising young people with hammers and chisels were chipping chunks out of the Berlin Wall and selling them, the French President François Mitterand travelled to Leipzig, where he met Egon Krenz, and to Kiev to see Gorbachev, in order to save what could no longer be saved. At first there was some reassurance, to both Paris and London, in the words Mitterand had heard from Gorbachev: 'If German unity comes, then there will be a two-line report in Pravda that a Soviet marshal is sitting at my desk.' If it is a characteristic of revolutions that state chancelleries are chasing behind events and lack the concepts with which to encompass them, then a European revolution had taken place in that German November.

Many of the leading dissidents in eastern Germany hoped for a chance to find a road between hated Stalinism and unloved capitalism. Their 'third way' soon proved an élitist dream, confined to editorial offices in the West and parsonages in the East. The great majority of the people wanted to be part of the West, both in outlook and with all its material advantages. Meanwhile Gorbachev had discreet inquiries made in Bonn whether Germany would help the Soviet Union through the winter.

Was another Potsdam conference to decide on the fate of the Germans? 'We don't need four midwives', Chancellor Kohl coldly commented. The salient point was that the US administration, more precisely President George Bush and

Chipping away the past.
Berliners have brought their own hammers, on New Year's Eve 1989, to deliver some symbolic blows to the ferro-concrete of the wall that has divided their city since 1961. An East German guard in his Russian-style winter headgear looks through a hole near the Brandenburg Gate, not to put a stop to proceedings but merely to satisfy his curiosity.
[PHOTO: GUY LE QUERREC]

Secretary of State James Baker, did not seek a continuation of the four-power system but wanted it replaced by the unification of Germany – admittedly on American terms. Chancellor Kohl was still thinking on a ten-year scale; in a ten-point declaration in the German Bundestag he spoke of federation – and after those ten years, perhaps, unification.

Four weeks after the breaching of the wall the world's two most powerful men agreed to discuss in person what was to be done and how to avoid confrontation. They started on board ship in a gale off Malta, but eventually moved onto firm ground. It was as if the ancient gods of the Mediterranean had sent them a warning not to step to the edge of the abyss again for the sake of Germany. Americans and Russians soon came to the decision not to seek a German peace treaty but a European settlement. While the Communist regimes from Warsaw to Budapest and Bucharest were toppling like dominoes, history was actually being driven by millions of people who no longer accepted the leaden dictatorships they had had to suffer for four decades. Each day on average some three thousand young people moved from eastern to western Germany, wishing to run their own lives and refusing to wait until everything was signed, sealed and delivered.

If things had been up to state chancelleries they would have run a slow course, from one conference to another. But mass demonstrations in Leipzig simply and directly stated what it was all about: 'If the DM won't come to us, we'll go to the DM.' While the West German Left was still hoping that some 'GDR identity' might be saved, and with it some 'Third Way', the Grand Old Man of the SPD, Willi Brandt, stepped in front of the cameras and repeated a slogan which his wife had whispered to him: 'What belongs together will grow together.' Federal President von Weizsäcker observed wryly that it must not 'run wild together', but when Chancellor Kohl addressed a huge crowd in nocturnal Dresden a few days before Christmas 1989 it was clear to everybody that unity must come. Everywhere there were hastily sewn flags in the old green-and-white colours of Saxony or black, red and gold flags from which the old state emblem – hammer and compasses – had been cut out. On motor cars the international plate DDR was changed to D by covering up the other letters. Later on most Germans confirmed that they were moved to tears by the events.

When the first free elections were held on 18 March 1990 an overwhelming majority voted for the end of the GDR and for German unity. The former Communist state party, the SED, the Socialist Unity Party, had changed its name even before the end of 1989 and now called itself the Party of Democratic Socialism, PDS. In the elections it obtained less than 20 per cent of the vote. All the other parties wanted German unification, and they wanted it soon, even though no one could say when and under what circumstances it would be achieved. This, the most desirable outcome, appeared attainable only via a route fraught with danger. It could only happen if the Soviet Union would accept the loss of its outer empire. And this must not cause the fall of Gorbachev or a shake-up of the Soviet Union. All the odds were against it.

There was no longer the coalition of the victors as in 1945, but the idea of the 'Baker boys' in the US State Department, the '2 + 4' formula, gained acceptance as a way forward. This meant that the two German states were to settle their affairs with each other, while the four powers, who in international law still held responsibility for Germany as a whole in their hands, would set the external framework amongst themselves and with the Germans. Demands from Rome and Warsaw to be actively involved were politely rejected.

Negotiations progressed briskly from early May to mid-July 1990. German credits and economic aid persuaded the Russians to stop procrastinating: they would have liked to keep the external questions of unification open for another five years. Parallel negotiations about conventional arms control and confidence-building measures provided a protective roof. At the London summit at the beginning of July 1990 a ground-breaking NATO statement was adopted: in unusually flowery language this extended 'a brotherly hand' to the countries of the Warsaw Pact and, more importantly, announced a thorough revision of nuclear strategy. When Chancellor Kohl brought the

negotiations with Gorbachev to a conclusion in the Caucasus in mid-July 1990, he came back with the Soviet leadership's consent not only to the unification of Germany but also to the membership of the whole of Germany in the North Atlantic Alliance. Soviet troops, Gorbachev assured him, would leave Germany within four years. At midnight on 2 October 1990 the flags of the GDR were hauled down everywhere. In front of the Reichstag in Berlin, to the accompaniment of Georg Friedrich Handel's music, then the national anthem and finally lighter music, the black, red and gold flag of Germany was hoisted.

Daily life soon turned somewhat grey again. Nevertheless, the 'National People's Army' and the notorious Frontier Guards of the GDR were soon dissolved and all stocks of MIG-29 fighter aircraft, armoured fighting vehicles and ammunition handed over. Deployment plans for a blitz-invasion of Western Europe were found, as well as a complete set of road signs in Roman and Cyrillic scripts for the route to the Atlantic. In Honecker's command bunker were three pairs of marshal's epaulettes which the head of state, in the event of war, was to have presented to himself and his army leaders. These were no longer needed. The minefields were cleared, what remained of the 'Iron Curtain', over 800 miles of it from Lübeck to Bohemia, was used for scrap.

Meanwhile the big enterprises of the former GDR turned out to be in poor shape, many of them beyond repair. Instead of a more or less functioning industrial economy, as conjured up by the statistics falsified by the regime and believed by the West, there was an industrial rubbish heap. The aim of privatizing

A short walk (above opposite) takes 81-year-old August Gemerod, for the first time in many a long year, from East German Grossburschla, behind him, to his old home of Altenburschla in the West, now that the barriers are down.
[PHOTO: DOMINIK OBERTREIS]

Three-wheeler to freedom. East Germans wave (right) as they reach Helmstedt, the former border crossing on the autobahn from Berlin to the West. The design of their vehicle and of the Trabants behind it are testimony to the economic failings of the DDR.
[PHOTO: G. LINZENMEIER]

Brandenburg Gate, *New Year's Eve, 1989. Young Germans have found a good grandstand from which to watch the fireworks. By now it is clear that nothing less than unity will do after what was, in effect, the fall of the East German Communist regime the month before.*
[PHOTO: GUY LE QUERREC]

Stasi headquarters in Berlin (opposite), now the offices of the body investigating the activities of this chief tool of the former DDR police state. Some of those combing the 180 kilometres of files and 35 million index cards have done the job before, but for the other side. The CIA obtained key material from Stasi records in return for big payments when the regime collapsed.

[PHOTO: J. H. DARCHINGER]

The last Russian tanks leave Berlin (right) by rail in 1994, nearly fifty years after the first rolled in.

[PHOTO: BARBARA KLEMM]

these industrial remains and selling them to efficient purchasers from the West for the most part was possible only if large state subsidies were granted in exchange for guarantees of jobs. The social system of the GDR, based as it was on factories and their semi-feudal environment of suppliers and social facilities, broke up. Because of the speed of events the inhabitants of the five eastern 'New Länder' had to assume the entire legal framework of the Federal Republic, including overadministration and overtaxation. Most of the old cadres had to go, but many were left in newspaper offices, local government, schools and universities, and these made no secret of their bitterness towards the West and their own 'ostalgia'. The old-new PDS cadres turned their resentment and self-pity into a political programme.

'State Security' had, during its final days, done all it could to expunge the traces of its activity. Mountains of files were burnt or went into the shredder. But the CIA got hold of many, with copies remaining in Moscow. What was left was enough to set up, under the directorship of the former pastor and dissident Joachim Gauck, an information and legal aid authority whose task it was to scrutinize the SED state and, above all, its machinery of oppression. It emerged that the Stasi had 102,000 officers plus an estimated 500,000 full-time domestic informers and up to two million occasional informers and stool pigeons – this in a country of seventeen million. This ratio easily surpassed both the Gestapo's and the KGB's. What is more, it is estimated that 20,000 West Germans spied for them, too.

From western Germany now came the political parties, the big media, a lot of officials, a few politicians such as the popular Minister-President of Saxony, Professor Kurt Biedenkopf, but also fortune-seekers and asset-strippers. Above all, there was a heavy flow of money, about 160 billion marks year after year, in transfer payments. Contrary to Bonn's expectations, reunification did not pay for itself, and because at first there seemed no need to raise taxes in the West, willingness to accept them soon declined. East Germans now enjoyed the same rights as West Germans, and their old-age pensions and unemployment benefits were paid out of West German funds – which soon led to lasting over-spending, bitterness and recriminations.

The face of East Germany was changing. Houses were colourwashed, old town halls were restored, telephone cables were laid, effluent was cleared up, ancient factories were pulled down or replaced by new ones. After just a few years one could barely recognize where the boundary had run. But in people's minds divisions were left which went deeper than the traditional differences between the German tribes. Time kept Germans waiting for its healing powers to start to work. The English tabloid press had conjured up alarming spectres of a 'Fourth Reich', French intellectuals worried about a 'Quatrième Empire'. Instead Germany's unification turned out to be a long, painful and costly process.

Claudia Schiffer, *(left) one of the three or four supermodels whose faces have continually stared out from the glossy magazines over the last ten years.*

Nastassja Kinski, *(opposite top) daughter of the actor Klaus Kinski and star of such films as* Tess *and* Paris, Texas. *Her empathy with the camera has been compared to Marilyn Monroe's.*

Wim Wenders, *(opposite below right) a leader of the new wave of German film directors in the 1980s and 90s, famous in particular for* Paris, Texas *and* Angels over Berlin.
[PHOTO: MARTIN FRANK]

Karl Lagerfeld *(opposite below left) in his trademark dark glasses comes out on the catwalk with his models to receive applause for his haute-couture collection for Chanel, shown at the Louvre at the beginning of 1999.*
[PHOTO: VERDY]

Mata Hari, *a ballet based on the life of the First World War spy shot by the French, premiered by the Stuttgart Ballet in 1993. The Brazilian Marcia Haydée dances* *the part of the spy and her partner is Ivan Cavallari. Since 1976 she has been director of the Stuttgart Ballet.*
[PHOTO: FÖRSTERLING]

Wagner in the 1990s. *The English singer John Tomlinson as the one-eyed god Wotan and Hanna Schwarz as his consort Fricka in* Das Rheingold, *the first part of the Ring Cycle, at Bayreuth in 1994.*
[PHOTO: KIEFER]

All the same, politicians in Bonn realized that Germany's European neighbours demanded reassurance. Alluding to the title of a book about the Bismarck era, Chancellor Kohl emphasized that Germany was not going to become, once again, a 'restless empire'. Reduction of the German armed forces to an upper limit of 370,000 men – soon to be reduced to 340,000 on financial grounds – restatement of the renunciation of weapons of mass destruction and the inclusion of the German forces into mixed formations, such as the German-French-Belgian-Spanish 'Eurocorps', the German-American corps, and the German-Dutch corps, were all part of this policy of reassurance. The German contribution to the coalition against Iraq's Saddam Hussein consisted primarily of a cheque for over 17 billion DM, while no mention was made of armed assistance. Bonn was almost too modest: the defence minister praised Germany's 'culture of restraint', foreign minister Genscher even found in the NATO treaty of 1949 a prohibition of action 'out of area' – something none of the other Allies had until then heard of and that, subsequently, was not confirmed by the Federal Constitutional Court. It took some time to realize that in the unquiet years following the Cold War more was being expected from Germany than mere expressions of dismay, and best wishes for world peace.

Within the European Community everything soon focused on the massive project of crowning market union with currency union, on creating a common currency and entrusting it to a European Central Bank to be established in Frankfurt. The Germans viewed the project with mixed feelings. They were proud of the mark, whose strength reflected their achievements since 1945, and of the Bundesbank, a staunch defender of stability against politicians' never-ending demands for easy money. They hesitated to enter into an indissoluble currency union with countries whose currencies they had watched melting away thanks to political irresponsibility and economic opportunism. Their grave doubts were shared by the Bundesbank itself which declared with a conspicuous lack of enthusiasm that the whole thing was a political project and therefore had to be decided on political grounds. But for François Mitterand – who demanded the Euro as the price for reunification, thus hoping to take France out of the shadow of the Bundesbank – and but for Helmut Kohl – who was driven by fear of Germany being isolated – the project would probably have foundered on its internal and external contradictions. In the end the Bundesbank agreed to its own decapitation.

Post-1990 Berlin, a city full of nervous energy but moving nowhere in particular, in its ambiguity reflects the state of Germany. The two halves of the city, no longer separated, don't look at each other, don't share the same newspapers or the same tasks, and even their party politics are very different. The fusion of Berlin and the surrounding land of Brandenburg, when put to a referendum, was rejected, because 'Ossis' did not like to live with 'Wessis' and vice-versa. In the east, the recycled Communists set the tone; in the west, the old political establishments join together in a grand coalition to keep the ex-Communists away from the levers of power. In the heart of Berlin, the waste lands around Potsdamer Platz and north to the Brandenburg Gate are rapidly filling up with glass, steel, and concrete piles housing world-class hotels and the offices of some multi-national companies. Developers and banks, seduced by the early post-unification euphoria and tax breaks into building much office space, now find it unsellable. German construction workers, having been priced out of the market by their unions, are idle and resentful. The new Chancellery rises north of the Reichstag, while down Unter den Linden the old Soviet Embassy, that was constructed after the war to house the Soviet Proconsul in Germany for ever and ever, is rented out to companies who like to give their guests a special frisson. But the portions of caviar served there are much smaller than they used to be.

With the Jews and the Junkers gone, and most industrial headquarters as well as factories firmly settled in the west, Berlin will not relive the 1920s. But with most of the Federal Government moving there at the end of the century, it will be the hub of politics, a workshop of ideas – complemented by a psychiatric ward. The Bundestag moves from Bonn in 1999, into the pathetic old Reichstag building, still showing the scars of its fire in 1933 and the shelling in 1945, but patched up by the British architect Norman Foster, who has also added a glass cupola in an attempt to balance once more its ornate bulk. Some of its members may, from time to time, ponder its changes of home.

Gossip columnists are slowly moving their gaze from Düsseldorf and Munich to Berlin. Smart shops are filling elegant arcades in the centre, hoping for rich customers, though most of those who come at present speak Russian and pay cash. West Germans do not venture much beyond the money-no-object glitz of the reconstructed *mitte*, with Borchard's and Lutter and Wegener's the favourite places for dinner. However, the decayed Prenzlauer Berg quarter is being colonised by Germans in search of la vie bohème and the international jet-set.

A decade after the collapse of the Soviet empire Germany, like Berlin, is still undergoing profound change, while Europe is still in transition. The Soviet Union by now is half forgotten, Russia perceived only as a weird shadow in the east, unable to resist NATO's dreaded expansion towards it. The governments of Germany's eastern neighbours vacillate between reformist Communists and middle-class anti-Communists; they too are on the move, on the way up, with hopes of further NATO extension and, even more, of admission to the European Union and its prosperity zone. Unity took a long time to have an impact on party politics and the composition of the government. The towering figure of Helmut Kohl created the illusion that continuity prevailed. Meanwhile, in the east, disillusionment grew, as did unemployment. All of German industry was forced to streamline production, to become 'cleaner and meaner', shedding jobs left and right and, in a silent alliance with trade unions, sending workers into early

Turkish gastarbeiter *emptying dustbins, the sort of work that Germans find less desirable. There are now over two million Turkish citizens in Germany, and to the problem of racist attacks on them by neo-Nazis has been added another caused by the growth of Turkish-Kurdish enmity.*

retirement. This in turn has made the Federal budget almost unmanageable. The Germans are still agonizing over whether globalization is a blessing or a curse, and a mood of pessimism (boosting the Greens) and a continuing demand for welfare protectionism (boosting the Social Democrats) prevail in the country. The multinationals of industry and the banking world are fleeing from overregulation and overtaxation between the Rhine and the Oder to more welcoming shores. Most politicians, however, find it difficult to accept that in economic terms the fully independent nation state is a thing of the past, and that their power is reduced accordingly.

Another problem, having a considerable bearing on nationality and unemployment, is that of the gastarbeiter and immigration. Guest workers or gastarbeiter, was the euphemism for the constant influx of foreign labour into Germany over the last four decades. When the Wall went up the flow of young, well-trained and highly motivated East Germans came to a halt. But in order to sustain the pace of economic growth, under the pressure of industry and state – the latter looking for dustmen, the former for unskilled workers – the labour exchanges had to look elsewhere for cheap labour. The high wages paid in Germany compensated the black-haired southern Europeans – from Italy's 'Mezzogiorno', for instance – for the rain, the food and loneliness. After the Italians came Serbs and Croats from Marshal Tito's Yugoslavia. A little later Turks followed from Anatolia bringing with them their eastern ways and Muslim religion, about which some Germans entertained mixed feelings.

At the time of the second oil crisis in 1980 those willing to return could cash in their premiums, but few were ready to

leave. They preferred to continue living in Germany with the idea that, somehow, some time, they would return home, set up a little business and look after the grandchildren. Meanwhile their own children were growing up in Germany, speaking better German than their parents, merging into German petit bourgeois society, joining football clubs, opening shops, restaurants, garages and driving taxis. Of the more than 1.5 million Turks in Germany when the Cold War ended, more than 300,000 lived in Kreuzberg, a Berlin suburb, complete with their own banks, newspapers, travel agencies, schools and mosques.

No German government ever forcefully addressed the need for a 'melting pot' or 'salad bowl' approach, so resentment and tension grew, aggravated by the fact that the handouts of the German welfare state continued to attract hundreds of thousands from all over the world, sometimes the needy and downtrodden, sometimes merely the clever ones who knew how to claim oppression and seek asylum. It was only after an agonising public debate and much protest from local authorities, left and right, that in 1993 the Bundestag voted through legislation intended to stem the tide – as other European nations had done before. The spectre of the Nazi past was ever ready to be unleashed upon a timid public by resolute minorities, and this made it almost impossible to define immigration, citizenship and national interest and bring them into a sustainable pattern more in line with the norms of neighbouring countries. Since the Schengen agreement in 1994 on open borders among continental EU counties, the Germans have been forced to follow a more sober line.

It was the fundamental shift from optimism to pessimism,

Boris Becker *(far left), the youngest-ever men's singles champion at Wimbledon in 1985, aged 17. He went on to win it again in 1986 and 1989. Here he is in action at the US Open in 1985.*
[PHOTO: GERD LUDWIG]

Franziska van Almsick *(opposite top), the outstanding German woman swimmer of the 1990s. Born in East Germany, she is seen here training in Barcelona for the 1992 Olympics, aged only 14. In 1993 she became the first woman to win six gold medals at the European Championships, three individual and three relay.*
[PHOTO: REHDER]

Jürgen Klinsmann *(opposite centre) running towards the Colombian goal during the 1990 World Cup final in Italy, that Germany went on to win. In the 1994 contest he captained the German team in the USA. At club level he played in the top flight at home, in Italy and in England.*
[PHOTO: MARTIN HELLMANN]

Steffi Graf *(opposite below), seven times Wimbledon women's singles champion, whose earnings from tennis now exceed those of Martina Navratilova, if endorsements and sponsorship are excluded.*
[PHOTO: WÄRNER]

Michael Schumacher *(opposite), the greatest Formula One driver of his generation, who has won well over thirty races so far, latterly driving for Ferrari who pay him a salary of £20 million a year.*
[PHOTO: STEPHAN ENDERS]

together with a mood of boredom after sixteen years of Helmut Kohl, that produced the landslide election victory of the Left in September 1998. Notwithstanding the 'new middle' or 'third way' propaganda of the election campaign, a red-green government was formed almost instinctively in Bonn, parallel to the first fully-fledged coalition government of the Social Democrats with the recycled Communists in the north-eastern Land of Mecklenburg-Vorpommern. Oskar Lafontaine came to power not only as finance minister, but also as leader of the SPD and thus master of patronage, bringing with him his fellow 'sixty-eighters' after their long march through the institutions. Some of them haven't forgotten that capitalism is the enemy. However, on 11 March 1999 Lafontaine resigned from all his offices, declared himself a *privatmann* without even trying to give any serious reasons. His failure was caused by the economy, by reality and by himself, and perhaps even by a somewhat different agenda on the part of the chancellor, Gerhard Schröder. Meanwhile in the Chancellery, it seems a German version of Britain's Blairism – whatever that is – is being worked out. The Greens have mutated from chaotic opposition into being pillars of the establishment, from sandals and knitted socks to three-piece suits, Armani ties and the rhetoric of continuity. The government has promised to allow widespread dual citizenship, thus putting at risk internal European cohesion, while at the same time the new minister of the interior has stated bluntly that every acceptable level of immigration has long been passed. The balance of an industrial society demands constant immigration, yet the country refuses to decide whether rigorous melting-pot integration is the answer, or uneasy multi-ethnic co-existence.

In a situation of high unemployment, socialist policy and global recession, together with the advent of the Euro run by the European Central Bank in Frankfurt, will Europe's welfare states, largely immune to streamlining or reform, ruin the common currency, or will the common currency force politicians into surrender and the public into austerity? There is no European government to bring fiscal policies into line; European nations continue to be driven by their different traumas and dreams; and the frame of reference for politics is still, outdated or not, the nation state. The common currency represents a break with history, but also a blow against globalization. Certainly it will make or break the European venture, and determine much of the fate of Germany.

The Reichstag's new dome *designed by the British architect Norman Foster, with a ramp spiralling up to the public viewing platform round an inverted cone of mirrors deflecting daylight into the debating chamber below. It reinvigorates the 1890s* *classicism of the rest of the building, and the hope is that the Bundestag will likewise combine tradition and innovation in this, its new Berlin home. Peace in her chariot on top of the Brandenburg Gate is a style of symbol from a very different age.* [PHOTO: BERND SETTNIK]

BIBLIOGRAPHY

Ash, Timothy Garton, *In Europe's Name.* Germany and the Divided Continent. 1994.

Bark, Dennis L.; Gress, David R., *A History of West Germany.* Volume 1: From Shadow to Substance 1945-1963. Volume 2: Democracy and its Discontents 1963-1988. 1989.

Benz, Wolfgang, *Encyclopedia of German Resistance to the Nazi Movement.* 1996.

Benz, Wolfgang, *The Holocaust.* 1999.

Bertram, Christoph, *Europe in the Balance.* Securing the Peace Won in the Cold War. 1995.

Beschloss, Michael R.; Strobe, Talbott, *At the Highest Levels.* The Inside Story of the End of the Cold War. 1993.

Botting, Douglas, *In the Ruins of the Reich.* 1985. (Quotations from the British Colonel on p. 212 and the German police official on p. 214, Chapter 7.)

Bracher, Karl Dietrich, *Turning Points in Modern Times.* Essays on German and European History. 1995.

Bullock, Alan, *Hitler and Stalin. Parallel Lives.* 1990/91.

Channon, Sir Henry (Chips), *Diaries.* 1967.

Cole, J.A., *My friend Michel.* 1955. (Quotations from British official on pp 218 and 221, Chapter 7.)

Craig, Gordon A., *Germany 1866-1945* (Oxford History of Modern Europe). 1978.

Craig, Gordon A., *Europe since 1914.* 1972.

Eyck, Erich, *Bismarck and the German Empire.* 1964.

Fest, Joachim, *Hitler.* 1992.

Genscher, Hans Dietrich, *Rebuilding a House Divided.* A Memoir by the Architect of Germany's Reunification. 1998.

Goebbels, Joseph, *Diary, 1925-26.* 1962.

Goebbels, Joseph, *Diaries, 1939-1941.* 1982.

Gorbachev, Michail, *The Demise of the Soviet Union.* 1991.

Haffner, Sebastian, *Ailing Empire.* Germany

An exciting ride. *(opposite) Ordinary Germans have enjoyed the thrills of the fairground throughout this century (see the half-title page); most though, would have preferred something a little more gentle than the roller-coaster ride that has been the story of the nation's last hundred years.*

from Bismarck to Hitler. 1991.
Haffner, Sebastian, *The Meaning of Hitler*. 1983.
Hills, Denis, *Tyrants and Mountains*. 1992.
Hobsbawm, Erich J., *The Age of Extremes*. A History of the World, 1914-1991. 1996.
Jones, L.E., *I Forgot to Tell You*. 1959.
Jünger, Ernst, *Storm of Steel*. 1921.
Kennan, George F., *Memoirs of a Diplomat*. 2 vols. 1967.
Kennan, George F., *At a Century's Ending*. Reflections 1982-1995. 1996.
Kennedy, Paul, *The Rise and Fall of the Great Powers*. 1988.
Kissinger, Henry, *Diplomacy*. 1995.
Kissinger, Henry, *A World Restored*. 1973.
MacCauley, Martin, *The German Democratic Republic since 1945*. 1983.
Macdonald, Lyn, *Voices and Images of the Great War*. 1988. (Quotation from Fritz Heinemann in Chapter 3.)
Mandelbaum, Michael, *The Dawn of Peace in Europe*. 1995.
Mowrer, E., *Germany Puts the Clock Back*. 1932.
Nipperdey, Thomas; Nolan, Daniel, *Germany from Napoleon to Bismarck 1800-1866*. 1996.
Marsh, David, *Germany and Europe*. The Crisis of Unity. 1994.
Pflanze, Otto, *Bismarck and the Development of Germany*. Vol. 1-3. 1990.
Padgett, Stephen (ed.), *Adenauer to Kohl*. The Development of the German Chancellorship. 1994.
Pond, Elizabeth, *Beyond the Wall*. Germany's Road to Unification. 1993.
Rauschning, Hermann, *Hitler Speaks*. 1939.
Schoenbaum, David; Pond, Elizabeth, *The German Question and other German Questions*. 1996.
Schulze, Hagen, *Weimar*. Deutschland 1917-1933. 1982.
Schulze, Hagen, *Germany*. A New History. 1998.
Schwarz, Hans Peter, *Konrad Adenauer: A German Politician and Statesman in a Period of War, Revolution and Reconstruction*. 2 Vols. 1991
Sereny, Gitta, *Albert Speer, His Battle with the Truth*. 1995.
Speer, Albert, *Inside the Third Reich*. 1970.
Stürmer, Michael, *Das Ruhelose Reich*. Deutschland 1866-1918. 1983.
Stürmer, Michael, *Die Grenzen der Macht*. Begegnung der Deutschen mit der Geschichte. 1992.
Stürmer, Michael; Teichmann, Gabriele; Treue, Wilhelm, *Striking the Balance*. Sal. Oppenheim jr. & Cie. A Family and a Bank. 1994.
Szabo, Stephen, *The Diplomacy of the German Unification*. 1992.
Taylor, A.J.P., *Bismarck, the Man and the Statesman*. 1955.
Weinberg, Gerhard L., *A World at Arms*. A Global History of World War II. 1994.
Winter, Jay; Baggett, Blaine, *1914-18, The Great War and the Shaping of the 20th Century*. 1996. (Quotations from Karl Gorzel and Gerhard Gürtler in Chapter 3.)
Zelokow, Philip; Rice, Condolezza, *Germany Unified and Europe Transformed*; A Study in Statecraft. 1995.

ACKNOWLEDGEMENTS

The following have kindly granted us permission to use the photographs on the pages listed below:

Ursula Arnold, Berlin, 244, 245, 264
Austrian Archives, Christian Brandstätter, Wien, 20t, 86, 141, 183, 184, 188
Rolf Ballhause, Plauen, 135, 146
Bayerische Staatsbibliothek, München, 118-119, 124
Berlinische Galerie, Landesmuseum für Moderne Kunst, Photographie und Architektur,128tl/Heinrich Zille Erbengemeinschaft, Bremervörde: 1, 8, 29b, 31, Bilderberg, Archiv der Fotografen, Hamburg, 259t, 263, 268, 281
Bildarchiv Preussischer Kulturbesitz, Berlin, 27, 28, 32, 40b,40t, 41b, 41t, 46-47, 57, 60r, 62, 67, 70, 80, 81, 89, 99, 106-107, 106, 110-111, 112-113, 115, 128tr, 131t,134, 139, 142, 143, 144b, 162, 164, 176l, 176r, 180, 182t, 194, 198, 200, 202t, 210-211, 212, 214, 220, 222, 225b, 230, 231, 232, 234-235, 242, 251, 253 / 132mr Hugo Erfurth/DACS, London 1999
Bundesarchiv, Koblenz, 12-13(70/49/29), 13(75/68/2A), 15(70/77/26), 39(17974), 49(15121), 58, 61l(N1022/501), 61r(S30285), 75t, 85(102-3388), 87(75/68/127 A), 92-93(98/9/34), 94, 114b(72/62/1), 116-117(71/109/44), 121(102/84), 122(76/84/17A), 123, 137(97/42/30A), 147(79/96/3), 156(102/14471), 158(152/11/12),165, 175b, 189, 191b (97/66/18), 191m (97/66/2.3), 191t (97/66/2.3), 194-195(286/82317)
Josef H. Darchinger, Bonn, 217, 248, 249, 257, 272
Deutsches Historisches Museum, Berlin, 19, 22-23, 24, 29t, 66b, 68, 69, 73, 112l, 151, 196-197, 216
Deutsches Museum, München, 71, 84
Deutsche Presse-Agentur, Stuttgart, 274(B2800epaAFP), 275 bl, 276(A2411), 276-277(C3319), 280tl(A2P36), 280m, 280b(A2954), 284 EPA/PA, 282-283
Ernst-Thorman-Archiv, Eichwalde, 140
Lux Feininger/Fotografische Sammlung Essen, 132l

Foto Atelier Louis Held, Weimar, 32, 63, 132tr, 132 br
Erika Furtmayer, 25tr
Gabriele Münter- und Johannes Eichner-Stiftung, München, 56
Gedenkstätte Deutscher Widerstand, Berlin, 206tl, 206tr, 206br
Galerie Alex Lachmann, Köln, 201
Rolf Gillhausen, Hamburg, 227
Haus der Geschichte der Bundesrepublik Deutschland, Bonn/Barbara Klemm/Die Frankfurter Allgemeine Zeitung, 256, 260
Monica und Walter Heilig, Berlin, 88, 96l
Historisches Archiv Krupp, Essen, 17, 38, 42-43, 64, 65, 66t, 82, 98
Hulton Getty, London, 5, 48, 52, 55, 78-79, 96, 97, 102, 103, 104, 105, 108-109, 125, 126b, 126t, 127l, 127r, 148-149, 157, 192l, 192r, 193, 193l, 204, 208-209
Imperial War Museum, London, 90b, 91, 101
Barbara Klemm, Die Frankfurter Allgemeine Zeitung, 254, 256, 260, 272
Landesmedienzentrum, Hamburg, 6-7, 16, 21, 25b, 35, 42t, 136, 202b, 203, 219
Robert Lebeck, Jau-Dignac-Loirac, 229
Lee Miller Archive, Chiddingly, 209
Leni Riefenstahl Produktion, Poecking, 182b
Lotte Jacobi Archives, Dimond Library, University of New Hampshire, 128b, 131bl, 131bm, 131br
Magnum Photos, London, 205, 207, 262, 266-267, 270-271,275 br, 278-279
Liese-Lotte Meffert, Hildburghausen, 172, 173t, 173m, 173b, 226
Roger Melis, Berlin, 250tr
Münchner Stadtmuseum/Fotomuseum, 130
Museum für Kunst und Gewerbe, Hamburg/Hugo Erfurth/DACS, London 1999, 30
Museum Ludwig, Köln, 233
Payer Familienarchiv, 20b, 95

Photo Archive C. Raman Schlemmer, Oggebbio, Italy/The Oskar Schlemmer Theatre Estate I-28824 Oggebbio, 129
Photo Galerie Bucher, Berlin 1870-1910, Janos Frecot, 76
Die Photographische Sammlung/SK Stiftung Kultur-August Sander Archiv, Köln; DACS, London 1999, 138 144t
PPS-Galerie FC Grundlach, Hamburg, 240, 241
Private Collection, Berlin, 53
Walther Rathenau Gesellschaft e.V., Bad Homburg, 117
Rheinisches Bildarchiv, Köln, 54, 133
Roger-Viollet, Paris, 10-11
Sächsische Landesbibliothek Staats-und Universitätsbibliothek Dresden, Deutsche Fotothek, 186-187, 213, 215, 218
Sybille Seidl-Obermayer, 26tl, 26b
DER SPIEGEL, Hamburg, 4, 145, 154, 155, 160, 161, 166, 167, 168-169, 171, 174, 175t, 177, 178, 179b, 179t, 181, 185, 190, 225t, 236-237/224,XXP
STERN, Hamburg, 250, 252
Stadtarchiv München, 159, 219 (R1763V15A)
Stiftung Automuseum Volkswagen, Wolfsburg, 239l, 239r
Süddeutscher Verlag, Bilderdienst, München, 34b, 34t, 36-37, 44t, 50, 51, 72, 77, 83, 90t
Thyssen AG Archiv, Duisburg, 120-121(260 22/2)
Clarita von Trott zu Solz, 206b
Ullstein Bilderdienst, Berlin, 2-3, 45, 59, 60l, 74-75, 114t, 152, 163, 170, 221, 223, 238, 243, 246-247, 255 (IVB report), 261 (BAR), 275t (Bildarchiv Peter Engelmeier), 284 (MEDIUM)
Visum, Hamburg, 258, 259, 269, 280l
Gehard Weber, Grimma, 265
Yad Vashem Photo Archives, courtesy of USHMM Photo Archives, 199t, 199m
Zentrale Stelle der Landesjustizverwaltungen, courtesy of USHMM Photo Archives, 199b

INDEX